Workbook

HOW 13: A Handbook for Office Professionals

James L. Clark
Professor Emeritus, Business Division
Pasadena City College

Lyn R. Clark
Chair: Computer Applications
and Office Technologies Department
Los Angeles Pierce College

SOUTH-WESTERN
CENGAGE Learning

Australia • Brazil • Japan • Korea • Mexico • Singapore • Spain • United Kingdom • United States

SOUTH-WESTERN
CENGAGE Learning·

ISBN-13: 978-1-133-58663-0
ISBN-10: 1-133-58663-5

South-Western, Cengage Learning
5191 Natorp Boulevard
Mason, OH 45040
USA

Cengage Learning is a leading provider of customized learning solutions with office locations around the globe, including Singapore, the United Kingdom, Australia, Mexico, Brazil, and Japan. Locate your local office at: **international.cengage.com/region**.

Cengage Learning products are represented in Canada by Nelson Education, Ltd.

For your course and learning solutions, visit **www.cengage.com**.

Purchase any of our products at your local college store or at our preferred online store **www.CengageBrain.com**.

Printed in the United States of America
1 2 3 4 5 6 7   15 14 13 12

Contents

Preface for *HOW 13* Workbook

The worksheets in this book, *Workbook for HOW 13*, have been developed to correlate specifically with the principles in *HOW 13: A Handbook for Office Professionals, 13th edition*. Each section in this workbook corresponds with a chapter in *HOW 13*. In fact, the reference to the section containing the information needed to complete each worksheet is shown in parentheses in the heading of the worksheet, for example, Grammar Overview (1-1). The first number in parentheses refers to the chapter, and the second number refers to the section within the chapter.

Workbook for HOW 13 is divided into five parts, with some parts containing several sections. Instructions for completing the worksheets in each section precede the exercise materials. Answers or solutions to the initial learning activities are given in Part 5. Other keys and solutions are contained in the *Instructor's Manual and Key*, which is available online and on the *Instructor's Resource CD* (ISBN 9781133588221).

Students may use this workbook independently or in an organized class activity. If the worksheets are to be completed independently, students should first complete the Familiarization Exercise for *HOW* (pages 3–10). Then they should use the information presented in *HOW 13* to complete the worksheets. The worksheets are perforated so that students may remove them from the workbook and turn them in to the Instructor.

Class sets for distribution of the key may be made from printouts of the files on the *Instructor's Resource CD* or its online version, should the instructor wish to do so. For students completing the worksheets independently, the keys may also be made available online through a course management system or postings on an instructor's Web site.

If *Workbook for HOW 13* is to be used as a regular classroom learning activity, the Word projection files on the *Instructor's Resource CD* may be used to present the major principles before the corresponding worksheets are completed. These files may be accessed in Word and projected on a screen through a data projector. If a computer and a data projector are unavailable, the Word projection files may also be printed and used as masters to create transparencies for use with an overhead projector.

Regardless of the instructional method employed, the practice materials contained in *Workbook for HOW 13* will reinforce the knowledge and skills needed to prepare business documents.

Assessments are contained on the *Instructor's Resource CD* that may be used to measure student learning outcomes for the punctuation, capitalization, number-usage, and document formatting principles reinforced in *Workbook for HOW 13*. Six assessments have been designed to evaluate students' ability to integrate language applications with the preparation of business letters and memorandums. Each of the assessments contains two documents, either (1) a memorandum and a letter or (2) two letters.

We invite you to contact us directly if you have any questions or comments about *HOW 13* or any of its ancillary materials.

James and Lyn Clark
E-mail: lynclarkpc@hotmail.com
(818) 701-9770
(818) 772-8108 (fax)

Part 1

Name_____ Date _____

Familiarization Exercise for *HOW*

Instructions: Use *HOW* to locate the correct answers to the following items. Place the letter or letters corresponding to the correct answer in the answer column provided. Indicate in the second column the number of the section (or page number when a section number is not given) where you found your answer.

To locate information, turn first to the Contents page and locate the chapter in which the information is contained. Use the tabs printed on the side of the pages to reach the beginning of the chapter where you will find the Solution Finder. This alphabetical listing of chapter topics shows the section number in which the corresponding information is located. Use the page header guides to turn to the section number you need. You may also use the comprehensive Index at the back of the book to locate information.

	Answer	*Section*

1. If you wished to know the correct format for a dash in word processing copy, which chapter of *HOW* would you consult?

   a. Grammar and Usage
   b. Punctuation
   c. Hyphenating and Dividing Words
   d. Abbreviations and Symbols   _____ _____

2. If you were writing an e-mail message and needed to know whether to use *as* or *like* in a sentence, which chapter of *HOW* would you consult?

   a. E-Mail Messages, Business Letters, and Memorandums
   b. Grammar and Usage
   c. Elements of Writing Style
   d. Spelling, Proofreading, and Editing   _____ _____

3. If you wanted to know the two-letter postal abbreviation for Wyoming, which chapter would you consult?

   a. Grammar and Usage
   b. Capitalization
   c. Abbreviations, Acronyms, and Symbols
   d. Address Format and Forms of Address   _____ _____

4. If you wanted to know how to address a letter to the mayor of your city, which chapter would you consult?

   a. Capitalization
   b. E-Mail Messages, Business Letters, and Memorandums
   c. Address Format and Forms of Address
   d. Elements of Writing Style   _____ _____

5. If you wished to know how to locate information on the Internet, which chapter would you consult?

   a. Manual and Electronic File Management
   b. E-Mail Messages, Business Letters, and Memorandums
   c. The Internet and Its Resources
   d. Address Format and Forms of Address   _____ _____

6. If you wanted to obtain information on how to prepare an itinerary, which chapter of *HOW* would you consult?

   a. Employment Application Documents
   b. E-Mail Messages, Business Letters, and Memorandums
   c. Reports and Other Business Documents
   d. Elements of Writing Style

   _____ _____

7. If you wished to know how to deemphasize an idea in a written document, which chapter of *HOW* would you consult?

   a. Elements of Writing Style
   b. Grammar and Usage
   c. Proofreading and Editing
   d. E-Mail Messages, Business Letters, and Memorandums

   _____ _____

8. If you wanted to know whether the word in an e-mail message should be spelled *affect* or *effect*, which chapter of *HOW* would you consult?

   a. Grammar and Usage
   b. E-Mail Messages, Business Letters, and Memorandums
   c. Proofreading and Editing
   d. Words Often Confused and Misused

   _____ _____

9. If you were interested in learning how to format listings in various business documents, which chapter of *HOW* would you consult?

   a. Hyphenating and Dividing Words
   b. Employment Application Documents
   c. Reports and Other Business Documents
   d. E-Mail Messages, Business Letters, and Memorandums

   _____ _____

10. If you were in search of procedures to check your keyboarded documents to ensure that they matched an original copy, which chapter of *HOW* would you consult?

    a. Elements of Writing Style
    b. Grammar and Usage
    c. Manual and Electronic File Management
    d. Spelling, Proofreading, and Editing

    _____ _____

11. Which one of the following sentences has the correct ending punctuation mark?

    a. Will you please send us your check by the end of the month?
    b. Will you please send us your check by the end of the month.

    _____ _____

12. Business organizations and divisions are usually divided into departments. How would you handle the capitalization of department names? Indicate which of the following sentences is/are correct. Select all correct answers.

    a. Our department of human resources hired three new accountants.
    b. Our Division is planning to enlarge its facilities.
    c. We will forward the forms to the Research Department next week.
    d. When can we expect to receive the reports from the Accounting Department?

    _____ _____

4

13. Related numbers are written in the same format. According to *HOW*, which of the following sentences has/have been expressed correctly? Select all correct answers.

    a. Our 4 salespersons sold 32 houses this week.
    b. We will be able to fill your order for 26 chairs, 9 dining tables, and 4 sofas.
    c. Of the 12 entrees listed, only four were priced under $10.
    d. Last year our subscribers increased from 2 million to 2,800,000.

    _____ _____

14. Some compound numbers are always hyphenated; others are not. Locate the correct rule in *HOW*. Then indicate which of the following numbers is/are expressed correctly. Select all correct answers.

    a. twenty seven
    b. one hundred nineteen
    c. eighty-three
    d. two hundred fifty-seven
    e. one-hundred forty-three

    _____ _____

15. Pronouns are used in the subjective case under certain circumstances. Select all the correct circumstances from the ones described below.

    a. As the complement of a *being* verb
    b. Following a preposition
    c. As the subject of a sentence
    d. After *to be* when this infinitive does not have a subject
    e. As the subject of any infinitive other than *to be*

    _____ _____

16. In comparing adjectives, which of the following sentences is/are written correctly? Select all correct answers.

    a. John writes letters more better than I.
    b. This men's suit line is the most handsome one I have seen this season.
    c. Our reception area is more cheery since it has been redecorated.
    d. The hard disk on your computer is more nearly full than the one on mine.

    _____ _____

17. Which of the following geographical locations is/are capitalized correctly? Select all correct answers.

    a. Our next flight to New York City will leave at 10:05 a.m.
    b. We took float trips down the Colorado and Snake rivers.
    c. Last year the State of Colorado initiated new election procedures.
    d. Most of our new business has come from the South.

    _____ _____

18. Select the correct format for capitalizing and expressing the name of the following book.

    a. *HOW: A Handbook For Office Professionals*
    b. HOW: A Handbook for Office Professionals
    c. How: a Handbook for Office Professionals
    d. HOW: A Handbook for Office Professionals
    e. *HOW: A Handbook for Office Professionals*
    f. HOW: A HANDBOOK FOR OFFICE PROFESSIONALS

    _____ _____

19. Which **one** of the following sentences shows a short direct quotation punctuated correctly?

    a. "All overtime hours have been canceled", said Mr. Stevens.
    b. "All overtime hours have been canceled" said Mr. Stevens.
    c. "All overtime hours have been canceled," said Mr. Stevens.
    d. "All overtime hours have been canceled;" said Mr. Stevens.

    _____ _____

Familiarization Exercise for *HOW*

20. Which **one** of the following sentences shows a parenthetical expression punctuated correctly?

    a. You may in addition, order these products from our Web site.
    b. You may, in addition, order these products from our Web site.
    c. You may in addition order these products from our Web site.
    d. You may in addition; order these products from our Web site.

    _____ _____

21. Which of the following salutations would be correct according to *HOW* if you were asked to address a letter to R. Lewis?

    a. Dear Mr. Lewis   c. Dear Mrs. Lewis
    b. Dear R. Lewis   d. Dear Ms. Lewis

    _____ _____

22. According to the rules for forming noun plurals, which of the following words is/are spelled correctly? Select all correct choices.

    a. attornies   d. monkies
    b. notaries   e. companys
    c. valleys   f. secretarys

    _____ _____

23. Which of the following uses of *among* and *between* is/are correct? Select all correct choices.

    a. Please distribute these supplies among the two departments.
    b. This information should remain between the three of us.
    c. Place the lamp between the two tables.
    d. The client's invoice was found among the legal documents.

    _____ _____

24. Locate in *HOW* the correct two-letter postal abbreviation for the state of Massachusetts. Which **one** of the following answers is correct?

    a. MA   c. MC
    b. MS   d. MT

    _____ _____

25. Specific rules govern subject-verb agreement for sentences beginning with *There* and subjects indicating portions. Locate this section in *HOW*. From this section determine which of the following sentences is/are expressed correctly. Select all correct choices.

    a. There is three people in the lobby waiting to see Dr. Lyons.
    b. Almost one half of the packages has been shipped.
    c. There is only one other explanation for the error in this customer's statement.
    d. Some of the contracts were destroyed in the fire.

    _____ _____

26. Which of the following statements is/are true about e-mail messages? Select all correct answers.

    a. E-mail messages may be used to replace all business letters and memorandums as long as the recipient has an e-mail address.
    b. E-mail messages are secure and protected from network hackers as they make their way through the Internet.
    c. E-mail messages are sent through both organizational networks and the Internet.
    d. Creating and sending e-mail messages through the Internet is more convenient and economical than using conventional mailing methods.

    _____ _____

27. Which one of the following dates is expressed correctly?

    a. Please send us your check by March 22nd.
    b. We need your check by the 22 of March.
    c. The audit was conducted on March 22nd, 2010.
    d. May we have your reply by March 22.

    _____ _____

28. In the modified block letter style, the date may be placed in all the following positions except one. Use *HOW* to determine which one of the positions listed below is **incorrect**.

    a. Aligned with the right margin
    b. Centered
    c. Begun at the center of the page
    d. Begun at the left margin

    _____ _____

29. Which of the following statements is/are true about dividing words at the end of a line? Select all correct choices.

    a. The last words appearing in two consecutive lines in the middle of a paragraph may never be divided.
    b. The last word of a paragraph may never be divided.
    c. The last word appearing on a page may never be divided.
    d. The last word in the first line of a paragraph may never be divided.

    _____ _____

30. Sometimes professional titles are capitalized; other times they are not. Which of the following sentences is/are written correctly? Select all correct choices.

    a. May I please have an appointment to see the President of your company?
    b. Please ask Professor Ripley to call me.
    c. Sally Abramowitz, the President of Allied Enterprises, attended the conference.
    d. Yes, we did receive a response from the vice president of the United States.

    _____ _____

31. Which of the following uses of *principal* and *principle* is/are correct? Select all correct choices.

    a. The principle of our school resigned yesterday.
    b. You must reinvest this principal within 90 days.
    c. Please take time to review these accounting principals.
    d. My principle concern is that we retain the same high quality in our products.

    _____ _____

32. Sometimes words appearing with numbers or letters are capitalized; other times they are not. Which of the following sentences is/are written correctly? Select all correct choices.

    a. The insured, Jeremy Sanders, policy 381294, sent his premium payment on October 11.
    b. Ask Ms. Mann to delete line 5 from the first paragraph.
    c. Our committee is scheduled to meet in Room 52 at 1:30 p.m.
    d. The table is located on Page 4.

    _____ _____

Familiarization Exercise for *HOW*

33. Which one of the following dates is punctuated correctly?

    a. By August 15, we must complete our inventory.
    b. By August 15, 2011 we must complete our inventory.
    c. By Tuesday August 15, 2011, we must complete our inventory.
    d. By Tuesday, August 15, 2011, we must complete our inventory.

    _____ _____

34. Sometimes compound adjectives are hyphenated; other times they are not. From the information contained in *HOW*, indicate which of the following sentences is/are correct. Select all correct choices.

    a. Your thoroughly-documented report has been read by the research staff.
    b. Because your records are up-to-date, we have been able to contact members who have not paid this year's annual dues.
    c. Use 4- by 6-inch cards for this invitation.
    d. Only three high-school students applied for the scholarship.

    _____ _____

35. Which of the following statements is/are true about the format of an attention line in a letter? Select all correct choices.

    a. The attention line may be typed after the salutation.
    b. The attention line may be included in the inside address.
    c. The attention line must always be underlined.
    d. The word *attention* may or may not be followed by a colon.

    _____ _____

36. In indexing names to be filed in alphabetical order, which of the following statements is/are true? Select all correct choices.

    a. Hyphenated last names are considered as separate filing units.
    b. Suffixes and titles are not used as filing units unless they are needed to distinguish between or among identical names.
    c. Two-word first names are considered as a single filing unit.
    d. Middle initials are not considered filing units.

    _____ _____

37. What are the dimensions of a No. 10 envelope?

    a. 6.5 inches by 3.63 inches
    b. 9.5 inches by 4.13 inches
    c. 7.5 inches by 3.88 inches
    d. 5.94 inches by 4.63 inches

    _____ _____

38. Which of the following Internet search sites is considered to be the most popular one on the Web?

    a. Google
    b. Yahoo!
    c. Bing
    d. Ask

    _____ _____

39. If you were to write the governor of your state, which form of address would you use for the salutation?

    a. Dear Mr. Harris:
    b. Dear Governor:
    c. Esteemed Honorable Sir:
    d. Dear Governor Harris:
    e. Dear Excellency:

    _____ _____

40. Which of the following statements is/are true about placing delivery notations in a business letter? Select all correct choices.

    a. Delivery notations always appear in all capital letters.
    b. Delivery notations may appear in a combination of uppercase and lowercase letters *or* in all capital letters.
    c. Delivery notations may appear a double space below the date.
    d. Delivery notations may appear a double space above the inside address.
    e. Delivery notations may appear directly below the copy notation.

    _____ _____

41. Most verbs form their parts in a regular way (*ask, asked, asked*), but others do not follow the regular pattern. From the information contained in *HOW*, indicate which of the following combinations is/are correct. Select all correct choices.

    a. go   went   gone
    b. catch   catched   catched
    c. pay   payed   payed
    d. do   done   done
    e. throw   threw   thrown

    _____ _____

42. Which of the following sentences is/are expressed correctly in the capitalization of academic subjects, courses, or degrees? Select all correct choices.

    a. Will you enroll in History 12 next semester?
    b. I plan to take a course in Mathematical Analysis.
    c. When will you earn your Associate in Arts degree?
    d. What grade did you earn in your conversational Spanish class?

    _____ _____

43. Select the listing below that contains the information included in second-page headings for business letters and memorandums.

    a. Complete address of addressee
    b. Page number only, centered
    c. Name of addressee, name of sender, page number
    d. Name of addressee, page number, date

    _____ _____

44. Which of the following amounts of money is/are expressed correctly? Select all correct choices.

    a. We received invoices for $101.87, $395.00, and $62.50 today.
    b. The postage for your two mailings was 87 cents and $1.73.
    c. Has the wholesale price of your pens increased from 89 cents to 99 cents?
    d. The construction costs for this building were $3,000,000.

    _____ _____

45. Which of the following statements is/are correct about using the dictionary to locate the proper spelling of words. Select all correct choices.

    a. When the dictionary offers two spellings for a word in the same entry, use the first spelling.
    b. When the dictionary shows compound words spelled as one word and two words in different entries, use the spelling for the first entry.
    c. The spellings of irregular plural nouns appear in the dictionary directly after the root word in the entry.
    d. The spellings of all verb forms appear in the dictionary directly after the root word in the entry.

    _____ _____

Familiarization Exercise for *HOW*

46. Which of the following movie titles is/are expressed correctly? Select all correct choices.

    a. Next week "Father of the Bride" will be shown on television.
    b. Next week <u>Father of the Bride</u> will be shown on television.
    c. Next week FATHER OF THE BRIDE will be shown on television.
    d. Next week *Father of the Bride* will be shown on television.

    _____ _____

47. According to the general rules for expressing numbers, which of the following statements is/are true? Select all correct choices.

    a. Numbers *ten* and below are usually written in word form; numbers above *ten* are usually written in figure form.
    b. Approximations above *ten* are always written in figures.
    c. Numbers above *ten* may not be used to begin a sentence.
    d. Round numbers in the millions or billions are usually expressed in a combination of figures and words.

    _____ _____

48. Which **one** of the following compound sentences containing a transitional expression is punctuated correctly?

    a. All our sales representatives are attending a sales meeting in Chicago, therefore, no one will be available to call on your company until next week.
    b. All our sales representatives are attending a sales meeting in Chicago, therefore no one will be available to call on your company until next week.
    c. All our sales representatives are attending a sales meeting in Chicago; therefore no one will be available to call on your company until next week.
    d. All our sales representatives are attending a sales meeting in Chicago; therefore, no one will be available to call on your company until next week.

    _____ _____

49. Which of the following statements is/are **not true** about forming possessives? Select all correct choices.

    a. Nouns not ending with a pronounced *s* form the possessive by adding *'s*.
    b. All nouns may show possession.
    c. When two or more persons own a single item, show possession only on the last person.
    d. Ownership on compound nouns is shown on the main word, e.g., *sister's-in-law car*.

    _____ _____

50. Which of the following uses of *lose* and *loose* are correct? Select all correct choices.

    a. Did you loose any money in the stock market this year?
    b. The latch on the back door is too loose.
    c. When did you lose your watch?
    d. This lose screw must be tightened.

    _____ _____

Check your answers with those given on pages 341–342 before continuing with the exercises in this workbook.

Familiarization Exercise for *HOW*

Part 2

Name _____ Date _____

Section 1 Grammar and Usage

Grammar Overview (1-1)

Practice Guide 1

Instructions: In the blank at the right, write the part of speech the <u>underscored</u> word represents: noun, verb, adjective, adverb, pronoun, conjunction, preposition, or interjection.

1. The medical <u>building</u> is located on Ventura Boulevard.   1. _____

2. How many miles do you <u>drive</u> daily to and from the office?   2. _____

3. Have <u>you</u> submitted your monthly expense report?   3. _____

4. Leslie <u>and</u> Sean have volunteered to work overtime.   4. _____

5. Our <u>new</u> shipment of video games will arrive on Monday.   5. _____

6. <u>Oops</u>, I should have checked these records more carefully!   6. _____

7. Kevin has worked <u>steadily</u> on this project for three months.   7. _____

8. <u>Through</u> your efforts we were able to obtain the contract.   8. _____

9. We <u>submitted</u> your petition to the court yesterday.   9. _____

10. Our sales representatives will receive new <u>laptops</u> next month.   10. _____

11. Please let <u>me</u> know your appointment schedule for next week.   11. _____

12. Jared <u>or</u> Tony can give you the information you need.   12. _____

13. Which one of our representatives calls on this client <u>regularly</u>?   13. _____

14. Most <u>of</u> our employees have signed up for stock options.   14. _____

15. These <u>discount</u> prices will be in effect only until June 30.   15. _____

16. <u>No</u>, our company was not involved with this building contract!   16. _____

17. We ordered the book last month, <u>but</u> we have not yet received it.   17. _____

18. How many <u>scholarships</u> were awarded to students this year?   18. _____

19. Almost 40 people <u>attended</u> our last investment seminar.   19. _____

20. Please check thoroughly <u>into</u> this customer's complaint.   20. _____

21. All the figurines in this cabinet should be cleaned <u>carefully</u>.   21. _____

22. His <u>latest</u> novel will be available for purchase by July 1.   22. _____

23. Only <u>she</u> can provide you with the information you need.   23. _____

24. <u>The</u> property in which you were interested was sold yesterday.   24. _____

25. Your <u>consideration</u> of others' feelings is certainly apparent.   25. _____

Check your answers with those given on page 343 before completing the next exercise.

Name _____ Date _____

Practice Guide 2 (1-2)

Instructions: In the following sentences, first <u><u>double underline</u></u> the verb or verb phrase and then <u>underline</u> the simple or compound subject.

Helpful Hint: Place the sentence in subject-verb order. Begin by identifying the verb or verb phrase. Then ask "Who?" or "What?" and answer one of these questions by supplying the verb or verb phrase.

Example: Many of our <u>employees</u> in Dallas <u><u>have agreed</u></u> to move to our new facility in Fort Worth.

Identify the verb phrase <u><u>have agreed</u></u>, and then ask "Who?" or "What?" have agreed? <u>Employees</u> have agreed….

1. The committee has met several times this week.

2. Hamburgers and french fries are served daily from 6 a.m. until 12 midnight in this McDonald's location.

3. The yellow copy paper in the supply room has been placed on the wrong shelf.

4. The new laptop for our department from Toshiba was damaged during transit.

5. Either the office manager or her assistant should have this information on her computer.

6. Our son-in-law will take an active part in the business.

7. How many gallons of water should I place in the tank?

8. The carload of fresh oranges will be delivered tomorrow morning.

9. Brad and Melissa have moved their offices to the new building.

10. Please answer these e-mail inquiries this afternoon.

11. Our agency is proud of its reputation for excellent service and dependability.

12. Three members of the Board of Directors agreed to support our proposal.

13. E-mail me the meeting agenda as soon as possible.

14. This information should be kept confidential between you and me.

15. Our new clothing line was designed by one of Mr. Simonian's students.

16. The agent sent separate contracts to Mark and me.

17. How did you respond to his question?

18. Please audit these accounts before March 1.

19. In my estimation, Ms. Garcia is the best-qualified person for the position.

20. You certainly have made great progress during the past month.

21. Your understanding of our new medical plan benefits is different from mine.

22. The architect and the builder did not fulfill their contracts.

23. Were you angry with John for not approving your budget request?

24. During the past year, our sales and profits have declined steadily.

25 Our new breakfast and lunch menus have attracted more dining customers.

Check your answers with those given on page 343.

Name _____ Date _____

Noun Plurals (1-4)

Practice Guide 3

Instructions: Write the plural form for each noun below in the blank provided at the right of each item.

1. policy _____

2. church _____

3. radio _____

4. life _____

5. Montgomery _____

6. tomato _____

7. curriculum _____

8. statistics _____

9. mumps _____

10. brigadier general _____

11. yes and no _____

12. cupful _____

13. bookshelf _____

14. brother-in-law _____

15. basis _____

16. pants _____

17. 9 _____

18. roof _____

19. attorney _____

20. waltz _____

21. alto _____

22. cargo _____

23. this and that _____

24. monkey _____

25. analysis _____

Check your answers with those given on page 344 before completing the next exercise.

Name _____ Date _____

Practice Guide 4 (1-4)

Instructions: Write the plural form for each noun given below. Use the blank at the right of each item.

1. alumnus _____

2. per diem _____

3. county _____

4. box _____

5. Koltz _____

6. A _____

7. parenthesis _____

8. lessee _____

9. father figure _____

10. father-in-law _____

11. valley _____

12. RN _____

13. Ms. Ross _____

14. datum _____

15. Mickey Mouse _____

16. going-over _____

17. t _____

18. jockey _____

19. Japanese _____

20. Mr. Ramirez _____

21. embargo _____

22. yourself _____

23. chassis _____

24. half _____

25. German _____

Check your answers with those given on page 344 before completing the next exercise

Name _____ Date _____

Practice Guide 5 (1-4)

Instructions: In the following sentences, underline any errors in the use of noun plurals. Write the correct form in the blank at the right. If a sentence is correct, write *OK* in the blank line.

1. Road-surfacing repairs are scheduled to begin in the San Fernando and San Gabriel Vallies on July 1.

1. _____

2. Have the cargos been loaded on all the ships scheduled to sail today?

2. _____

3. Did you find both halfs of the torn $100 bill?

3. _____

4. Which pest-control company did you call to rid our warehouse of the mouses?

4. _____

5. We have yet to receive bill of ladings for any of these shipments.

5. _____

6. We no longer accept trade-ins on any computer purchases.

6. _____

7. Please write your 7's more legibly.

7. _____

8. Several financial crisis forced the company into bankruptcy.

8. _____

9. Do not accept IOU's instead of cash, check, or credit card payments.

9. _____

10. Disregard any of the information contained in parenthesis.

10. _____

11. What percent of incoming freshman this semester have qualified to enroll in English Composition?

11. _____

12. Please ensure that all new employees complete W-4's.

12. _____

13. The two companys have yet to agree on the terms of the merger.

13. _____

14. We issue annually new picture ID's to all our employees.

14. _____

15. The Hillarys have purchased the home we had listed on Elm Street.

15. _____

16. The mosquitos in this beautiful meadow prohibit our using it for weddings and other outdoor events.

16. _____

17. There are too many zeroes in this number for it to be correct.

17. _____

18. Yesterday the city council members unanimously voted themselfs pay increases.

18. _____

19. Several alumnuses have made large contributions to the college scholarship fund.

19. _____

20. Our economicses courses are offered in the College of Business.

20. _____

Check your answers with those given on page 344 before completing the next exercise

Name _____ Date _____

Practice Guide 6 (1-4)

Instructions: Based on the context of the following letter, first underline all nouns that should be written in plural form. Then write the correct spellings in the blank lines given at the right. The same plural may appear more than once.

Dear Mr. Johnson:

According to our staff of analyst, there are several basis on which your tax were determined. Several analysis from three of our staff member are enclosed.

As your tax accountant, I advise you to appeal individually the assessed valuation of two property; the other seven property appear to have been assessed correctly. If our firm can assist you with these proceeding, please call one of our attorney to set up an appointment within the next two week.

To protest the two assessment, we will need to collect sufficient datum to show the value of other duplex in the area. Both attorney who specialize in this area would be able to help us. One of the major criterion will be the average price of comparable real estate sale during the past six month. Another factor will be the assessed valuation of other such property in both the Brea and Simi Valley. Survey of three or four real estate agency should provide the appropriate information to assist us with these two case.

We believe that we can have the assessment on both these duplex lowered considerably to reduce your tax.

Sincerely yours,

1. _____
2. _____
3. _____
4. _____
5. _____
6. _____
7. _____
8. _____
9. _____
10. _____
11. _____
12. _____
13. _____
14. _____
15. _____
16. _____
17. _____
18. _____
19. _____
20. _____
21. _____
22. _____
23. _____
24. _____
25. _____

*The answers to this exercise appear in the **Instructor's Manual and Key** for **HOW 13: A Handbook for Office Professionals,** 13th edition.*

Noun Plurals

Name _____ Date _____

Noun Possessives (1-5)

Practice Guide 7

Instructions: So that each of the following sentences is expressed correctly, write in the blank at the right the proper form of the word(s) shown in parentheses.

1. Our (son-in-law) successful business is conducted solely through the Internet.

1. _____

2. This store carries quality (child) clothing at reasonable prices.

2. _____

3. (Everyone else) paycheck had been received on time.

3. _____

4. Yesterday our receptionist gave the doctor a (week) notice.

4. _____

5. Two members of the (personnel manager) association agreed to speak to our class.

5. _____

6. The (Ross) and (López) mountain cabin was not damaged during the recent severe snowstorm.

6. _____

7. The (girl) softball team will participate in the championship playoffs.

7. _____

8. The file you requested is kept in (Mr. Beaty) office.

8. _____

9. (Dora) and (Phil) offices are located in Suite 454.

9. _____

10. This (company) stock has declined sharply during the past six months.

10. _____

11. The store manager moved (lady) apparel from the second floor to the third floor.

11. _____

12. You are still responsible for paying four (month) interest on this loan.

12. _____

13. (Mary) receiving this scholarship was no surprise to me.

13. _____

14. (Mrs. Jones) petition has been submitted to the court.

14. _____

15. The (chief of police) answer did not satisfy the press.

15. _____

16. (Alumnus) children receive preferential consideration for admission to our college.

16. _____

17. (ITT) investment in new equipment this year amounted to $18 million.

17. _____

18. The (lease) expiration date is July 31.

18. _____

19. You may purchase both (man) and (boy) clothing at this Web site.

19. _____

20. (Martha) and (Don) house was sold yesterday.

20. _____

Check your answers with those given on page 344 before completing the next exercise.

Practice Guide 8 (1-5)

Instructions: In the following sentences, underline any errors in the use of noun possessives. Write the correct form in the blank at the right. If a sentence is correct, write *OK* in the blank.

1. All womens' wearing apparel has been moved to the first floor.   1. _____

2. This computer's CD/RW drive needs to be replaced.   2. _____

3. Jesse's and Sue's e-mail address is JSMcCune2006@yahoo.com.   3. _____

4. During the past year, our companys profits increased 17 percent.   4. _____

5. If the tenant does not pay his rent by July 15, give him a 30 days' notice to move.   5. _____

6. Our new office is scarcely a stones throw from the old one.   6. _____

7. Bob hesitating to accept our offer leads me to believe he may be negotiating with other firms.   7. _____

8. All these students term papers have been graded.   8. _____

9. What percent of this company stock is your brother-in-laws?   9. _____

10. Be sure to send Ms. Walsh commission checks to her new address.   10. _____

11. Adams and Barbaras offices are located on the second floor.   11. _____

12. All our fire stations are ready to respond on a moments notice.   12. _____

13. We spent the entire afternoon at our attorneys giving depositions.   13. _____

14. Mr. Stevens appointment with Dr. Rose has been scheduled for Tuesday, June 2, at 2 p.m.   14. _____

15. Both your companys and our companys downsizing has caused major unemployment in our community.   15. _____

16. Who witnessed Mr. Smith's signing the contract?   16. _____

17. Most of the editor in chief suggestions related to the design of the book.   17. _____

18. Because of manufacturing difficulties, we are experiencing a weeks delay in shipping all orders.   18. _____

19. Only three of our regional managers' have submitted their reports.   19. _____

20. Already six of these truck's engines have been rebuilt.   20. _____

Check your answers with those given on page 345 before completing the next exercise.

Name _____ Date _____

Practice Guide 9 (1-5)

Instructions: Based on the context of the following letter, first underline all the nouns that should be written in the possessive form. Then write the correct spelling of each in the blank lines at the right.

Dear Ms. Hoffman:

Because of your companys outstanding payment record, we are extending an invitation to you to increase your credit limit. This months charges on your account reached $5,600, $600 beyond your present limit. If you wish to extend your credit line to $7,500, all we need is your Purchasing Departments approval and Mrs. Kellys signature on the enclosed application.

Next month we will be distributing our holiday sales catalog. This seasons merchandise is even more exciting than last seasons. You will see by your salespeoples enthusiasm that we have the best product line in our history. Childrens toys are more advanced than ever before with electronic game toys promising to be best sellers. Also, for this year the number of items in boys and girls apparel has nearly doubled.

By distributing our catalog early in August, we hope to get a two months head start on the season. With everyones cooperation we can have record-breaking sales this year. Our managers new shipping program can have any of the catalog merchandise at your door with only five working days notice.

To encourage buyers early orders, we are offering a 25 percent discount on all babys clothing and furniture ordered during September. Similar discounts are being offered on mens clothing and ladys lingerie. Take advantage of Septembers savings; place your order when the holiday catalog arrives. Turn todays savings into future profits.

1. _____

2. _____

3. _____

4. _____

5. _____

6. _____

7. _____

8. _____

9. _____

10. _____

11. _____

12. _____

13. _____

14. _____

15. _____

16. _____

17. _____

18. _____

19. _____

20. _____

Sincerely,

*The answers to this exercise appear in the **Instructor's Manual and Key** for **HOW 13: A Handbook for Office Professionals,** 13th edition.*

Name _____ Date _____

Verbs (1-6 Through 1-14)

Practice Guide 10

Instructions: In the following sentences, underline any errors in the use of verb parts or tenses. Write the correct form in the blank at the right. If a sentence is correct, write *OK* in the blank.

1. The client payed his outstanding balance yesterday.

1. _____

2. Joleen has called all the patients to remind them of their appointments tomorrow.

2. _____

3. As soon as we receive your payment, we are shipping your order.

3. _____

4. Dr. Warner also teachs courses at a nearby college.

4. _____

5. We received your revised order after we already shipped your original one.

5. _____

6. If home sales continue at the same rate, we will have sold all the homes in this construction phase even before ground is broken.

6. _____

7. Sales in the Northern Region increased steadily since we opened our new office in Billings.

7. _____

8. This baggage claim area has laid idle for the past 24 hours.

8. _____

9. More and more, small companies are useing accounting software to prepare their financial records.

9. _____

10. Neither applicant has yet submitted his résumé.

10. _____

11. During the past year, our sales in this state have growed from $1.2 million to $1.8 million.

11. _____

12. Do you know when the city council will chose a new chief of police?

12. _____

13. Our spring sale has begun on March 18 and will continue until March 31.

13. _____

14. During the past few months, representatives from both sides have lain the groundwork for the new labor contract.

14. _____

15. Last week the decorator hanged draperies in all the model homes.

15. _____

16. Our credit union loans money to its members at lower interest rates than those offered by other sources.

16. _____

17. We cannot afford to loose any more of our present market share.

17. _____

18. I have spoke personally to several of our employees about applying for the management opening.

18. _____

19. Do not leave any papers or litter laying around in the conference room after the meeting.

19. _____

20. Has anyone verifyed the accuracy of these figures?

20. _____

Check your answers with those given on page 345 before completing the next exercise.

Name _____ Date _____

Practice Guide 11 (1-6 Through 1-14)

Instructions: In the following sentences, underline any errors in subject-verb agreement. Write the correct form in the blank at the right. If a sentence is correct, write *OK* in the blank line.

1. Pork and beans are a favorite side dish among our customers.

1. _____

2. Our supply of blank CD/RW discs are rapidly diminishing.

2. _____

3. Every student, instructor, and administrator is expected to evacuate the building when the fire alarm sounds.

3. _____

4. The administrative staff and the president is planning to attend the board meeting this afternoon.

4. _____

5. Someone in our Human Resources Department need to resolve this issue.

5. _____

6. A check for the first night's stay or a credit card number are all you need to hold this reservation.

6. _____

7. Most of the salespersons in our Portland office has been with the company more than five years.

7. _____

8. I believe either you or Alex has won the sales contest.

8. _____

9. There is at least four candidates on this list whom we should interview for the opening in our Payroll Department.

9. _____

10. The committee were arguing continually during the meeting about which accounting software to purchase.

10. _____

11. The number of worldwide text messages sent daily are rising rapidly.

11. _____

12. If I was you, I would certainly take advantage of this promotional opportunity.

12. _____

13. Nearly 60 percent of the students enrolled in our college needs to take a computer literacy course.

13. _____

14. The secretary-treasurer of our small company approve all purchases over $1,000.

14. _____

15. Everything in these boxes need to be placed on the shelves by the opening of the store tomorrow morning.

15. _____

16. Whenever our supervisor leaves the office, Danielle acts as if she were in charge.

16. _____

17. Each of the applicants have been notified that additional scholarships are available through the grant program.

17. _____

18. A detailed description of possible side effects are included with each filled prescription.

18. _____

19. Neither of them have submitted a request to transfer to our new office in St. Paul.

19. _____

20. An unusually large number of stockholders has requested extra copies of our annual report.

20. _____

Check your answers with those given on page 345 before completing the next exercise.

Name _____   Date _____

Practice Guide 12 (1-6 Through 1-14)

Instructions: If the verb in the following sentences is used correctly, write *OK* in the blank line to the right of the sentence. If the verb is used incorrectly, underline the error and write the correct form in the blank line.

1. Have you wrote e-mail messages congratulating the two new agents on their sales for the first quarter?

1. _____

2. The tract of these new homes were laid out to attract buyers with growing families.

2. _____

3. Our client has already spoke to an agent in your firm.

3. _____

4. The patient asked if he could lay down on the cot.

4. _____

5. Has the criteria been ranked in the order of their importance?

5. _____

6. There is several alternatives you may wish to consider.

6. _____

7. Neither of them wish to postpone his vacation until August.

7. _____

8. One fourth of the crystal glasses in this shipment were broken.

8. _____

9. Dr. Sanders is one of those doctors who knows a great deal about law.

9. _____

10. Our stock of felt-tip pens have disappeared from the supply cabinet.

10. _____

11. He had forgot about his doctor's appointment until his assistant reminded him.

11. _____

12. Until yesterday the sign-in book had laid on top of the reception area counter.

12. _____

13. All the water in the coolers on the second and third floors have been drunk.

13. _____

14. Between the two bookcases was a locked cabinet.

14. _____

15. Neither you nor the other accountant have been absent once this past year.

15. _____

16. Each sofa, chair, and table in the reception area of our hotel need to be replaced.

16. _____

17. The staff was arguing loudly about who was responsible for the $110,000 error in overpayment of commissions.

17. _____

18. One of the mothers have agreed to bring donuts for the class to celebrate the third-grade students' high scores on the English proficiency examination.

18. _____

19. All our bills for this month have already been payed.

19. _____

20. Either Michael or Ashley is to receive the commission for this sale.

20. _____

21. Have the Board of Directors approved this purchase?

21. _____

22. There is still a number of options we need to explore before we can institute a new loan-tracking system.

22. _____

23. Andrew has drove nearly 15,000 miles during the past three months calling on all the doctors in his territory.

23. _____

24. Either you or I am responsible for closing the store this week.

24. _____

25. The stock market has sank 107 points within the past two days.

25. _____

26. I e-mailed you this information after the 2013 financial information was compiled.

26. _____

27. Bob worked in our Research Department since 2005.

27. _____

28. Have the committee submitted their report?

28. _____

29. None of the antiques was damaged during the earthquake.

29. _____

30. By the opening of the fall semester, we will have installed the software updates to all our classroom computers.

30. _____

Check your answers with those given on pages 345–346 before completing the next exercise.

Name _____ Date _____

Practice Guide 13 (1-6 Through 1-14)

Instructions: As you read the following paragraphs, first underline all the verb forms that are used incorrectly. Then write the correct answers in the blanks at the right.

To: Mr. Anderson

In national medical journals, we have ran several ads describing our new disposable thermometers. Although the number of responses we have received to these ads have been great, the staff is in disagreement as to whether this advertising mode should be continued. One of the officers feel strongly that we have exhausted the market reached by the medical journals. She believes local distribution channels or direct mail advertising are more effective than national advertising.

Hospitals is the main users of our disposable thermometers. Our supply of these thermometers are almost depleted because one of the clerks in our main office had forgot to notify the factory to manufacture an additional supply. We have spoke to him about this matter, and he has took steps to prevent this error from occurring again. In the clerk's defense, however, we must consider that a large number of these disposable thermometers had laid in our warehouse for more than four months without our filling any orders from this supply. All the orders was filled directly from the factory.

Dr. Morgan is one of those doctors who has supported the use of disposable thermometers since their introduction. He believes that every doctor's office, medical clinic, and hospital need to use this kind of thermometer; it is more sanitary and economical than the conventional thermometer. Dr. Morgan has brung out this concept in a number of the speeches he has given at national

1. _____

2. _____

3. _____

4. _____

5. _____

6. _____

7. _____

8. _____

9. _____

10. _____

11. _____

12. _____

13. _____

14. _____

15. _____

medical conventions. We are fortunate to have the support of a

person who are so well-known in the profession.

16. _____

We are looking forward to this product becoming a top seller.

17. _____

Although advertising in medical journals has payed for itself, two

members of the staff prefers alternate methods of advertising.

18. _____

Neither of them, though, have yet offered specific advertising

19. _____

plans. When the media for future advertising has been selected,

we will let you know.

20. _____

*The answers to this exercise appear in the **Instructor's Manual and Key** for **HOW 13: A Handbook for Office Professionals,** 13th edition.*

Name _____ Date _____

Pronouns (1-15 Through 1-18)

Practice Guide 14

Part 1. Subjective- and objective-case pronouns. From the choices given in parentheses, select the correct pronoun form. Write your answer in the blank line at the right of each sentence.

1. (We, Us) students are planning a surprise party for Ms. Morinaka.   1. _____

2. Be sure to give a copy of the sales receipt to Ron or (I, me, myself).   2. _____

3. Speaking of Mr. Reynolds, that was (he, him) on the telephone.   3. _____

4. Mr. Ryan is more likely to receive the promotion than (I, me).   4. _____

5. I would not want to be (she, her) when our sales manager discovers the error.   5. _____

6. Dr. Boyer asked (we, us) nurses to work overtime during the epidemic.   6. _____

7. The person at the end of the hall could not have been (he, him).   7. _____

8. The receptionist mistook my brother to be (I, me).   8. _____

9. I would prefer to send the letter to Ms. Cook rather than (she, her).   9. _____

10. We, John and (I, me), plan to attend the convention.   10. _____

Check your answers with those given on page 346 before completing the following exercise.

Part 2. Subjective- and objective-case pronouns. If a pronoun is used correctly in the following sentences, write *OK* in the blank line. If a pronoun is used incorrectly, underline the error and write the correction in the blank line.

1. Between you and I, I believe this new microchip will revolutionize the industry.   1. _____

2. Did you say that the top salesperson was her?   2. _____

3. I was taken to be her at the company holiday party.   3. _____

4. The person who selected the equipment must have been him.   4. _____

5. Copies of the announcement were sent to us, Paul and myself.   5. _____

6. Dr. Rich asked Teri and I to reschedule his appointments for the remainder of the week.   6. _____

7. Ms. Allison knows as much about this contract as I.   7. _____

8. Three accountants—Bob, Arlene, and me—attended the convention in Chicago.   8. _____

9. If you were me, what decision would you have made?   9. _____

10. I would not want to be he under these circumstances.   10. _____

Check your answers with those given on page 346 before completing the following exercise.

Part 3. *Who* and *whom* pronouns. From the choices given in parentheses, select the correct form. Write your answer in the blank line at the right of each sentence.

1. Our company needs an engineer (who, whom) understands construction design.   1. _____

2. Do you know (who, whom) Mr. Reece selected as his assistant?   2. _____

3. We do not know (who, whom) the real estate agent could have been.   3. _____

4. John is a person (who, whom) I believe will perform well under pressure.   4. _____

5. (Whoever, Whomever) acts as chair of the committee will have an advantage.   5. _____

6. Elizabeth Jones is the person (who, whom) we believe will be elected.   6. _____

7. (Who, Whom) did Bryan recommend for the position?   7. _____

8. Ms. Hill is courteous to (whoever, whomever) enters the office.   8. _____

9. Please list the names of the staff members (who, whom) you think will participate in the contest.   9. _____

10. My supervisor, (who, whom) you met yesterday, has been promoted to general manager.   10. _____

11. (Whoever, Whomever) arrives at the hotel first should check on our reservations.   11. _____

12. Call me as soon as you learn (who, whom) has been awarded the contract.   12. _____

13. Mr. Dorman may have been the agent (who, whom) we contacted originally.   13. _____

14. I cannot imagine (who, whom) you thought him to be.   14. _____

15. I do not know (who, whom) the newest member of the board could be.   15. _____

Check your answers with those given on page 347 before completing the next exercise.

Name _____ Date _____

Practice Guide 15 (1-15 Through 1-18)

Instructions: In the following sentences, underline any errors in pronoun usage. Write the correct form in the blank at the right. If a sentence is correct, write *OK* in the blank line.

1. The judge assigned to the case could be her.
   1. _____

2. None of we stockholders were interested in purchasing additional shares.
   2. _____

3. Please ask all patients to check in with either Jessica or me.
   3. _____

4. Yes, two of our employees, Steve and her, have requested transfers to our Orange County office.
   4. _____

5. You may give a copy of this brochure to whomever requests one.
   5. _____

6. Greg is a person that always seems to have a complaint about any change in procedures.
   6. _____

7. On the telephone Cassidy is often thought to be me.
   7. _____

8. Between you and I, I believe the price of this stock will drop even lower.
   8. _____

9. When will the company issue it's next dividend to stockholders?
   9. _____

10. Several instructors asked Mark and me to help them create interactive Web sites for their classes.
    10. _____

11. Donna always takes longer lunch breaks than me.
    11. _____

12. The vice president has requested we managers to attend an emergency meeting tomorrow morning.
    12. _____

13. You may obtain this information from either one of our investment counselors, Ms. Wong or he.
    13. _____

14. Ms. Lloyd delivered the signed contracts to the attorney herself.
    14. _____

15. Only those applicants whom you believe would be willing to travel should be called for return interviews.
    15. _____

16. The company is giving new hires the same benefit package as we.
    16. _____

17. Be sure to ask all patients for there insurance cards.

17. _____

18. Only two of the applicants who we interviewed seemed qualified for the position.

18. _____

19. Alan Whitman, Melanie Lipman, and myself have been selected to serve on the interview committee.

19. _____

20. Andrea works for a company which deals exclusively with recycling preowned computers.

20. _____

Check your answers with those given on page 347 before completing the next exercise.

Practice Guide 16 (1-15 Through 1-18)

Instructions: In the following sentences, underline any errors in pronoun agreement. Write the correct form in the blank at the right. If a sentence is correct, write *OK* in the blank line.

1. Some members of the production team had not completed its assignments from our previous meeting.

   1. _____

2. Each of the council members involved in the fraud has been asked to submit their resignation.

   2. _____

3. Shari Thomas, who recently earned her master's in accounting, has applied for a position with Ernst & Young.

   3. _____

4. Please post signs asking everyone to clear their tray and dishes from the table before leaving the employee lunchroom.

   4. _____

5. Cameron is one of those computer enthusiasts who spend much of his free time browsing the Internet.

   5. _____

6. Because Andrea is chair of the editorial committee, please give your suggestions to them.

   6. _____

7. If somebody requests more information about our products, refer them to me.

   7. _____

8. Dylan Investment Company has already sent us copies of their annual report.

   8. _____

9. Only one of the bidding companies will guarantee their work beyond one year.

   9. _____

10. Speak-Eze Corporation plans to introduce their new voice-recognition software for home computer users next week.

    10. _____

11. Madison is one of those persons who are always willing to help others solve his or her problems.

    11. _____

12. Either Samantha or Emily will take her vacation the first week in June.

    12. _____

13. Toy sales, which are usually at its high during the holiday season, have dropped nearly 10 percent.

    13. _____

14. If anything is missing from this gem collection, please list them on this form.

    14. _____

15. Our president is one of those executives who believe in praising his employees for a job well done.

    15. _____

16. Since neither company guaranteed their work, the county refused to accept either bid.

    16. _____

17. Will everyone please return their car pool forms by May 15.

    17. _____

18. Anyone who has completed all their assignments may take the final examination early.

    18. _____

19. My assistants will be able to help you with this report, so please provide him and her with appropriate instructions.

19. _____

20. Neither Ms. Hastings nor Ms. Carson has read their e-mail messages today.

20. _____

Check your answers with those given on page 347 before completing the next exercise.

Pronouns

Name _____ Date _____

Practice Guide 17 (1-15 Through 1-18)

Instructions: Based on the context of the following letter, first underline all pronouns that are used incorrectly. Then write the correct pronouns in the blank lines.

To the Staff:

    During the next month, us nurses must renew our parking permits. Be sure to bring your permit to either Mr. Feinberg or myself before April 30. Mr. Feinberg is in the office longer hours than me, so perhaps you may find leaving your parking permit with him more convenient than leaving it with me. The person issuing the new parking permits will be him.

    All of us—you, the other nurses, and I—will be prohibited from parking in the visitors' parking lot. This restriction will be imposed because our chief administrator, Ms. Takagi, has received numerous complaints about the crowded condition of this lot. It was her who decided that this lot would be closed to all staff members, no matter whom the individual may be or what his or her position may entail. The hospital security staff has been instructed to issue tickets to whoever they find parked there.

    I realize that a number of the staff may be annoyed with Ms. Takagi's decision. Under these circumstances I would not want to be her. Between you and I, though, I believe that our chief administrator had no other alternative.

    Ms. Takagi has asked we employees to park in Lot C, which is located in our high-rise parking facility. An additional security guard, who Mr. Feinberg employed recently, will patrol this employee parking area during the evening hours. The new security officer, Joseph Davis, has asked Mr. Feinberg and I to inform you of his

1. _____

2. _____

3. _____

4. _____

5. _____

6. _____

7. _____

8. _____

9. _____

10. _____

11. _____

12. _____

13. _____

14. _____

15. _____

presence. He will be pleased to help whomever needs his

assistance with any parking problems. Joseph is a person whom I

believe will be an excellent addition to our hospital staff.

If you have any questions about the new parking regulations,

please be sure to consult me personally.

*The answers to this exercise appear in the **Instructor's Manual and Key** for **HOW 13: A Handbook for Office Professionals,** 13th edition.*

Pronouns

Name _____ Date _____

Adjectives (1-19 Through 1-24)

Practice Guide 18

Instructions: In the following sentences, underline any errors in the use of adjectives. Write the correct form in the blank at the right. If a sentence is correct, write *OK* in the blank line.

1. Before purchasing a home, our client wishes to lease an one-bedroom apartment in the area.

1. _____

2. We wish to have a more lighter oak finish for these cabinets.

2. _____

3. The programmer we hired last month is less knowledgeable than any programmer in the department.

3. _____

4. This is the fullest the theater has been since the musical production *Life on Broadway* began.

4. _____

5. Although Jennifer did not feel good all week, she did not miss a day's work.

5. _____

6. The starting salary for nursing assistants at Bayview Hospital is $12 a hour.

6. _____

7. Of all the contestants, Matthew seems to be the least confident.

7. _____

8. Nicole felt worser this afternoon than she did this morning, so she left early today.

8. _____

9. I feel badly that you did not receive information about this scholarship before the filing deadline date.

9. _____

10. Heather keyboards faster than anyone in the office.

10. _____

11. Although this new musical has an historical perspective, it is definitely a modern production.

11. _____

12. The most prompt response to our inquiry came from the Baltimore Chamber of Commerce.

12. _____

13. We have found that e-mail is a more better way to communicate with our clients on the East Coast.

13. _____

14. In this state license fees for registering out of state cars are prohibitive.

14. _____

15. For this construction project, we must erect a 12 foot fence around the site.

15. _____

16. Our office just listed a eight-unit apartment house on Superior Street.

16. _____

17. The more popular cribs on the market today are manufactured by Baby Town.

17. _____

18. If we are to compete in this market, we must create more unique television commercials.

18. _____

19. The dissension among the partners is becoming noticeabler every   19. _____
    day.

20. In this condominium complex, the two-bedroom unit has more   20. _____
    square footage than any unit.

Check your answers with those given on page 347 before completing the next exercise.

Name _____ Date _____

Adverbs (1-25 Through 1-29)

Practice Guide 19

Instructions: In the following sentences, underline any errors in the use of adverbs. Write the correct form in the blank at the right. If a sentence is correct, write *OK* in the blank line.

1. Joshua checked these sales figures less careful than he should have.

1. _____

2. Our fund-raiser for the new library has nearly netted $2.3 million.

2. _____

3. Both agents certainly should receive some compensation for their assistance with the sale.

3. _____

4. The red-and-white letters looked well against the black background.

4. _____

5. Who has been with the company longer—David, Brittany, or Jonathan?

5. _____

6. Do not discuss the proposed merger with nobody.

6. _____

7. Our department expects to shortly receive the two color printers we ordered.

7. _____

8. I have scarcely had an opportunity to review this report.

8. _____

9. Fresh fruits and vegetables are delivered regular to our restaurants throughout the city.

9. _____

10. Most of the students who graduate from our law school do good on the state bar examination.

10. _____

11. Your laptop computer seems to process more slower than mine.

11. _____

12. This research team's findings have scratched the surface barely.

12. _____

13. We cannot hardly believe that the company is moving all its operations to another state.

13. _____

14. Although I appreciate your kind remarks, you shouldn't feel badly about my not receiving the promotion.

14. _____

15. Is the air-conditioning system in our building working good?

15. _____

16. This news commentator claims to be the more widely listened to of all.

16. _____

17. Most of us were real disappointed to learn of our president's resignation.

17. _____

18. I haven't received no information about the new products we will be featuring.

18. _____

19. Let us hope that these contract negotiations will run smoothlier than the last ones.

19. _____

20. Please ask our attorneys to carefully evaluate all the clauses in this contract.

20. _____

Check your answers with those given on page 347 before completing the next exercise.

Adverbs

Prepositions (1-30 Through 1-33)

Practice Guide 20

Instructions: In the following sentences, underline any errors in the use of prepositions. Write the correct form in the blank at the right. If a sentence is correct, write *OK* in the blank line.

1. Between the three of us, we should be able to complete the inventory by the end of this weekend.

1. _____

2. Has the committee finally agreed upon the location for the new warehouse site?

2. _____

3. The final plans for the new medical center are quite different than what I had expected.

3. _____

4. There seems to be a discrepancy among the expense report and the receipts submitted.

4. _____

5. Most of these suggested policy changes are identical to the recommendations we have already submitted to the executive committee.

5. _____

6. Does the company plan on expanding its operations to locations outside the United States?

6. _____

7. According to the new contract, all salary increases are retroactive from January 1.

7. _____

8. All of the computers in our department have online access to the Internet.

8. _____

9. Our offices are located in the building directly opposite of Westlake Square.

9. _____

10. Pick up your visitor's badge at the window just inside of the main entrance to the building.

10. _____

11. Do you know who took the dictionary off of this counter?

11. _____

12. With all the loud shouting, we could hardly help from hearing the customer's angry remarks.

12. _____

13. Did you receive the fax from Megan?

13. _____

14. Is the date and time set for the meeting convenient to you?

14. _____

15. Both of these recommendations have been submitted to the board of education for approval.

15. _____

16. Before beginning the final draft, please ensure that these grant proposals are in compliance to the specifications prescribed in the instructions.

16. _____

17. If you become angry at one of the clerks, do not display your feelings in front of the other employees.

17. _____

18. Between themselves the committee members agreed to limit their meetings to no longer than two hours.

18. _____

19. All consultants in our employ are expected to conform to the dress standards set by our organization.

19. _____

20. We were able to buy off of Midtown Office Supply all its sale cartridges for our inkjet color printers.

20. _____

Check your answers with those given on page 348 before completing the next exercise.

Prepositions

Name _____ Date _____

Conjunctions (1-34 Through 1-38)

Practice Guide 21

Instructions: In the following sentences, underline any errors in the use of conjunctions. Write the correct form in the blank at the right. If a sentence is correct, write *OK* in the blank line.

1. We can either send you this information by fax or e-mail.

1. _____

2. Talking about becoming a doctor is one thing, but to become one is quite another.

2. _____

3. This year's profits are not so high as last year's.

3. _____

4. Our company manufactures not only stand-alone home stereo systems but also installs stereo systems in new-home construction projects.

4. _____

5. Neither Dana or Shannon has the combination to the vault.

5. _____

6. Before we can release the keys to the apartment, we will need both a certified check and to have the tenants sign the lease.

6. _____

7. Most of these new designs look like they were created by amateurs.

7. _____

8. For the meeting I am responsible for reserving the conference room and to prepare the agenda.

8. _____

9. Our new low-priced desk model laser printer has become so popular as our standard model.

9. _____

10. We would appreciate your filling out the enclosed questionnaire and to return it in the enclosed envelope.

10. _____

11. Our organization not only provides assistance to physically disabled children but also emotionally disturbed children.

11. _____

12. You may either receive your dividends monthly or reinvest them in the bond fund.

12. _____

13. Anthony felt that he not only scored well on the written examination but also the interview.

13. _____

14. Unfortunately, the molds for these new figurines did not turn out like we had hoped.

14. _____

15. This professor has neither the patience nor has she the understanding to work well with disabled students.

15. _____

16. We can either ship your order by Parcel Post or United Parcel Service.

16. _____

17. If you need assistance with your financial affairs you may wish to   17. _____
contact one of our consultants.

18. Providing information about our city and to assist visitors are the   18. _____
main functions of our bureau.

19. Please cancel all appointments for the second week in April,   19. _____
because the doctor will be out of the office.

20. Replace the printer cartridges just like the diagram illustrates.   20. _____

Check your answers with those given on page 348 before completing the next exercise.

Conjunctions

Section 2   Punctuation

The following pages contain 20 sets of exercises for the major uses of the comma, the semicolon, the colon, and the dash. These sets include *Practice Sentences,* a *Practice Paragraph,* and a *Reinforcement Letter.*

Each principle is labeled by name at the beginning of the exercise series. The section in *HOW* that explains the use of the principle is shown in parentheses.

For *Practice Sentences* use proofreaders' marks to insert punctuation marks where they are needed. (See Section 9–12 or the inside back cover of *HOW for* proofreaders' marks.) Only the punctuation mark illustrating the principle under consideration is to be inserted. After you have punctuated the sentences, check your answers on pages 348–358.

Practice Paragraphs use mainly the punctuation mark presented in the current section. Insert the necessary punctuation marks, and **label them using the abbreviations listed below.** Then check your answers on pages 348–358.

Punctuation Labels

Comma

Series	ser
Parenthetical	par
Direct Address	da
Appositive	app
Date	date
Address	add
Coordinating Conjunction	cc
Independent Adjective	ia
Introductory Clause	intro
Introductory Phrase	intro
Nonrestrictive	nr
Contrasting or Contingent Expression	cont ex
Omitted Words	omit
Clarity	cl
Short Quotation	sq

Semicolon

No Conjunction	nc
Coordinating Conjunction	cc
Transitional Expression	trans
Series	ser
Enumeration	enum

Colon

Enumerated or Listed Items	List
Explanatory Sentence	exp

Dash

Summary Statement	summ
Appositive with Commas	app
Emphasis	emph

An illustration of an edited *Practice Paragraph* appears below:

We, of course, are concerned about the production problems Deco Designs has

encountered during the past year. We cannot, however, allow its unpaid balance of $324 to

continue much longer. You can perhaps understand the difficult position in which suppliers

find themselves today. We, too, must meet our financial obligations. Therefore, we must

turn over this account for collection unless we receive payment by May 1.

Reinforcement Letters are cumulative; that is, once a punctuation principle has been covered in a previous exercise, it may appear in any of the following *Reinforcement Letters.* For the *Reinforcement Letters,* use proofreaders' marks to insert any necessary punctuation marks. Label each mark with the reason for its use by selecting one of the abbreviations shown on page 47. Check your answers with your instructor. One example of an edited *Reinforcement Letter* follows:

Dear Ms. Davis:

We appreciate receiving your April 8 letter. Because we want you to be pleased with your selection for many years to come, your china is available on an open-stock basis. If you need to replace a broken piece, you may do so at any time. Also, you may purchase additional pieces at your convenience.

Enclosed is a brochure describing your china pattern. This brochure features the available money-saving sets, and it also shows all pieces that may be purchased individually. If you are interested in purchasing additional sets or individual pieces, use the enclosed order form. You may include a check with your order, charge it on a bank card, or have it sent c.o.d.

We hope this information has been helpful to you. However, if you have any other questions, please let us know.

Sincerely yours,

Section 2 Punctuation

Comma Placement, Series (2-1)

Practice Sentences 1

1. Many doctors dentists and lawyers are among our clientele.

2. The administrative assistant in our office uses word processing spreadsheet and presentation software.

3. This particular travel group is scheduled to tour Arizona Nevada Utah and Idaho.

4. Your main duties will be to answer the telephone greet callers and respond to customer e-mail inquiries.

5. Trees shrubs and ground cover are needed to complete this landscaping project.

6. Call Jeremy Andrews offer him the job and ask him to begin work on July 1.

7. We changed all the locks barred the outside windows and installed a burglar alarm system last week.

8. The contractor obtained a permit purchased the building materials and hired several additional workers to complete the job within the specified three-week period.

9. Proofread the report make three copies and mail the original to Ms. Williams.

10. Sheila was late because she stopped at the office supply store the post office and the grocery store before arriving at the office.

Check your answers with those given on page 348 before completing the next exercise.

Practice Paragraph 1

We must e-mail Mr. Jones regarding our projected sales current expenses and profit picture. Ask him to let us know how our high inventory low sales volume and declining profits during the last quarter will affect our status for the entire year. Write the e-mail proofread it and send it.

Check your answers with those given on page 348 before completing the next exercise.

Reinforcement Letter 1

To: John Cole

    Our legal assistant collected the facts Mr. Phillips researched the case and Ms. Watson prepared the brief. This team of experts was instrumental in our receiving a favorable court decision. They are to be congratulated on their ability patience and success.

    Please continue to rely on Mr. Day for collecting the information Mr. Phillips for conducting the research and Ms. Watson for preparing the briefs. We will be able to develop a steady group of business industrial and professional clients by using the special talents of these three people.

*The answers to this exercise appear in the **Instructor's Manual and Key** for **HOW 13: A Handbook for Office Professionals**, 13th edition.*

Comma Placement, Parenthetical Expressions (2-2)

Practice Sentences 2

1. In fact Mr. Ryan has called our office several times to inquire about employment opportunities.

2. We feel nevertheless that you should honor your original commitment.

3. The committee has rejected his proposal fortunately.

4. Yes we are planning to revise the previous edition of our beginning algebra textbook.

5. Perhaps you would like to purchase online access to this encyclopedia.

6. The chapter was not in other words well presented and thoroughly documented.

7. Between you and me I would be surprised if Canton Industries bids on this project.

8. We are therefore placing a hold on your account until the past-due balance has been paid.

9. We will without a doubt ship your order to you in time for your fall sale.

10. You can indeed receive a full refund within 30 days if you are not fully satisfied with any of our products.

Check your answers with those given on page 349 before completing the next exercise.

Practice Paragraph 2

We as a rule do not employ inexperienced accountants. However Mr. Williams had so many excellent recommendations that we could not afford to turn down his application. Perhaps you will wish to meet him personally before assigning him to a supervisor. I can of course have him stop by your office tomorrow.

Check your answers with those given on page 349 before completing the next exercise.

Reinforcement Letter 2

To: David Post

Next month we will open new stores in Los Angeles San Francisco and Phoenix. Publicity releases consequently have already been sent to the major newspapers in these cities. In addition we will advertise a number of grand-opening specials that should attract a large number of customers.

Plans for opening our new stores are contained in the attached report. You may however wish to contact the store managers for further information on their sales promotions present merchandise inventory and progress in hiring personnel. Such additional information will perhaps be of help to you in your new assignment.

Your assistance needless to say will be important in assessing marketing trends in Los Angeles San Francisco and Phoenix. May we rely on you then for information regarding consumer preferences buying habits and purchasing power? The results of your research will indeed assist the staff in ensuring the success of these three new stores.

*The answers to this exercise appear in the **Instructor's Manual and Key** for **HOW 13: A Handbook for Office Professionals**, 13th edition.*

Comma, Parenthetical Expressions

Name _____   Date _____

Comma Placement, Direct Address (2-3)

Practice Sentences 3

1. Brett please reword the final paragraph of this e-mail message to refer to the attachment.

2. You may continue class with the assigned lessons shown in your syllabus.

3. Your staff is certainly efficient Mrs. Davis.

4. We can ladies and gentlemen promise you increased dividends for the next fiscal period.

5. Have you Gary decided on the dates for your vacation this year?

6. Yes fellow citizens of Spokane Senator Winfield's voting record is open for public scrutiny.

7. We plan to ask Ms. Stevens to complete the billing for this month.

8. Only you can help us solve this problem Dr. Bradley.

9. Will David Kloss be leaving for Michigan next week?

10. You friends and neighbors can help prevent further crime increases in this city.

Check your answers with those given on page 349 before completing the following exercise.

Practice Paragraph 3

Would you Ms. White please review the financial report. I would appreciate your doing so too Ms. Smith. Gentlemen please check with both Ms. White and Ms. Smith for their advice before making any further financial commitments.

Check your answers with those given on page 349 before completing the following exercise.

Reinforcement Letter 3

Dear Mrs. Smith:

    We welcome you as a charge account customer of the Valley Department Store. Enclosed are your two charge cards some information outlining our charge plan and a circular describing our special sale items for this month.

    You may be interested Mrs. Smith in the special women's clothing sale now in progress. In fact this sale is one of the best we have had this year. You can for example purchase many of our designer jeans at half price. We hope that you will be able to take advantage of these savings.

              Sincerely yours,

*The answers to this exercise appear in the **Instructor's Manual and Key** for **HOW 13: A Handbook for Office Professionals**, 13th Edition.*

Name _____ Date _____

Comma Placement, Appositives (2-4)

Practice Sentences 4

1. This new budget was proposed by our accountant Stan Hughes last week.

2. John's sister the author of a best seller has agreed to speak at one of our association meetings.

3. Senator Johnson a member of the finance committee favors our position.

4. John J. Lopez Jr. has requested our committee to provide additional funds for his program.

5. Was your latest article "Skiing in Colorado" accepted for publication?

6. Is it possible that they themselves are not confident of the outcome?

7. Janet Hodges our new assistant will be working in the office next to yours.

8. This book was written by Alice Porter and David Simms two prominent authorities on the subject of e-commerce.

9. Please refer any requests for further information to my assistant Bill Thompson.

10. One of our new clients Kligman Industries has recently been admitted to the New York Stock Exchange.

Check your answers with those given on pages 349–350 before completing the next exercise.

Practice Paragraph 4

We have just learned that our president Mr. Black will retire next June. He has been president of Data Products Inc. for the past ten years. My assistant received the news yesterday and believes that Stephen Gold PhD will be asked to fill the position. We will keep our employees informed of further developments through our monthly newsletter *Data Jottings*.

Check your answers with those given on page 350 before completing the next exercise.

Reinforcement Letter 4

Dear Mr. Ray:

Our newest project in the business communication area *Writing Résumés That Get Jobs* will be released within the next three months. Consequently we are in the process of preparing an advertising campaign for this project. One of the authors James Martin Jr. will be contacting you shortly about the special features of this program.

The authors editors and reviewers all expect this book to be one of our best sellers next year. There has been a need for a book of this type for some time. Hopefully our potential customers will recognize the considerable amount of effort that has gone into producing the kind of book for which they have indicated a need.

Mr. Sharp our advertising manager has asked his son Peter to work up some preliminary drawings for the artwork to advertise this new book. Peter has had considerable experience in this area and has done some other freelance work for our organization.

We will be able to meet with Peter as soon as he has had an opportunity to work up the preliminary drawings. He himself is not exactly sure when he can have them available. However I will contact you regarding a specific date time and place when we are ready for the initial conference.

Sincerely yours,

*The answers to this exercise appear in the **Instructor's Manual and Key** for **HOW 13: A Handbook for Office Professionals**, 13th edition.*

Name _____ Date _____

Comma Placement, Dates and Time Zones (2-5)

Practice Sentences 5

1. The merger took place on February 28, 2013.

2. On July 26 we will expect to receive your check for $720 to cover your past-due account.

3. Did you say that the president's address will be broadcast at 8 p.m. EST?

4. The contractor expects the shopping center to be completed by October 2015.

5. We have made arrangements for the conference to be held on Thursday June 12 2014.

6. By April 15 the bulk of our income tax work will have been completed.

7. Our records show that on November 4 2012 your association filed for tax-exempt status.

8. Your subscription to this vital magazine ends with the July 2014 issue.

9. American Airlines Flight 390 is scheduled to land in Chicago at 8:40 a.m. CST.

10. On Wednesday December 6 2016 the company will have been in business for a century.

Check your answers with those given on page 350 before completing the next exercise.

Practice Paragraph 5

We will meet on April 1 to plan the opening of two new branch offices scheduled for Tuesday May 3

and Thursday May 19. These offices are the first ones we have opened since August 22 2012. We will

need to plan these openings carefully because we will be directly responsible for two additional openings

in September 2015 and April 2016.

Check your answers with those given on page 350 before completing the next exercise.

Reinforcement Letter 5

Dear Charles:

We are pleased to announce that the next convention for hotel managers will be held from Tuesday September 30 2014 until Friday October 3 2014 at the West Hotel in Chicago.

The convention committee recognizes that the next convention was originally scheduled for September 2015. However the convention committee felt that the date should be moved forward since so many of our members had expressed an interest in meeting annually. We hope Charles that this change in convention plans will fit into your schedule.

We would very much like to have you speak at one of our morning meetings. Ed Bates our program chair suggested that you might be interested in describing the new reservations plan you developed for the Holiday Hotels. Would you be able to address the membership on this topic on October 2?

Please let me know by February 18 if you will be able to accept this invitation.

Sincerely,

*The answers to this exercise appear in the **Instructor's Manual and Key** for **HOW 13: A Handbook for Office Professionals**, 13th edition.*

Name _____ Date _____

Comma Placement, Addresses (2-6)

Practice Sentences 6

1. Please return your application to New Age Photo Publishing 6200 Walnut Avenue Salem Oregon 97302.

2. Mrs. Harvey presently resides at 98 Spring Lane Los Angeles California 90041-2027.

3. We will visit London England and Paris France during our tour.

4. Our company owns a number of condominium complexes in Honolulu, Hawaii.

5. The tour agent sold us tickets to Albuquerque, New Mexico in error.

6. Our closest branch office is located at 2150 Madison Avenue Knoxville Tennessee 37912-5821.

7. Please complete this form and mail it to Mrs. Alice Stocker Office Manager Smythe & Ryan Investment Counselors 3370 Ravenwood Avenue Suite 120 Baltimore Maryland 21213-1648.

8. This customer's new address is Box 360 Rural Route 2 Bangor Maine 04401-9802.

9. Dallas Texas has been selected as the site for our next convention.

10. All these articles are imported from Madrid Spain.

Check your answers with those given on pages 350–351 before completing the following exercise.

Practice Paragraph 6

We sent the information to Mr. David Hope Manager Larry's Clothing Store 2001 Adams Street SW Atlanta Georgia 30315-5901. The information should have been sent to Mr. Hope's new address in Columbus Ohio. It is 2970 Olive Avenue Columbus Ohio 43204-2535.

Check your answers with those given on page 351 before completing the following exercise.

Reinforcement Letter 6

Ladies and Gentlemen:

Please reserve for me two gift subscriptions under your special holiday plan. The subscriptions are for one year and should begin with your January 2014 issue.

One gift subscription should be sent to Mrs. Alice Daily 65 Martha Road Apt. 11A Boston Massachusetts 02114-1210. The other one should be sent to Mrs. Ann Green 421 30th Street Pittsburgh Pennsylvania 15219-3728.

I would appreciate your sending the bill for these subscriptions to my office. The address is Tower Building 500 Washington Street Suite 201 San Francisco California 94111-2919.

Please acknowledge receipt of this order. In addition I would appreciate your sending gift cards to both Mrs. Daily and Mrs. Green telling them of their gift subscriptions that are to begin on January 1 2014.

Sincerely yours,

The answers to this exercise appear in the **Instructor's Manual and Key** *for* **HOW 13: A Handbook for Office Professionals**, *13th edition.*

Name _____ Date _____

Comma Placement, Coordinating Conjunctions (2-7)

Practice Sentences 7

1. Three major accounting reports are due in January and two of them must be prepared for presentation to the Board of Directors.

2. The meeting was scheduled to adjourn at 3 p.m. but we had not finished all the business by then.

3. You may transfer to our Chicago office or you may remain here in Cincinnati.

4. Most of the applicants cannot keyboard 60 words a minute nor can they use our word processing software.

5. Marie was offered a promotion last week but did not accept it.

6. A new edition of this textbook is in the publication process and it will be available for the fall semester.

7. We hope that Mr. Moore will be able to attend the convention and that he will be our guest for the banquet on May 5.

8. Tom will finish the project himself or he will arrange for his assistant to complete it.

9. Bob will no longer have to travel to Akron nor will he have any accounts in that district.

10. Janet has been promoted twice and is now eligible for a third advancement.

Check your answers with those given on page 351 before completing the next exercise.

Practice Paragraph 7

We have checked our records and find that you are correct. Our deposit was mailed to your branch office but no record of this deposit was entered into our check record. Our records have been corrected and we appreciate your help in solving this problem. We hope that we have not caused you any inconvenience and that we may rely upon your help in the future.

Check your answers with those given on page 351 before completing the next exercise.

Reinforcement Letter 7

Dear Mr. Harris:

We are pleased to announce that in the near future we will be opening several new branch offices. The first one is scheduled to open in Tacoma Washington on June 1 2014. Other offices are planned for Indianapolis Indiana and Tampa Florida.

You may mail all future orders to the Tacoma office and we will fill these orders from there. Just fill out one of the enclosed order blanks and your order will be processed immediately upon receipt. We plan to serve our customers more rapidly and efficiently in this way.

Mr. Parks the former manager of our Portland branch will be in charge of the Tacoma office. He will be able to assist you with future orders and follow through on their delivery. We cannot promise you a three-day delivery date for regular orders but I can assure you that most orders will reach you within a week. Of course we will continue to provide our express overnight service for an additional shipping fee.

We hope that you will take advantage of ordering from our Tacoma office and that this new development in our company will expedite deliveries to your store.

Sincerely yours,

*The answers to this exercise appear in the **Instructor's Manual and Key** for **HOW 13: A Handbook for Office Professionals**, 13th edition.*

Comma Placement, Independent Adjectives (2-8)

Practice Sentences 8

1. Mr. Sommers is known to be a pleasant patient supervisor.

2. Was your real estate agent able to locate an affordable five-bedroom home for the Lopezes?

3. The red brick building on the corner of Main and Third Streets is scheduled to be demolished next week.

4. The Hardys own an elegant secluded hotel in the Berkshires.

5. This afternoon one of the customers broke an expensive crystal vase.

6. Ms. Rice's ambitious greedy attitude makes the other agents feel uneasy.

7. Our new electronic payroll system has caused considerable confusion.

8. Your outgoing cheerful manner has brought you many friends.

9. One of our wealthy well-known alumni has donated $1 million for the new library wing.

10. We will still need to purchase a large oak desk for the reception area.

Check your answers with those given on page 351 before completing the following exercise.

Practice Paragraph 8

Your informative well-written report was submitted to the board of education yesterday. You will certainly be permitted to purchase some inexpensive modern equipment on the basis of the facts presented. I am sure the board will agree that the present facilities do not reflect a realistic practical learning environment for business students.

Check your answers with those given on page 352 before completing the following exercise.

Reinforcement Letter 8

Dear Mr. Winters:

I am pleased to recommend John Davis for a position with your accounting firm. He has been in our employ for three years and we are sorry to see him leave our company.

Mr. Davis is an intelligent hardworking young man. His pleasant congenial manner has also contributed to our organization. Unfortunately our small company is unable to offer him the opportunities for advancement to which a person of his ability is entitled.

Mr. Davis has been in charge of accounts receivable for the past year. His duties included posting purchases to individual accounts entering customer payments and making appropriate journal entries in our computerized accounting program. Our accounting supervisor Mr. Long has often remarked about Mr. Davis's prompt efficient handling of the duties that were assigned to him. He has contributed greatly to the smooth operation of the entire department.

I am pleased to be able to recommend such a capable young man to you. Do not hesitate to let me know if you should require any additional information about Mr. Davis.

Sincerely yours,

*The answers to this exercise appear in the **Instructor's Manual and Key** for **HOW 13: A Handbook for Office Professionals**, 13th edition.*

Comma, Independent Adjectives

Comma Placement, Introductory Clauses (2-9)

Practice Sentences 9

1. When you see Bill ask him to e-mail me his response.

2. While you were in New York the committee published its findings.

3. Before you leave for Denver will you be able to finish the financial reports?

4. As stated previously we plan to renew our contract with you next month.

5. Because Mr. Logan wishes to move to Indianapolis he has requested a transfer to our plant there.

6. If so may we count on you to ship the merchandise by November 14?

7. While Ms. Smith was consulting with her attorney her car was stolen.

8. Provided we receive a budget increase next year you may add an additional person to your staff.

9. If you are unable to keep your appointment please notify our office at least 24 hours in advance.

10. As explained above this refrigerator has a one-year warranty on all parts and labor.

Check your answers with those given on page 352 before completing the next exercise.

Practice Paragraph 9

When you receive the material please review it carefully and return it to our office within two weeks. If possible note all changes in red. As soon as we receive your corrections we will be able to submit the manuscript to the printer. We expect that if the current production schedule is maintained the book will be released early in March.

Check your answers with those given on page 352 before completing the next exercise.

Reinforcement Letter 9

To: Henry Small

I recommend that we network the desktop computers in our Sales Department. Although expensive a network will save money and improve efficiency over a period of time.

I believe that if the present number of customer orders and inquiries continues we will need to modify update and streamline our current procedures to maintain our reputation for good service. If we network our computers our sales staff will become more productive. They will have access to information possessed by other employees and they will be able to keep up more easily with the increasing workload in this department. Where possible I myself would be willing to assist the staff in making any necessary changes.

May I have your approval to investigate further the possibility of installing a network to link our desktop computers? As soon as I hear from you I will be able to contact the various equipment vendors for specific price quotations.

*The answers to this exercise appear in the **Instructor's Manual and Key** for **HOW 13: A Handbook for Office Professionals**, 13th edition.*

Name _____ Date _____

Comma Placement, Introductory Phrases (2-10)

Practice Sentences 10

1. To continue this project we will need $2 million in additional funding next year.

2. Seeing Tom's mistake Kate corrected his calculations.

3. After viewing the architect's drawings, Dr. Ruston made several suggestions regarding the placement of the electrical outlets.

4. Near the top of the new listings you will find the Hills' home.

5. For your information we are including the records of last month's sales.

6. During the next month we must decrease our inventory by at least 30 percent.

7. After the meeting a number of us plan to have dinner together at a nearby restaurant.

8. To be interviewed for this position an applicant must be fully qualified.

9. Until the end of the month no one may take additional vacation time.

10. In the future our buyer expects to increase the number of product lines carried by our suburban stores.

Check your answers with those given on page 352 before completing the next exercise.

Practice Paragraph 10

For the past 100 years our bank has served the needs of the people of Hartford. At the present time we wish to attract more depositors to our institution. To attract new customers to the Bank of Connecticut we have established a premium plan. Hoping that such an incentive will draw a large group of new depositors we have provided a number of gift items to be given away with the opening of new accounts for $1,000 or more.

Check your answers with those given on pages 352–353 before completing the next exercise.

Reinforcement Letter 10

To: Karen Hill

With the purchase of additional computing equipment we will need to compile a series of form paragraphs to answer our routine correspondence. I recommend that when Mr. Black returns from vacation he should be assigned the responsibility of analyzing our previous correspondence and composing a series of form paragraphs to handle routine matters. If possible Mrs. Day should be requested to assist him.

Once the form paragraphs have been compiled they can be stored on the computer. Then when the need for a routine response arises the assistant may retrieve and personalize the message. This method of answering routine correspondence will save a great deal of time and we will be able to cut costs by eliminating a considerable amount of repetitive keying.

The most prominent office systems magazine *Office Systems and Procedures* has been running a series of articles on speech-recognition programs. In this series the authors describe the many different uses for voice-input software. They also describe the advantages and disadvantages of the various programs marketed by major software manufacturers. Attached are reprints of this series and I hope that you will have an opportunity to read them before our meeting.

I look forward to meeting with you on Monday August 4 to discuss the specific steps we should take to improve our handling of correspondence and reports. As you suggested I will be in your office at 10 a.m.

*The answers to this exercise appear in the **Instructor's Manual and Key** for **HOW 13: A Handbook for Office Professionals**, 13th edition.*

Comma, Introductory Phrases

Name _____ Date _____

Comma Placement, Nonrestrictive Phrases and Clauses (2-11)

Practice Sentences 11

1. Mr. Sims who is responsible for reviewing all appeals will make the final decision.

2. Each person who enrolls in the college will receive a schedule of classes.

3. Her latest article which appeared in last Sunday's local paper discusses family budgeting.

4. All students applying for a scholarship must attend the meeting on Wednesday.

5. Your order has already been shipped although I tried to cancel it.

6. May I have copies of the materials that were distributed at the last meeting.

7. Mr. Young who has attended many of our seminars is a licensed real estate broker.

8. May I have a copy of our latest financial report which was distributed at the last meeting of department heads.

9. We have decided to hold our conference at the Shadow Oaks Inn regardless of its expensive meals and remote location.

10. Our new company president planning to make major organizational changes first consolidated the six top executive positions into four.

Check your answers with those given on page 353 before completing the next exercise.

Practice Paragraph 11

The new community library which is located on South Main Street is presently recruiting employees to serve the public during the evening hours. Mr. Harris is looking for staff members who would be willing to work from 5 to 9 p.m. on weekday evenings. He would be pleased to receive your recommendations if you know of any qualified individuals who would be interested in such a position. We would appreciate your recommendations within the next few days since Mr. Harris must hire the evening staff by May 10 before the library opens on May 13.

Check your answers with those given on page 353 before completing the next exercise.

Reinforcement Letter 11

Dear Mr. Little:

Now is the time to obtain the necessary protection for your family protection in terms of providing them with the life insurance needed by American families today.

We have several insurance plans that may be of interest to you. One of our most popular ones for young people is our home mortgage insurance. This plan which has been in existence for over 40 years provides families with home insurance protection in the form of life insurance.

Our regular life insurance program as you can see from the enclosed brochure has been designed for the family that wishes to receive protection as well as provide for future savings and investment. During the lifetime of the policy it accumulates a cash value which may be withdrawn upon the expiration of the policy or may be used for extended life insurance coverage. Also you may borrow at a low interest rate against the value of your policy should you need to do so.

Another one of our plans provides term insurance coverage. This plan allows you Mr. Little to purchase the greatest amount of protection for your family during the time that it is most needed. By selecting this plan you will be able to obtain higher benefits at less cost when your family is young and its needs are greater.

Mr. Mills who has been one of our agents for more than ten years would be able to discuss further with you the advantages of our various programs. Please call Mr. Mills at 555-0881 and he will set up an appointment to meet with you.

Sincerely yours,

*The answers to this exercise appear in the **Instructor's Manual and Key** for **HOW 13: A Handbook for Office Professionals**, 13th edition.*

Comma, Nonrestrictive Phrases and Clauses

Comma Placement, Contrasting and Contingent Expressions (2-12)
Comma Placement, Omitted Words (2-13)

Practice Sentences 12

1. The format not the content of the report made it unacceptable.

2. The sooner we receive your completed application forms the sooner we can process you for employment.

3. Tickets will be made available July 1 but only to members of the homeowners' association.

4. The more often you access and explore Internet sites the more adept you will become in using the Internet as a source of information.

5. I intend to write a full report not just a simple e-mail outlining all the circumstances involved in this transaction.

6. Tom will leave for vacation on July 9; Jennifer August 15; Michael August 22; and Katelyn August 29.

7. Just today we sold six of these advertised living room suites; yesterday three; and the day before two.

8. The Sales Department received 18 copies of the report; the Personnel Department 12; and the other departments 8.

9. Last month we received two orders of supplies; this month only one.

10. Four new expressways will be completed in 2015; three in 2016; two in 2017.

Check your answers with those given on page 353 before completing the next exercise.

Practice Paragraph 12

Last week our agent sold six homes this week just four. Mr. Stevens maintains that our construction site is not appealing to home buyers. His argument is plausible yet weak. Other builders in the area have been more successful in their marketing efforts. The more competition Mr. Stevens encounters the more his sales efforts seem to decline.

Check your answers with those given on page 353 before completing the next exercise.

Reinforcement Letter 12

Dear Ms. Stadthaus:

We appreciate receiving your order for 12 dozen of our Model 18 frying pan sets.

Because the Model 18 set has been so popular as a summer sale specialty we have not been able to keep up with the demand for this item. We have a number of these sets on hand but not 12 dozen. At the present time we would be able to supply you with 4 dozen.

Mr. Jones who is in charge of our Production Department promises us an additional supply of these pans within the next two weeks. He realizes that the more of these sets that we can manufacture during the next month the more of them we can sell during the summer sales.

The 4 dozen sets on hand can be shipped to you immediately; the remaining 8 dozen by April 18. Please let us know by e-mail (jlopez@remco.com) or by fax (626-555-3427) whether or not you wish us to make this partial shipment. We look forward to hearing from you within the next few days.

Sincerely yours,

*The answers to this exercise appear in the **Instructor's Manual and Key** for **HOW 13: A Handbook for Office Professionals**, 13th edition.*

Comma, Contrasting and Contingent Expressions
Comma, Omitted Words

Name _____ Date _____

Comma Placement, Clarity (2-14)

Practice Sentences 13

1. We have dealt with this company for many many years.

2. A long time before she had spoken with the company president.

3. Whoever wins wins a $2,000 jackpot and a trip to Hawaii.

4. Ever since Mr. Salazar has kept a careful record of his expenses.

5. We were very very disappointed with the final recommendations given by the consultant.

6. Students who cheat cheat only themselves.

7. Three months before our sales manager had been offered a position by one of the leading manufacturers on the East Coast.

8. Whoever skydives skydives at his own risk.

9. Even before he had shown an interest in that area.

10. After this time will seem to pass more quickly.

Check your answers with those given on page 354 before completing the next exercise.

Practice Paragraph 13

All the meeting was was a discussion of Mr. Green's plan to move the plant. Mr. Green has presented this same plan many many times. A few weeks before another committee totally rejected his proposal. Ever since he has looked for another group to endorse his ideas.

Check your answers with those given on page 354 before completing the next exercise.

Reinforcement Letter 13

To: Mr. John Allen

We were very very disappointed to learn that you will not be able to deliver the main address at our sales conference in January. As you know the staff was extremely impressed with your last speech in Dallas. Ever since many of them have requested that we ask you to conduct the general session in January.

I understand Mr. Allen why you cannot attend our meeting. As national sales manager you must visit other regional sales meetings also. What it is is too great of a demand on one person's time.

We appreciate the many times in the past when you have addressed our Southern Region and we look forward to the time when you will be able to do so again.

*The answers to this exercise appear in the **Instructor's Manual and Key** for **HOW 13: A Handbook for Office Professionals**, 13th edition.*

Comma Placement, Short Quotations (2-15)

Practice Sentences 14

1. "Please be sure to remove that sign" said Mr. Grey.

2. "How long" asked Ms. Foster "will it take to replace the hard drive?"

3. The receptionist answered "no" very sharply and rudely.

4. Mr. Hughes said "Everyone must agree to sign his or her own contract."

5. "Not this time" was the answer given by many of our past donors.

6. "Are you finished" asked Scott "with that catalog?"

7. The witness reaffirmed "That man is the one who stole my car."

8. "Please finish this report by Friday, May 5" said Dr. Reynolds.

9. All the union members agreed "to abide by the judgment of the union leaders throughout the negotiations."

10. "Mr. David Brown" said Ms. Burns, the Department of Human Resources head "has been hired for the vacancy in your department."

Check your answers with those given on page 354 before completing the following exercise.

Practice Paragraph 14

Mr. Dallas answered the reporter's question with a simple "yes." His philosophy appeared to be "A bird in hand is worth two in the bush." The reporter then asked "Do you believe this labor contract will be ratified within the next week?" Mr. Dallas answered confidently "I believe the terms of the contract will be accepted by a clear majority." "I am sure" added Ms. Hill "that the employees will be especially pleased with the additional insurance benefits offered."

Check your answers with those given on page 354 before completing the following exercise.

Reinforcement Letter 14

Dear Mr. Ryan:

Ask yourself "Did the Wilson Paper Company fill my last order accurately and promptly?" The answer is "yes." Ask yourself again "Did the Wilson Paper Company provide us with the promotional material we requested?" Again you must reply "yes."

We have carried out our part of the bargain Mr. Ryan. We have supplied you with the merchandise you ordered and the brochures you requested. Now in turn won't you be fair with us?

Your account is presently 60 days past due. We have sent you two reminders but have not received a check for $435 to cover our last statement. We can perhaps understand why you have not made payment but we cannot understand why you have not answered our letters. If there is some reason why you cannot make payment at the present time please let us know.

We have asked ourselves "Is this the way Ryan's Office Supply has done business in the past?" "Not according to our previous records" our accountant said. So won't you be fair to both your credit record and to us by mailing your check for $435 in the enclosed envelope.

Sincerely yours,

*The answers to this exercise appear in the **Instructor's Manual and Key** for **HOW 13: A Handbook for Office Professionals**, 13th edition.*

Semicolon Placement, No Conjunction (2-17)

Practice Sentences 15

1. Our company has released a new series of products for purchase at its Web site we feel they will receive a favorable response from the online market.

2. Ms. Stephens will file the rewritten reports she wishes to cross-reference some of them.

3. Andrea collated Kim stapled.

4. Attach the revised instructions to an e-mail message I will review them later.

5. Steve has begun work on a new project he will be out of the office for the next three weeks.

6. I dusted furniture Tim cleaned the showcase Linda vacuumed—all just before the store opened.

7. Bill has not finished his sales report for Thursday's meeting he will work late tonight to complete it.

8. We received your application today the committee will make its decision regarding your loan within two weeks.

9. The thief entered he grabbed the jewelry he exited swiftly.

10. Sales for July and August hit an all-time low they increased somewhat during September November recorded the highest sales for 2014.

Check your answers with those given on page 355 before completing the following exercise.

Practice Paragraph 15

We need someone to meet with the Atlas Corporation representatives. Please call Mr. Green ask him to be in my office by 10 a.m. tomorrow morning. He knows Piedmont he knows commercial real estate he knows prices. Mr. Green would be my first choice for the job Ms. Jones would be my second choice my final choice would be Mr. Bruce.

Check your answers with those given on page 355 before completing the following exercise.

Reinforcement Letter 15

To: Carol Smith

We are pleased with the results of the new commission plan that was initiated this year we hope that you will endorse it also.

During the past year our sales have increased 40 percent and this increase is reflected in the salaries earned by our staff. As our sales manager stated at last year's stockholders' meeting "By offering our sales force the opportunity for higher salaries through commissions we will be able to increase substantially our sales during the next year."

I believe our sales manager Jim Black was correct this sales increase appears to be related directly to our placing the staff on a commission basis. We do realize too that our economy has experienced favorable conditions during the past year.

I recommend that we continue our present commission plan it appears to provide the proper incentive for our staff. Please let me know Ms. Smith if you agree with this recommendation.

*The answers to this exercise appear in the **Instructor's Manual and Key** for **HOW 13: A Handbook for Office Professionals**, 13th edition.*

Semicolon, No Conjunction

Semicolon Placement, With Conjunction (2-18)

Practice Sentences 16

1. James Hogan who is originally from Nevada has written a book about tourist sights in Las Vegas and he plans to have it translated into several languages for purchase by foreign visitors.

2. Cliff Lightfoot our supervisor has been ill for several weeks but he plans to return to the office next Wednesday November 19 in time for our committee meeting.

3. We have purchased new carpeting and furniture for all the offices and we expect to have them completely redecorated by the end of the month.

4. We cannot Ms. Baron repair the DVD player under the terms of the warranty nor can we under the circumstances refund the purchase price.

5. Nevertheless the committee must meet again next Friday but today we will cut short the agenda.

6. Many of our employees live nearby and they often ride bicycles to work.

7. Unfortunately three of our large moving vans have mechanical problems but according to the latest information we have received they will be back in service next Monday morning.

8. I believe Ms. Edwards that the contract will expire next week and that it has been scheduled for renewal.

9. You may of course keep your original appointment or you may reschedule it for another time during March.

10. Our last investment program was so successful that it netted a 9 percent return but we cannot guarantee that our next program or any other program planned for the future will do as well.

Check your answers with those given on page 355 before completing the next exercise.

Practice Paragraph 16

We were pleased to learn Mr. Bell that you have opened a new store on West Main Street and you may be sure that we look forward to establishing a mutually profitable business relationship. Our new line of stationery greeting cards and other paper products should be of interest to you and we will have our sales representative in your area Jack Dale phone you for an appointment to view them. He can leave a catalog with you or he can take you personally to our showroom which it is located only 3 miles from your store.

Check your answers with those given on page 355 before completing the next exercise.

Reinforcement Letter 16

Dear Mr. Mason:

We have written you three letters requesting payment of our last invoice 187365 for $98.84 but as of the close of business today we have not yet received your check or an explanation why this invoice has not been paid.

During the past year we have appreciated your business we cannot understand though why you have not made payment on this invoice. You as a businessman realize the importance of maintaining a high credit rating and the damage that nonpayment can do to your credit reputation.

We now find it necessary to place your account in the hands of a collection agency. Save yourself the embarrassment of a damaged credit rating mail your check in the enclosed envelope today. If we receive payment by Friday May 11 there is still time to avoid legal action.

Sincerely yours,

*The answers to this exercise appear in the **Instructor's Manual and Key** for **HOW 13: A Handbook for Office Professionals**, 13th edition.*

Semicolon, With Conjunction

Semicolon Placement, With Transitional Expressions (1-19)

Practice Sentences 17

1. Our sales have declined substantially this year therefore we are planning a new promotional series.

2. Ms. Lee is in the process of arranging next week's schedule however your hours will remain the same.

3. We will not close our store for remodeling on the contrary we will be open longer hours to accommodate our clientele.

4. The foundation is building a large new hospital wing consequently we will have office space for this community project.

5. All the sixth-grade classes will need new math textbooks moreover they will need workbooks to accompany them.

6. Send us an outline and three chapters of your proposed novel then we will let you know whether we will be able to publish it.

7. Our company no longer manufactures pencil sharpeners however we are enclosing the names and addresses of several companies that do.

8. Mr. Cooper vice president of Western Bank will not be able to attend our meeting consequently we will need to find a replacement speaker.

9. Our computer network was down yesterday for more than eight hours thus the distribution of payroll checks will be delayed until tomorrow.

10. Several of our salespersons are being transferred to the Chicago area therefore they will need your assistance in locating homes or apartments.

Check your answers with those given on page 356 before completing the next exercise.

Practice Paragraph 17

Our order for 24 sets of china arrived yesterday however more than half the sets have broken pieces. These china sets are a featured item for our May sale thus we would appreciate your sending an additional 14 sets to replace the broken ones. Please ship these replacements immediately so that they will arrive in time for our sale.

Check your answers with those given on page 356 before completing the next exercise.

Reinforcement Letter 17

To: Kristin Harris

We have received e-mail messages from two of our retailers they are complaining about our service in the Boston area. These retailers have not seen our representative for several months therefore their supply of our products has become depleted.

During our special discount sale neither of these retailers was contacted. They were unable to take advantage of our reduced prices consequently they are considering dropping our line unless some specific action is taken.

I have checked into this matter and found that our representative in this area has had a declining sales record during the past two years. His supervisor believes that he is not devoting the time necessary to cover all the accounts in his territory in fact his supervisor suspects that this representative is in the process of establishing his own business while at the same time retaining his position with our company.

As you know Kristin our sales in Boston have been declining steadily and as a result we cannot afford to lose any dealers in this area. I suggest therefore that you contact the two dealers personally and work out a procedure to retain their business. Also I suggest that you work closely with the supervisor in this area to establish a procedure for restoring our sales efforts.

Please let me know the outcome of your actions I am eagerly awaiting your reply.

*The answers to this exercise appear in the **Instructor's Manual and Key** for **HOW 13: A Handbook for Office Professionals**, 13th edition.*

Name _____ Date _____

Semicolon Placement, Series and Enumerations (2-20 and 2-21)

Practice Sentences 18

1. Our family has lived in Miami Florida Houston Texas and Portland Oregon.

2. Attending the meeting were David Stevens president of North Hills Academy Agnes Moore assistant principal of Rhodes School and Vera Caruso director of Flintridge Preparatory School.

3. We plan to initiate a new sales campaign for example we will flood the local media with advertisements offering discounts on several items in our product line.

4. Several factors have contributed to this problem namely labor shortages wage increases and frequent strikes.

5. Joleen has done all the fact-finding for this case Jim has verified her findings and Paul will take the case into court next Wednesday morning.

6. Staff members from San Fernando California Phoenix Arizona and Reno Nevada plan to attend the Western Regional meeting.

7. The quiz cards asked the contestants to tell what important events occurred on July 4 1776 October 24 1929 and November 22 1963.

8. We have changed a number of our former procedures for example we no longer approve requisitions in this office.

9. Several of our agents have already exceeded the $5 million mark in real estate sales this year namely Charles Brubaker Dana Walters Phillip Gordon and Lisa Stanzell.

10. Corporate offices will be moved to Dayton Ohio sales territories will be expanded from eight to ten and the position of sales manager will be elevated to vice president.

Check your answers with those given on page 356 before completing the next exercise.

Practice Paragraph 18

Our next student travel tour will include visits to London England Madrid Spain and Frankfurt Germany. Two years ago we received 200 applications for our European tour last year we received nearly 400 and this year we expect more than 700 students to apply for this tour. This tour is one of the most popular ones we offer because the Smith Foundation underwrites many of the costs namely hotel accommodations meals and surface transportation.

Check your answers with those given on page 356 before completing the next exercise.

Reinforcement Letter 18

Dear Jason:

In 2011 our convention was held in Philadelphia Pennsylvania in 2012 it was held in Atlanta Georgia and in 2013 it was held in Dallas Texas. The selection of our 2014 convention site has been narrowed down to three cities namely Los Angeles San Francisco and Denver.

The majority of the planning committee favors Denver however hotel accommodations appear to be more favorable in the other two locations. As soon as the committee has had an opportunity to look into the matter further I will let you know the specific location for the 2014 convention.

For one of the program sessions we have been able to obtain four excellent speakers to serve on a resource panel but before we can publicize the names of our resource panel we must yet receive written confirmation from one of them. So far Ms. Ann Jones vice president of First National Bank Mr. Richard Lee treasurer of Security Savings Federal Bank and Dr. Robert Long professor of management at Illinois State College have formally accepted our invitation. Our fourth resource person Mr. James Fountain has tentatively accepted our invitation also.

As you can see plans are well under way for the 2014 convention. We are very close to selecting a site I am sure that we will have a decision within the next two weeks. Many of our speakers have been confirmed and I believe we will be able to provide a tentative program by the end of July. In the meantime if you have any comments or suggestions for the convention committee please let me know.

Sincerely yours,

*The answers to this exercise appear in the **Instructor's Manual and Key** for **HOW 13: A Handbook for Office Professionals**, 13th edition.*

Semicolon Placement, Series and Enumerations

Colon Placement, Formerly Enumerated or Listed Items (1-23)
Colon Placement, Explanatory Sentences (1-24)

Practice Sentences 19

1. Please order the following supplies bond paper laser printer paper and writing pads.

2. Several people called while you were out Marguerite Rodríguez from Atlas Corporation Robert Wong from the Accounting Department Lynne Hale from Thompson Industries and Jerry Horowitz from the home office.

3. Carmen has examined this case thoroughly from every viewpoint she has studied all the evidence gathered by the investigators and reviewed the court decisions in similar cases.

4. Included with this statement are bills for January 4 January 8 February 1 and February 7.

5. You may select merchandise from either of these catalogs Spring 2014 or Summer 2014.

6. Employees with the highest rating for the month of February were Naomi Chahinian Bertha Granados and Kelly Crockett.

7. Our buyer ordered the following items last week from your spring line shirts jeans shoes belts and jackets.

8. Two of our subsidiaries have shown considerable growth during the past year Belmont Industries and Feldson Manufacturing Company.

9. Four of our products in this series are being discontinued we have had too many difficulties servicing them.

10. You will need to hire 14 temporary employees for our spring sale namely 3 cashiers 5 salespersons and 6 inventory clerks.

Check your answers with those given on page 357 before completing the next exercise.

Practice Paragraph 19

   New offices were opened in the following cities last year Albany Billings Dayton and Fresno. We had planned to add additional offices in Portland and San Antonio the high cost of financing has delayed the openings of these offices until next year. Both the planning and the development of the new offices have been handled by five persons in our home office Bill Collins Brad Morgan Susan Smith Carol White and David Williams.

Check your answers with those given on page 357 before completing the next exercise.

Reinforcement Letter 19

Dear Mrs. Farmer:

We appreciate receiving your order. As you requested we are shipping the following items immediately

> 1 carton bond copy paper, 8.5″ × 11″
>
> 1 carton laser printer paper, 8.5″ × 11″
>
> 1 print cartridge for HP LaserJet 8540 printer
>
> 2 USB drives, 8 GB capacity

You may place any future orders by telephone just call our toll-free number (800) 618-4932. Ask for one of the following salespersons Mary Small Bill Green or Ann Smith. If the items you order are in our current catalog they will be sent to you the same day you place your order. On the other hand allow at least ten days for delivery of noncatalog items namely ink cartridges for printers tape cartridges for labelers and supplies for other office equipment manufactured prior to 2007.

We are enclosing a copy of our latest catalog it may be helpful to you in placing future orders. We look forward to doing business with you and toward developing a successful business relationship.

Sincerely yours,

*The answers to this exercise appear in the **Instructor's Manual and Key** for **HOW 13: A Handbook for Office Professionals**, 13th edition.*

Colon Placement, Formerly Enumerated or Listed Items
and Explanatory Sentences

Dash Placement—Parenthetical Elements, Appositives, and Summaries (2-29)

Practice Sentences 20

1. Former employers and instructors these are the only names you should supply to prospective employers as references.

2. A number of urgent e-mail messages one from Mary Thompson two from Laura Woo and two from Michael Benton still need to be answered.

3. Several major factors increased interest rates higher property values and a general business slowdown have caused a real estate decline in this area.

4. The administrative staff hoping to boost employee morale increase sales and raise profit levels instituted a bonus-commission plan.

5. Sunburst Apollo Courtyard and Apple Blossom these four china patterns will be featured during our August sale.

6. Any number of private delivery services Federal Express United Parcel Service DSL etc. can provide you with overnight service to Cincinnati.

7. All our staff members with possibly only one or two exceptions are certified public accountants.

8. You may choose from a variety of colors black navy gray white bone red pink yellow brown taupe emerald and sky blue.

9. Three commercial online service providers AT&T Time Warner Cable and Verizon are being evaluated by our manager.

10. Word processing spreadsheet and database any applicant we interview must have recent training or experience in these kinds of software programs.

Check your answers with those given on page 357 before completing the next exercise.

Practice Paragraph 20

Crestview Wood Finishing manufacturers of French doors and windows main entrance doors and window boxes has been serving our community for more than 25 years. Our quality workmanship which can be seen in the lustrous wood finish elegant hardware and precision fit of our doors and windows is guaranteed for five years. Stop by our showroom to view our new display of French doors and windows.

Single pane double panes beveled or frosted you may choose any of these glass types for your French

doors or windows.

Check your answers with those given on pages 357–358 before completing the next exercise.

Reinforcement Letter 20

To: Susan Brady

This morning our bank president Phillip S. Hoover announced that Continental Bank will merge with

United Federal Bank. The merger will become effective on January 1 and all Continental Bank offices will

officially become part of United Federal Bank. At that time Continental Bank will cease to exist however

every effort will be made to make this transition as smooth as possible for both our customers and our

employees.

The Devonshire Branch the Mission Hills Branch and the Chatsworth Branch these three Sun Valley

branches will be closed as a result of the merger with United Federal Bank. Because United Federal

Bank has existing branches in these areas the Continental Bank branch offices are no longer needed.

Between January 1 and February 28 the branches designated to close will maintain normal

operations for all customers. All three branch managers Gail Davis Tony Garcia and Chris Ellis will begin

transfer and shutdown operations on March 1. These managers besides notifying customers transferring

accounts to other branches and vacating the premises will need to reduce their staffs by 50 percent and

give proper notice to those employees who will no longer have positions with the bank. All displaced

personnel who remain with the bank through March 31 the target date for the branch office closings will be

awarded an attractive severance package.

As vice president of real estate and development you will need to determine the disposition of the furniture

equipment and facilities. Please keep me informed Susan of your progress in this regard.

*The answers to this exercise appear in the **Instructor's Manual and Key** for **HOW 13: A Handbook for Office Professionals**, 13th edition.*

Section 3   Capitalization

Practice Sentences, Practice Paragraphs, and Reinforcement Letters

The following materials contain five sets of exercises for the major principles governing the capitalization of nouns. These sets include *Practice Sentences,* a *Practice Paragraph,* and a *Reinforcement Letter.*

Each principle under consideration is labeled by name at the beginning of the exercise series. The section in *HOW that* explains the use of the principle is shown in parentheses.

For *Practice Sentences* use the proofreaders' mark for capitalization under each letter to be capitalized; that is, place three short underscores below the letter to be capitalized. Follow the procedure shown in the following example:

Mary richter ordered a model 5879 calculator for each member of the staff in our

accounting department.

For those sentences requiring quotation marks, italics, or underscores use proofreaders'

marks to show these marks of punctuation directly on the copy. See the following illustration:

I read with interest your article more vacation for less money that appeared in the march

issue of arizona highways.

Practice Sentences deal only with the principle or principles under consideration. After you have completed each exercise, check your answers on pages 358–360.

Practice Paragraphs illustrate further the capitalization principle or principles under consideration. Use the procedures described for *Practice Sentences* to complete the exercises. Check your answers on pages 358–360.

Reinforcement Letters are cumulative; that is, once a capitalization principle has been covered in a previous exercise, it may appear in the *Reinforcement Letters.* Use the same procedures outlined for the *Practice Sentences* and the *Practice Paragraphs* to edit the *Reinforcement Letters.* Check your answers with your instructor.

Practice Guides

Seven additional sets of exercises on capitalization follow the *Practice Sentence-Practice Paragraph-Reinforcement Letter* series. These *Practice Guides* correspond to the previous exercises and have been designed to give additional, more intensive practice in the application of the capitalization principles under consideration.

Specific instructions for the completion of each *Practice Guide* are given at the beginning of the exercise material. For solutions to these exercises, check with your instructor.

Section 3 Capitalization

Capitalization, Proper Nouns and Adjectives (3-2)

Practice Sentences 1

1. Did you know that dr. chu's new offices are located in the medical arts building?

2. Are there any stores in the promenade shopping mall that sell franciscan china?

3. We will visit the caribbean on the cruise ship the viking queen.

4. During the storm the green tree bridge collapsed into the suwannee river.

5. Two of the old desktops in our firm are being replaced with hp touchsmarts.

6. For the banquet did you order caesar salad to accompany the beef stroganoff?

7. Our next convention will be held at the montclair hotel in the city of angels.

8. Miniblinds are a new version of the old-fashioned venetian blinds.

9. This year the dakota county fair will be held in norfolk.

10. All these sketches by john sreveski are done in india ink.

Check your answers with those given on page 358 before completing the next exercise.

Practice Paragraph 1

In april we will meet in the islands to discuss the reorganization of territories in alaska, california, hawaii, oregon, and washington. Reservations have been made for april 7 on an american airlines flight to honolulu. Either general motors or ford motor company cars may be rented from budget car rental for those agents attending the meeting.

Check your answers with those given on page 358 before completing the next exercise.

Reinforcement Letter 1

Dear ms. harris:

We were sorry to learn that you were disappointed with the performance of your travelwell luggage during your recent trip to the far east.

We agree that the zipper on your suitcase should not have broken. If you will take the suitcase and this letter to white's department store, the manager will have the zipper on your travelwell luggage repaired or your suitcase replaced free of charge.

We are sorry for the inconvenience you have been caused. As a token of our appreciation for your patience and to reaffirm your confidence in travelwell products, we are enclosing a $50 gift certificate that may be used toward your next purchase of any piece of travelwell luggage.

May we suggest you view our newest product, the travel-lite briefcase. Its lightweight feature and durability have made this briefcase one of our most popular products. See it for yourself at white's department store.

sincerely yours,

*The answers to this exercise appear in the **Instructor's Manual and Key** for **HOW 13: A Handbook for Office Professionals**, 13th edition.*

Proper Nouns and Adjectives

Capitalization, Abbreviations (3-3)
Capitalization, Numbered or Lettered Items (3-4)

Practice Sentences 2

1. Please deliver this c.o.d. order before 2 p.m.

2. The cpa examination will be given at usc next month.

3. Unfortunately, aa flight 82 has been delayed several hours.

4. Enclosed is payment for invoice 578391, which covers all the merchandise we purchased from you last month.

5. Please refer to page 28 of our current catalog to see an illustration of our model 1738 dvd player.

6. I believe the check I issued you, no. 347, was returned by the bank in error.

7. Notice that figure 3 on page 23 illustrates the increase in foreign car sales during the past two years.

8. I believe that paragraph 4 should be deleted from this report.

9. Have you notified the insured that policy no. 6429518-C will lapse next month?

10. Next week we will place our model 17 desk on sale.

Check your answers with those given on page 358 before completing the next exercise.

Practice Paragraph 2

The medical expenses resulting from your fall are covered by your policy, no. 846821. However, as stated in section B, paragraph 3, the company will cover medical costs only after the $100 deductible has been satisfied. If your medical expenses since January 1 have exceeded the deductible amount, please have your doctor fill out form 6B and return it in the enclosed envelope. If you have any questions, call me at (800) 759-6382 any weekday between 9 a.m. and 4 p.m.

Check your answers with those given on pages 358–359 before completing the next exercise.

Reinforcement Letter 2

Dear mrs. rice:

We have made reservations for you on united airlines flight 980 to new york city on march 18. Your flight will leave denver at 9:30 a.m., mst, and arrive in new york at 3:10 p.m., est. As shown on page 2 of the enclosed brochure, the tour will leave for europe the following day.

Please limit the weight of your luggage to 50 pounds. According to the enclosed policy, no. 48613, your luggage is insured up to $3,000 against loss or damage.

Once you arrive in new york, you will be met at jfk by a representative from our travel agency. She will take you to the wilson hotel where room 422 has been reserved for your overnight stay. Your tour guide will contact you there.

Do have a wonderful stay in europe. We appreciate your allowing us to make the arrangements for you.

sincerely yours,

*The answers to this exercise appear in the **Instructor's Manual and Key** for **HOW 13: A Handbook for Office Professionals**, 13th edition.*

Capitalization, Personal and Professional Titles (3-5)

Practice Sentences 3

1. When does the governor wish to schedule the conference?

2. We have sent all the extra copies of this book to professor Carlos Rodríguez.

3. The announcement was made by Mark Swenson, president of Georgetown Steel.

4. Please submit this application to our vice president, Joshua Wooldridge.

5. We request, professor, that all grade reports be returned by the end of next week.

6. Tomorrow mayor-elect Ann Brown will take office.

7. Each semester Byron Teague, assistant dean of instruction, must visit at least once the classes of all probationary instructors.

8. Only our director of human resources was invited to attend the meeting.

9. These orders are to be delivered to lieutenant colonel Bruno Furtado.

10. We hope that Barack Obama, the president, will accept the key to our city during his visit here.

Check your answers with those given on page 359 before completing the next exercise.

Practice Paragraph 3

    The purchasing agents' convention in miami was well attended this year. After a welcoming speech by mayor frank barnes, john lang, the president of williams manufacturing company, spoke on how inflation is affecting the inventories of many companies throughout the country. Also speaking on the same subject was professor roberta holt.

Check your answers with those given on page 359 before completing the next exercise.

Reinforcement Letter 3

Dear mr. ross:

As assistant to councilman john rogers, I, as one of my duties, schedule his appointments. On the day you wish to meet with him, he has an all-day meeting with alice day, auditor for springfield county. Following his meeting with ms. day, he will fly to washington, dc, to meet with george davis, senator from florida.

I expect councilman rogers to return on october 15. He is scheduled to arrive at dfw on united flight 76 at 9:15 a.m.

I know that as chairperson of his reelection campaign, you are quite eager to meet with him. Would you be able to meet in room 117 of the broadway building at 2 p.m. on october 15? Please call me at (661) 719-5555, ext. 523, to confirm this appointment or to set up a time for another one.

sincerely yours,

*The answers to this exercise appear in the **Instructor's Manual and Key** for **HOW 13: A Handbook for Office Professionals**, 13th edition.*

Capitalization, Literary or Artistic Works (3-6 Through 3-12)
Capitalization—Academic Subjects, Courses, and Degrees (3-13 and 3-14)

Practice Sentences 4

Note: The words appearing in brackets are titles of literary or artistic works.

1. We must purchase the book [a history of the americas] for our history 12 class.

2. Did you know that your subscription to [a music world of wonder] will expire with the next issue?

3. Theresa Flores, phd, has agreed to teach a conversational spanish class during the next semester.

4. Walt Disney's movie [the lion king] is available on digital video disc for your children's continual enjoyment.

5. Make an appointment to see Lisa Gartlan, md, for a physical examination.

6. Did you read [a look at teenage life in these united states] that appeared in the April issue of [outlook magazine]?

7. In June Mr. Magnuson will be awarded his master of science degree in engineering.

8. The group sang [singing in the rain] for its last number.

9. We are presently running ads in [the new york times] and [the wall street journal].

10. All the students in our theater arts 23 class went to see [phantom of the opera].

Check your answers with those given on page 359 before completing the next exercise.

Practice Paragraph 4

    I plan to interview fred case, phd, the author of the book [it's easy to make a million dollars]. This interview will be the basis for a feature article that will appear in the [people today] section of the sunday [chronicle]. I am interested to learn whether the ideas outlined in his book came from actual experience, research, or both. I understand, too, that the newly released movie, [how to make a million without really trying], is based on dr. case's book.

Check your answers with those given on page 360 before completing the next exercise.

Reinforcement Letter 4

Dear dr. carnes:

I was pleased to be able to meet with you to discuss the editorial problems we experienced with the manuscript for your latest book, [economics for the consumer]. Your production editor, mary jones, agrees with me that all the changes you suggested can be made easily so that the book will be applicable for use in marketing classes.

As far as publicity for the book is concerned, charles singer, director of advertising, suggested that we advertise the book in [the marketing educator], a periodical for instructors of marketing, general business, and consumer economics.

I am enclosing a copy of an article entitled [the consumer revolt—is it really here?] that appeared in the last issue of [new yorker] magazine. The author's ideas seem to be quite similar to yours, so I thought you might be interested in seeing it.

If I can be of any further editorial help to you, please let me know.

sincerely,

*The answers to this exercise appear in the **Instructor's Manual and Key** for **HOW 13: A Handbook for Office Professionals**, 13th edition.*

Capitalization, Organizations (3-15)

Practice Sentences 5

1. Please make your tax-deductible check payable to the national fund for the protection of american wildlife.

2. This bill was passed by the United States senate during its last session.

3. All personnel employed by the company and their families are ineligible to participate in the contest.

4. These forms must be approved by the accounting department before they can be forwarded to the payroll department.

5. Please ask our advertising department to make the changes shown on the enclosed copy.

6. Yesterday we learned that all county employees will receive a 5 percent pay increase.

7. Contact the department of human resources to assist you with solving this problem.

8. Only government employees are eligible to receive this discount.

9. The contracts must be ready for members of the board of directors to sign by June 4.

10. Are you a member of the national council of teachers of english?

Check your answers with those given on page 360 before completing the next exercise.

Practice Paragraph 5

    Bill Hughes has recently been promoted to head our public relations department. As a former president of both the chamber of commerce and the rotary club, he is well acquainted with many members of the business community. One of his main responsibilities in his new position at fairchild enterprises will be to promote the company among his business contacts.

Check your answers with those given on page 360 before completing the next exercise.

Reinforcement Letter 5

Dear mr. smith:

Thank you for your time and cooperation in helping us conduct the yearly audit of watson corporation. Your accounting department is among the most efficient and well-organized ones I have ever visited.

Hopefully your loan application to the small business administration will be approved. If you would like some advice or assistance in completing the loan application, you may wish to contact john jones, vice president of ryan corporation. He is quite knowledgeable in dealing with sba matters and would be able to answer any questions you may have. I have informed john that you may be calling him.

Please give my regards to your controller, peter swift. We appreciated his efforts during the audit to make our stay at watson corporation a pleasant one.

sincerely yours,

The answers to this exercise appear in the **Instructor's Manual and Key** *for* **HOW 13: A Handbook for Office Professionals***, 13*[th] *edition.*

Name _____ Date _____

Practice Guide 1: Capitalization—Proper Nouns and Adjectives (3-2)

Instructions: Proofread the following sentences for errors in capitalization of proper nouns or adjectives. Underline any errors, and supply the correct answer in the blank at the right. If a sentence is correct, write *OK* in the blank.

Example: Our offices are located in the Union Bank <u>building</u> on the   _____*Building*_____
corner of Broadway and State Street.

1. One of our most popular cruises takes travelers through the   1. _____
   Panama canal.

2. Within the Pittsfield area, we have at least four Italian Restaurants.   2. _____

3. Access the U.S. Postal Service Web site to locate the 9-digit ZIP   3. _____
   Codes for the enclosed list of addresses.

4. Your out-of-warranty Emerson Computer can be repaired by one   4. _____
   of our local authorized dealers.

5. You will need to cross the San Francisco Bay bridge to reach our   5. _____
   offices.

6. All these american corporations have been in existence for at least   6. _____
   50 years.

7. Please order an additional supply of letter-size Manila file folders.   7. _____

8. Prices for this year's models of Sony Digital Cameras have   8. _____
   dropped considerably.

9. Since our company has a number of clients in Chicago, I often visit   9. _____
   the windy city.

10. Alfredo's is best known for its delicious Chili con carne.   10. _____

11. A number of our clients have expressed an interest in taking a tour 11. _____
    down the Mississippi river.

12. Our design center features scandinavian furniture and modern art.   12. _____

13. This new fast-food chain serves only hamburgers, French fries,   13. _____
    and an assortment of beverages.

14. Clients may enjoy a cup of starbucks coffee during their   14. _____
    appointment with one of our investment counselors.

15. The camarillo fashion mall is scheduled to open on October 1.   15. _____

16. Although they appear to be made of wood, all these statues are   16. _____
    made of Plaster of Paris.

17. Our deluxe nut mixture consists of almonds, walnuts, cashews,   17. _____
    and Brazil nuts.

18. Dr. Lee has moved her offices to the Desert medical center.

18. _____

19. Salad dressing choices for our customers include Italian, French, Ranch, and Blue Cheese.

19. _____

20. Heavy storms over the Rockies have delayed most flights.

20. _____

21. With each entrée you have a choice of broccoli soup, caesar salad, or a visit to our salad bar.

21. _____

22. The Pasadena rose parade is shown each year on national television.

22. _____

23. We import only european-made clothing, shoes, and handbags.

23. _____

24. At our department store, you may obtain all available patterns of Lenox China.

24. _____

25. The xerox in our office needs to be serviced before I can make these copies.

25. _____

*The answers to this exercise appear in the **Instructor's Manual and Key** for **HOW 13: A Handbook for Office Professionals**, 13th edition.*

Name _____ Date _____

Practice Guide 2: Capitalization—Abbreviations (3-3), Numbered or Lettered Items (3-4)

Instructions: Proofread the following sentences for errors in capitalization of abbreviations and numbered or lettered items. Underline any errors, and supply the correct answer in the blank at the right. If a sentence is correct, write *OK* in the blank.

1. Our store hours are from 9 A.M. to 5 P.M. daily.

1. _____

2. All our scanners are fully illustrated and described on pages 78–86 of the enclosed catalog.

2. _____

3. Your check number 382 was returned by the bank for insufficient funds.

3. _____

4. We are moving our offices from suite 340 to suite 200 next month.

4. _____

5. Several people in our office are taking courses toward earning a ba degree.

5. _____

6. Do we have any additional Size 8 dresses in Style 4328?

6. _____

7. The premium on your fire insurance policy, number 18754BVN834, is due on March 1.

7. _____

8. You will be flying to Atlanta on Delta Flight 1074, which is scheduled to depart on time.

8. _____

9. This e-mail message was sent today at 12 noon, est.

9. _____

10. One of our computers, serial no. 18754390, will not boot up.

10. _____

11. The cpa examination is given biannually in Tampa.

11. _____

12. We have been rescheduled to meet in room 570 instead of room 420.

12. _____

13. Two of these orders are to be sent COD.

13. _____

14. Is the monthly rental fee correct as stipulated in paragraph 5, line 3, of the enclosed lease agreement?

14. _____

15. No. 440 in our wheelchair line will be discontinued as soon as the current stock is sold.

15. _____

16. Enclosed is a check to cover your invoice 8321 for $3,687.

16. _____

17. The Hewlett-Packard Officejet Pro printer, model K550, uses separate cartridges for printing in black and in other colors.

17. _____

18. Because of the dense fog, many planes have been rerouted to lax.

18. _____

19. Please refer to figure 4 on page 17 of the annual report for net earnings during the last quarter of the year.

19. _____

20. If you are interested in part-time employment, fill out and return form B in the enclosed envelope.

20. _____

21. This invoice was paid by check no. 472 last week.

21. _____

22. Because flight 1054 was overbooked, we were rerouted on flight 1283.

22. _____

23. These records belong to employee No. 576827, who is a supervisor at our Hartford plant.

23. _____

24. A summary of grammar rules appears in appendix A of this business communications text.

24. _____

25. John R. Jones, Soc. Sec. #576-41-9031, has signed the consent form for us to authorize a credit check.

25. _____

*The answers to this exercise appear in the **Instructor's Manual and Key** for **HOW 13: A Handbook for Office Professionals**, 13th edition.*

Name _____ Date _____

Practice Guide 3: Capitalization—Personal and Professional Titles (3-5)

Instructions: Proofread the following sentences for errors in capitalization of personal or professional titles. Underline any errors, and supply the correct answer in the blank at the right. If a sentence is correct, write *OK* in the blank.

1. When you complete the report, please forward a copy to Doctor Jeffrey Weisel.

1. _____

2. Such a decision will have to be made by the Vice President of Marketing.

2. _____

3. You will need to speak to sergeant Chris Nelson, the police officer who took the report.

3. _____

4. We expect, professor, to receive additional copies of this text by August 3.

4. _____

5. Barack Obama, president of the United States, will visit our city next month.

5. _____

6. Our new Vice President, Cameron Bentley, has arranged to visit all our branch offices during the next three months.

6. _____

7. Will rabbi Goldman be conducting the marriage ceremony?

7. _____

8. Our Director of Human Resources has announced that she will retire on June 30.

8. _____

9. This bill was initiated by the Senator from Indiana, John Simpson.

9. _____

10. Our scheduled shows, captain, that your next assignment is Flight 1042, on Tuesday, March 3, departing at 10:43 a.m.

10. _____

11. Copies of these reports should be sent to Governor-Elect Aaron Wagner before the end of the week.

11. _____

12. If you need additional information about our operations, just contact our general manager, Alice Duffy.

12. _____

13. At the next board meeting, our President, Gordon Hampton, will present plans to open branch offices in Santiago and Buenos Aires.

13. _____

14. All requests for budget transfers must be reviewed by Ms. Rodriguez, the Dean of Academic Affairs.

14. _____

15. Please forward all this mail to major Morgan at his new address.

15. _____

16. Mark W. Coulter, the Reverend at St. Luke's Trinity Church, is the beneficiary of this insurance policy.

16. _____

17. Ms. Foster's Grandmother, Estella Carter, named Ms. Foster executrix of her estate.

17. _____

18. We will be meeting with the mayor on this issue next week.

18. _____

19. Anita E. Gould, Professor of English, has been selected chairperson of the English Department.

19. _____

20. Charles E. Young, President of American Banking Services, has agreed to deliver the keynote address at the bankers' convention.

20. _____

21. You may, Mister Evans, wish to consult one of our attorneys about this matter.

21. _____

22. The dean of students has suggested we invite Senator Peter Goodwin to deliver this year's commencement address.

22. _____

23. When did queen Elizabeth make her last public appearance in May London?

23. _____

24. Since Former Mayor Clarence Chapman left office, he has had several offers from prestigious law firms in our city.

24. _____

25. The Academy Award-winning Actress, Heather Starr, has agreed to make a guest appearance on our show.

25. _____

*The answers to this exercise appear in the **Instructor's Manual and Key** for **HOW 13: A Handbook for Office Professionals**, 13th edition.*

Practice Guide 4: Capitalization—Literary or Artistic Works (3-6 Through 3-12)

Instructions: From the choices given below, select the correct one or ones. Write the corresponding letter or letters in the blank at the right.

1. Which of the following is/are correct to express the name of a
   newspaper?
   a. The Evening Outlook
   b. *The Evening Outlook*
   c. The evening outlook
   d. "The Evening Outlook"
   e. <u>The Evening Outlook</u>

   1. _____

2. How would you express the name of the following song?
   a. A Paradise of Happiness
   b. *A Paradise of Happiness*
   c. <u>A Paradise of Happiness</u>
   d. "A Paradise Of Happiness"
   e. "A Paradise of Happiness"

   2. _____

3. When referring to the appendix of a specific book, how would you
   express this reference?
   a. *Appendix*
   b. <u>Appendix</u>
   c. "Appendix"
   d. Appendix
   e. appendix

   3. _____

4. According to *HOW*, which of the following parts of speech are not
   capitalized in titles unless they (a) contain more than four letters or
   (b) appear as the first or last word?
   a. Nouns
   b. Pronouns
   c. Verbs
   d. Prepositions
   e. Adjectives

   4. _____

5. Which one of the following titles follows correctly the rules of
   capitalization for literary and artistic works?
   a. In this World of Music
   b. Learning through Proper Study Habits
   c. How to Learn What is Important in Looking for a Job
   d. So you Think You're In?
   e. A Guide to Understanding Literature

   5. _____

6. Which one of the following titles follows correctly the rules of
   capitalization for literary and artistic works?
   a. A Guide to Successful Lawn Care
   b. The Beginning of a New Era is Approaching
   c. What is Word Processing all About?
   d. The Computer Age: an Analysis of Today's Society
   e. Problems Of Urban Living

   6. _____

7. How would you express correctly the name of the following chapter   7. _____
   in a textbook?
   a. The Office Environment and Its Effect on Performance
   b. "The Office Environment and Its Effect on Performance"
   c. "The Office Environment and its Effect on Performance"
   d. <u>The Office Environment and Its Effect on Performance</u>
   e. *The Office Environment and its Effect on Performance*

8. How would you express correctly the name of the following book?   8. _____
   a. <u>The World Dictionary Of the German Language</u>
   b. *The World Dictionary of the German Language*
   c. "The World Dictionary of the German Language"
   d. <u>The World Dictionary of the German Language</u>
   e. *The World Dictionary Of The German Language*

9. Which of the following is written correctly to express the names of   9. _____
   these famous paintings?
   a. PINK LADY and BLUE BOY
   b. Pink Lady and Blue Boy
   c. "Pink Lady" and "Blue Boy"
   d. <u>Pink Lady</u> and <u>Blue Boy</u>
   e. *Pink Lady* and *Blue Boy*

10. How would you properly express the title of the following   10. _____
    unpublished report?
    a. Report on the Reconstruction of the Inner City
    b. <u>Report on the Reconstruction of the Inner City</u>
    c. REPORT ON THE RECONSTRUCTION OF THE INNER CITY
    d. "Report on the Reconstruction of the Inner City"
    e. "Report On The Reconstruction Of The Inner City"

*The answers to this exercise appear in the **Instructor's Manual and Key** for **HOW 13: A Handbook for Office Professionals**, 13th edition.*

Name _____ Date _____

Practice Guide 5: Capitalization—Literary or Artistic Works (3-6 Through 3-12)

Instructions: Proofread the following sentences. In the blank lines provided, rewrite each sentence, making any necessary changes in *capitalization, punctuation*, and *formatting*. The names of literary or artistic works are shown in brackets.

1. Professor Schwartz requested the class to read the book [a short history of the roman empire] by March 21.

   _____

   _____

2. The new newspaper column [to and from] that appears in the Sunday issue of the [pittsburgh tribune] has been an unexpected success.

   _____

   _____

3. Did you see the movie [an american werewolf in london].

   _____

   _____

4. When will we receive a copy of Professor Clybourne's lecture entitled [how long can interest rates go down].

   _____

   _____

5. In the [preface] the author explains how to use the textbook.

   _____

   _____

6. I read with interest your most recent article [changing trends in the housing industry] that appeared in last month's issue of [contractors' world].

   _____

   _____

   _____

7. The artist has called this painting [mood for a midnight dream].

   _____

   _____

8. His thesis [a statistical analysis of two approaches for analyzing consumer responses to newspaper advertising] was accepted by the committee last week.

_____

_____

_____

9. We hope that our new television series [for the love of law] will be as great a success as [nyc crime fighters] was.

_____

_____

10. When will you revise the pamphlet [can you hold a job].

_____

_____

11. Be sure to read the chapter [economic declines and depressions] that appears in the latest edition of our economics textbook [modern economic theories and philosophies].

_____

_____

_____

12. If you have any difficulty locating the information, be sure to consult the [index].

_____

_____

13. Last Sunday's sermon [it is up to you] left the congregation with a challenge.

_____

_____

14. When will our class view the movie classic [who's afraid of virginia woolf].

_____

_____

15. The column [brian williams reports] no longer appears in our local newspaper [the daily news].

_____

_____

*The answers to this exercise appear in the **Instructor's Manual and Key** for **HOW 13: A Handbook for Office Professionals**, 13th edition.*

Name _____ Date _____

Practice Guide 6: Capitalization—Academic Subjects, Courses, and Degrees (3-13 and 3-14)

Instructions: Proofread the following sentences for errors in capitalization of academic subjects, courses, and degrees. Underline any errors, and supply the correct answer in the blank at the right. If a sentence is correct, write *OK* in the blank.

1. Most of our english classes for nonnative speakers are offered in the evening hours.

1. _____

2. The instructor for our European history class is Paul D. Whalen, phd.

2. _____

3. Unfortunately, speech 31 is offered only during the spring semesters.

3. _____

4. You will be eligible for your bachelor of science degree next June provided that you complete the courses listed below.

4. _____

5. All our Conversational Spanish classes are usually filled during the first two weeks of registration.

5. _____

6. Before you may enroll in Accounting 1, you must take a Mathematics proficiency test.

6. _____

7. Two of our graduates have just been accepted into the Master's program at Loyola University.

7. _____

8. Business 8, introduction to business, will be offered Tuesdays and Thursdays from 8:30–10 a.m.

8. _____

9. You may wish to take a Music Appreciation class to fulfill this requirement.

9. _____

10. Two-year colleges offer only associate in arts degrees or associate in science degrees.

10. _____

11. A course in Business English will give you a better understanding of language principles.

11. _____

12. William J. Clark, md, will be the surgeon operating on your son next week.

12. _____

13. Our English Department offers several american literature courses.

13. _____

14. Business 85, Excel 2010, was inadvertently omitted in the listing of classes for the current class schedule.

14. _____

15. Our Nursing program was established at the college in 1989.

15. _____

16. You may fulfill the language requirement by taking any course in french, german, japanese, or spanish.

16. _____

17. Professor Taylor teaches three sections of principles of marketing each semester.

17. _____

18. Darryl's research topic deals with the origin and development of Greek mythology.

18. _____

19. Marian's Bachelor's degree is in marketing and management.

19. _____

20. Kevin Dickinson, DdS, has rented all this space for his new dental offices.

20. _____

21. The student wishes to know if her Greek Literature classes will satisfy any general education requirements.

21. _____

22. As a student of history, Robert has read most of the books listed in the professor's suggested reading list.

22. _____

23. Bryton College, a private career college, is the only college in this area that offers courses in Medical Office Procedures.

23. _____

24. History 12, history of the Americas, will be offered each semester and during the summer session.

24. _____

25. To complete the requirements for the Associate in Arts degree, you will need to complete at least 60 units in a prescribed program.

25. _____

*The answers to this exercise appear in the **Instructor's Manual and Key** for **HOW 13: A Handbook for Office Professionals**, 13th edition.*

Name _____ Date _____

Practice Guide 7: Capitalization—Organizations (3-15)

Instructions: Proofread the following sentences for errors in capitalization of organizational names and divisions. Underline any errors, and supply the correct answer in the blank at the right. If a sentence is correct, write *OK* in the blank.

1. Elizabeth Tanner obtained her master's degree from the Fisher school of accounting at the University of Florida.

1. _____

2. All contributions to the muscular dystrophy foundation are tax deductible.

2. _____

3. Our customer services department is open from 8 a.m. until 5 p.m., EST.

3. _____

4. All City offices will be closed on January 17, so you must file these papers before that date.

4. _____

5. Please make your check payable to the Arizona Association For The Preservation of National Forests.

5. _____

6. Under this program the federal government will guarantee the loan.

6. _____

7. Proposed revisions in the tax laws should come before congress during this session.

7. _____

8. When you have projected the costs of this advertising campaign, please report your findings to the manager of the sales and marketing department.

8. _____

9. All these federal housing projects are under the jurisdiction of the department of housing and urban development.

9. _____

10. You will need to submit this petition for a grade change to the office of academic affairs.

10. _____

11. Employees are eligible for health insurance benefits after six months of continuous employment with the Company.

11. _____

12. The board of directors' meeting has been rescheduled for March 4.

12. _____

13. Our survey included the Accounting Departments of more than 50 major United States corporations.

13. _____

14. When did the Supreme Court render a decision on this issue?

14. _____

15. All state employees were granted a 4 percent pay increase, retroactive to July 1.

15. _____

16. Members of the City Council have been unable to agree upon a plan to revitalize the downtown area.

16. _____

17. On Thursdays you may pick up your check in the payroll department between 2 and 3 p.m.

17. _____

18. Up-to-date population estimates are available from the bureau of the census.

18. _____

19. Please contact the school of engineering and computer science for more information about this major.

19. _____

20. Many Research Departments throughout the nation have used this software successfully to obtain long-term grants.

20. _____

21. Contact the department of highways for its construction plans in this area during the next five years.

21. _____

22. Students from high school and postsecondary music departments will be participating in this concert on May 1.

22. _____

23. You may obtain an application for employment from our human resources department.

23. _____

24. Ms. Donohue's latest experience is in the Product Development Department of Microsoft corporation.

24. _____

25. Our Service department stands ready to serve you every day of the week from 8 a.m. until 6 p.m.

25. _____

*The answers to this exercise appear in the **Instructor's Manual and Key** for **HOW 13: A Handbook for Office Professionals**, 13th edition.*

Section 4   Number Formats

Practice Sentences, Practice Paragraphs, and Reinforcement Letters

The following materials contain four sets of exercises for several major principles governing the expression of numbers. These sets include *Practice Sentences,* a *Practice Paragraph,* and a *Reinforcement Letter.*

Each principle under consideration is labeled by name at the beginning of the exercise series. The section in *HOW* that explains the use of the principle is shown in parentheses.

For *Practice Sentences* select from the alternatives in parentheses the correct choice for the expression of numbers. Underline your answers. Sentences deal only with the principle under consideration. After you have completed the exercise, check your answers on pages 360–362.

Practice Paragraphs illustrate further the number-usage principle under consideration. From the alternatives given in parentheses, select and underline the correct one. Check your answers on pages 360–362.

Reinforcement Letters are cumulative; that is, once a number-usage principle has been covered in a previous exercise, it may appear in the *Reinforcement Letters.* For the *Reinforcement Letters,* select the correct alternative in parentheses and underline your answer. Check your answers with your instructor.

Practice Guide

An additional set of exercises on numbers follows the *Practice Sentence-Practice Paragraph-Reinforcement Letter* series. The *Practice Guide* corresponds to the previous exercises and is designed to give additional, more intensive practice in the application of principles governing number style.

Specific instructions for the completion of the *Practice Guide* are given at the beginning of the exercise material. For solutions to these exercises, check with your instructor.

Section 4 Number Formats

Numbers, General Rules (4-1)

Practice Sentences 1

1. Mrs. Hayes invited (27, twenty-seven) people to the reception.

2. The committee will sponsor (6, six) candidates.

3. (36, Thirty-six) students will enter the competition.

4. Mr. Lucas will hire (10, ten) new clerks.

5. Dr. Francis will lecture on (5, five) symptoms of the common cold.

6. There are (38, thirty-eight) signatures on the roll sheet.

7. (86, Eighty-six) members of the club attended the convention.

8. Ms. Brown has flown (three million; 3 million; 3,000,000) miles since 2009.

9. The department has received (25, twenty-five) applications.

10. There are only (12, twelve) of these 45-inch HDTV-LED televisions left in stock.

Check your answers with those given on page 360 before completing the next exercise.

Practice Paragraph 1

Mr. Wells requested that we send him (seventy-five, 75) copies of our latest catalog. He is

conducting (three, 3) separate workshops at Eastern Business College and believes that more than

(twenty, 20) business teachers will sign up for each course. So that the business teachers can become

acquainted with the materials we have available, Mr. Wells would like to give each teacher a copy of our

catalog.

Check your answers with those given on page 361 before completing the next exercise.

Reinforcement Letter 1

Ladies and Gentlemen:

We appreciate your filling our order for (two hundred twenty-five, 225) Johnson serving tables. (Twenty-three, 23) pieces, however, were damaged in transit and cannot be sold in their present condition. Since (two, 2) separate transit companies handled the shipment of the tables, we cannot determine who is responsible for the damage.

We expect that more than (two hundred, 200) of our charge account customers will purchase the Johnson tables during our presale, which is scheduled to begin next week. Therefore, we would appreciate your rushing us an additional (twenty-three, 23) tables to replace the ones that were damaged. Also, please let us know what should be done with the damaged merchandise.

Sincerely yours,

*The answers to this exercise appear in the **Instructor's Manual and Key** for **HOW 13: A Handbook for Office Professionals**, 13th edition.*

Name _____ Date _____

Numbers, Related Numbers (4-2)

Practice Sentences 2

1. We have 26 computers, but (3, three) need to be repaired.

2. The number of visitors to this national park has increased from 980,000 last year to more than (1 million; 1,000,000) this year.

3. We have requested 25 books, 15 workbooks, and (2, two) instructor's manuals from the publisher.

4. Each of the (11, eleven) applicants gave (4, four) references.

5. Pat found 21 examples of this feature, but only (7, seven) were applicable to our company's needs.

6. There are (382, three hundred eighty-two) active members in this organization, but only (9, nine) are willing to be officers.

7. The prizes—15 television sets, 10 bicycles, and 20 gift certificates—will be awarded during the (2, two) days of our official opening.

8. The produce truck delivered 18 cartons of lettuce, 11 cartons of apples, and (8, eight) cartons of oranges.

9. Our company will manufacture and distribute between (1 million; 1,000,000) and (1.5 million; 1,500,000) of these pens this year.

10. Mrs. Hooper has requested 13 new employees for the (5, five) departments.

Check your answers with those given on page 361 before completing the next exercise.

Practice Paragraph 2

We appreciate your order for (eight, 8) digital cameras, (twenty-two, 22) DVD players, and (six, 6) portable television sets. At the present time, we have only (nine, 9) DVD players in our Dallas warehouse. We will check with our (three, 3) branch offices and our (two, 2) retail stores to determine whether they have available the remaining (thirteen, 13). In the meantime, we are shipping you (eight, 8) digital cameras, (nine, 9) DVD players, and (six, 6) portable television sets.

Check your answers with those given on page 361 before completing the next exercise.

Reinforcement Letter 2

Dear Bob:

We are expecting at least (one hundred, 100) people to attend our banquet planned for next Friday. Would you please have the hotel set up (fourteen, 14) circular tables, each one to accommodate (eight, 8) people. Although the total seating capacity will result in (one hundred twelve, 112), I would prefer to have the extra (twelve, 12) seats available in case the attendance rises to this level.

(Ninety-eight, 98) paid reservations have been received so far. I am especially pleased with the enthusiastic response we have received from people who are not members of our organization. In addition to the (seventy-three, 73) reservations received from our membership, we have received (nineteen, 19) reservations from business executives throughout the region and (six, 6) reservations from professors at nearby colleges.

I appreciate your handling the arrangements for the banquet and look forward to seeing you on Friday.

Cordially,

*The answers to this exercise appear in the **Instructor's Manual and Key** for **HOW 13: A Handbook for Office Professionals**, 13th edition.*

Name _____ Date _____

Numbers, Money and Percentages (4-4 and 4-5)
Numbers, With Words and Abbreviations (4-8)

Practice Sentences 3

1. The new listings may be found on (Page seven, Page 7, page 7).

2. Our insurance agent sent me a rider to (policy 83478, Policy 83478, Policy 83,478) in error.

3. Please refer to the restrictions; (Number three, Number 3, No. 3) is the most important one.

4. (Number 1886, No. 1886) battery chargers are no longer manufactured by our company.

5. The names of all participating dealers are listed in (Paragraph Eight, paragraph eight, paragraph 8, Paragraph 8).

6. The cash register receipt listed items for $1.98, $2.03, $3.01, and ($4, $4.00).

7. Enrollment figures for this year show a (6%, 6 percent, six per cent) increase over last year's.

8. These supplies vary in cost from (20 cents, $.20) to $2.35.

9. Our employer has given all workers an (8%, eight percent, 8 percent) pay increase.

10. The new price for these rulers will be (85 cents, eighty-five cents, $.85) each.

11. The highway repairs will cost between $980,000 and ($1 million; $1,000,000).

12. The city council has allotted (four million dollars, $4 million) for the housing project.

13. Ms. Lloyd has a (22%, 22 percent, 22 per cent) interest in the earnings of this company.

14. The wholesale price of these new pencils will be (30 cents, thirty cents, $.30).

15. There has been a (.4, 0.4) percent decrease in the current interest rate since last week.

Check your answers with those given on page 361 before completing the next exercise.

Practice Paragraph 3

A copy of your homeowner's policy, (policy 7832146, Policy 7832146), is enclosed. As you will note on (page one, page 1, Page 1), (line six, line 6, Line 6), the total company liability under this policy cannot exceed (Two Hundred Thousand Dollars; $200,000; $200,000.00). Please submit this year's premium of (Two Hundred Forty Dollars, $240.00, $240). Because increasing costs have forced us to raise our premium rates, this premium reflects an increase of (eight, 8) percent over last year's premium.

Check your answers with those given on page 361 before completing the next exercise.

Reinforcement Letter 3

Dear Mr. Black:

Although the (twelve, 12) batteries and (two, 2) drills arrived in good condition, we were sorry to learn that (three, 3) of our (Number 114, number 114, No. 114, no. 114) electric motors arrived in damaged condition. According to our records, we shipped you (Serial Numbers, serial numbers, Serial Nos., serial nos.) 832961, 832962, 832963, and 832964. Would you please let us know the serial numbers of the (three, 3) damaged motors.

We have credited your account for (Six Hundred Thirty Dollars, $630, $630.00) plus (Forty-three Dollars and Fifty Cents, $43.50) shipping for the damaged motors. Please keep in mind that you are eligible for a (ten, 10) percent discount on the price of the remaining motor. Also, should you wish us to replace the damaged motors, the (ten, 10) percent discount is still applicable on your reorder.

We were pleased to learn that the remainder of your order arrived in good condition. We are especially proud of the results the (no. 118, No. 118, Number 118, number 118) drill has achieved. Nearly (one hundred, 100) customers surveyed have told us of its superiority over other drills on the market.

Please return the damaged electric motors to our Chicago office. A prepaid shipping authorization is enclosed. If you wish us to replace the electric motors, just call (800) 555-7486.

Sincerely yours,

*The answers to this exercise appear in the **Instructor's Manual and Key** for **HOW 13: A Handbook for Office Professionals**, 13th edition.*

Name _____ Date _____

Numbers, Weights and Measures (4-6 and 4-7)
Numbers, Dates and Periods of Time (4-9 Through 4-12)

Practice Sentences 4

1. The Johnsons' new baby weighed (9 pounds, 12 ounces; 9 pounds 12 ounces; nine pounds, twelve ounces; 9 lbs. 12 oz.) at birth.

2. The engineer's report stated that the boulder weighed at least (three, 3) tons.

3. We will celebrate the fifth anniversary of our company on (June 3, June third, June 3rd).

4. Mrs. López will arrive at (6 P.M., 6 p. m., 6 p.m.).

5. Mr. Hodges will trim (8 inches, eight inches, 8") from each edge.

6. The package weighed (4 pounds, 2 ounces; 4 pounds 2 ounces; four pounds, two ounces; 4 lbs. 2 oz.).

7. (October 25, October 25th) has been set as the date for the next board meeting.

8. The orientation meeting was held at (9 o'clock a.m., 9 o'clock in the morning).

9. Your tour to South America will leave on the (1st of January, 1 of January, first of January) as scheduled.

10. During the past (18, eighteen) months, we have had two serious fires in our Toledo warehouse.

11. This invoice must be paid within (30, thirty) days to avoid interest charges.

12. In our state no one under (18, eighteen) may work in restaurants that serve alcoholic beverages.

13. Ms. Ige will be (33, thirty-three, thirty three) on her next birthday.

14. Our city will celebrate its (125th, one hundred twenty-fifth) anniversary in 2014.

15. Bob Sarafian, (63, sixty-three, sixty three), announced that he plans to take an early retirement at the end of the year.

Check your answers with those given on page 362 before completing the next exercise.

Practice Paragraph 4

When we were in Phoenix from (August 13, August 13th) until (August 24, August 24th), the average high temperature reading was (one hundred sixteen degrees, 116 deg., 116°, 116 degrees). On the (25 of August, 25th of August), the temperature reading dropped to (one hundred ten degrees, 110 deg., 110°, 110 degrees). We did enjoy our (twelve-day, 12-day) vacation but wished our stay had been a cooler one.

Check your answers with those given on page 362 before completing the next exercise.

Reinforcement Letter 4

Dear Mr. and Mrs. Reed:

We know that you will be pleased with your new home. With its (two thousand one hundred; 2,100; 2100) square feet of living space, you will find enjoyment and conveniences that will make it a real pleasure.

As you know, within your section we have built (sixteen, 16) town houses; at present (nine, 9) of them have been sold. We expect that within the next (eleven, 11) months, the remaining units will be occupied.

We are now in a position to offer you a special furniture value. At prices (thirty, 30) percent below retail value, you may purchase furniture you need for your new home. For example, you may purchase a (model 17, Model 17) Johnson dining room set, which retails for (Eight Hundred Seventy Dollars, $870, $870.00), for only (Six Hundred Dollars, $600, $600.00).

To purchase your new furniture, you need place only a (twenty, 20) percent down payment on your selections. The balance is due (thirty, 30) days after delivery of the furniture, or you may use one of our convenient financing plans. If you are interested in taking advantage of this offer and wish to have one of our decorators call, please return the enclosed postcard or call our office at (818) 555-3886.

Sincerely yours,

*The answers to this exercise appear in the **Instructor's Manual and Key** for **HOW 13: A Handbook for Office Professionals**, 13th edition.*

Name _____ Date _____

Practice Guide: Numbers—Figure and Word Style (4-1 Through 4-16)

Instructions: Proofread the following sentences for errors in numeral or word format. Underline any errors, and supply the correct answer in the blank at the right. If a sentence is correct, write *OK* in the blank.

Example: Since we posted this opening at our Web site Career Center,   _____23_____
we have received <u>twenty-three</u> résumés.

1. Members of the staff are making plans to celebrate next year the   1. _____
   50th anniversary of the college.

2. Your request for a thirty-day loan for $1,500 at 12 percent interest   2. _____
   has been granted.

3. Our company has occupied this suite of offices for the past   3. _____
   17 years.

4. If the meeting is still in session at 2 this afternoon, I will need to 4. _____
   leave early to catch my flight.

5. Would you please ensure that this proposal reaches the FedEx   5. _____
   office by four p.m.

6. If you wish to use these travel vouchers, you must book your flight   6. _____
   before the 31st of March.

7. Please send us a duplicate of Invoice #36583.   7. _____

8. Be sure to write the customer's check no. on the sales invoice.   8. _____

9. Our office is located approximately 30 km. outside London.   9. _____

10. Green Valley's specialty coffees are sold in one-pound packages   10. _____
    and K-Cup packs.

11. Although we suffered a 6% sales decline during the last quarter,   11. _____
    we showed a 2% increase in profits.

12. Damage to the city block area is estimated to be in excess of   12. _____
    $17,500,000.

13. Candy bars usually sell for 55 cents each, but one of our   13. _____
    neighborhood stores is selling three candy bars for $.99.

14. The twins' birth weights were recorded as 4 pounds, 14 ounces,   14. _____
    and 5 pounds, 2 ounces.

15. 43 orders are still waiting to be processed before we close today.   15. _____

16. Golden Star Realty's residential listings include 62 single-family residences, 18 condominium units, and three apartment complexes.   16. _____

17. This week I processed checks to Eagle Software for $657.85, $250, and $187.59.   17. _____

18. In the large banquet room, we can fit up to 30 60-inch round tables, which will each seat ten people.   18. _____

19. Homes planned for this new residential community will have from 3600 to 4850 square feet of living space.   19. _____

20. You will need to send 7 original copies of the proposal to the client.   20. _____

21. Nearly one hundred of these mailers were returned because of insufficient postage.   21. _____

22. Fifty two reservations are still needed to meet our guarantee for the president's retirement banquet.   22. _____

23. We will need 78 65-cent stamps to send out the remainder of these invitations to residents in our community.   23. _____

24. For the additional 14 Model AR110 wall air-conditioning units, please check our other 3 warehouses for availability.   24. _____

25. There are too many *zeros* in this total for the spreadsheet formula to be correct.   25. _____

*The answers to this exercise appear in the **Instructor's Manual and Key** for **HOW 13: A Handbook for Office Professionals**, 13th edition.*

Name _____ Date _____

Section 5 Hyphenating and Dividing Words

Compound Adjectives (5-2)

Practice Guide 1

Instructions: Make any necessary corrections to the underlined words in the following sentences. Write your answer in the blank provided at the right of each sentence. If the underlined words are written correctly, write *OK* in the blank line.

1. Please have all applicants for the administrative assistant position take a <u>five minute</u> keyboarding timed writing.

    1. _____

2. We must bring our customer records <u>up-to-date</u> by the end of this month.

    2. _____

3. At the present time, our company uses two different <u>word-processing</u> programs.

    3. _____

4. The <u>Boston-Miami</u> flight is scheduled twice daily on weekdays.

    4. _____

5. An <u>alarmingly-toxic</u> gas was feared to have been dispersed by the factory's exhaust system.

    5. _____

6. Next month we are scheduled to replace the two <u>slowest-printing</u> printers in our department.

    6. _____

7. The contractor plans to build <u>three and four-bedroom</u> homes on this piece of land.

    7. _____

8. Only <u>Oklahoma-University</u> students were issued tickets to the musical production.

    8. _____

9. All the company's <u>newly-acquired</u> land holdings are in Marin County.

    9. _____

10. Our manager, Mr. Allen, is one of the most <u>kind-hearted</u> people I have ever met.

    10. _____

11. Were you able to obtain a <u>30 year</u> loan on this property?

    11. _____

12. All our <u>charge-account</u> customers have already received advance notice of our July linen sale.

    12. _____

13. Tourists can view the <u>snow white</u> hills against the sky from the floor of the valley.

    13. _____

14. Too many <u>long-winded</u> speakers at this banquet could cause a low attendance at tomorrow night's banquet.

    14. _____

15. My present job is only <u>part time</u>.

    15. _____

16. The First Lady's recent visit to England bolstered <u>British-American</u> relations.

16. _____

17. At least 300 students from our college have applied for <u>interest free</u> loans.

17. _____

18. Three of these programs are <u>government-sponsored</u> and will expire at the end of 2014.

18. _____

19. The daughter Mildred is the <u>least-known</u> member of the prominent Kensington family.

19. _____

20. The <u>air conditioning</u> equipment in our building broke down yesterday.

20. _____

21. Did you show the <u>high and low-selling prices</u> of this stock in the report?

21. _____

22. Please see that these dresses are shipped to our <u>Main-Street</u> store.

22. _____

23. Our sales manager received a <u>well-deserved</u> promotion last week to vice president of sales.

23. _____

24. John's advertising campaigns seem to take on a <u>hit and miss</u> quality.

24. _____

25. Our company bids on both <u>large and small-scale</u> construction projects.

25. _____

26. Be sure to include at least three <u>redeemable-store coupons</u> in the ad.

26. _____

27. Each year our store sponsors a local <u>Little-League</u> team.

27. _____

28. Please use <u>larger-size</u> poster board for the displays.

28. _____

29. How many <u>basic-accounting</u> classes are being offered this fall?

29. _____

30. This semester we plan to offer several <u>distance learning</u> courses through the Internet.

30. _____

Check your answers with those given on page 362 before completing the next exercise.

Name _____ Date _____

Practice Guide 2

Instructions: Make any necessary corrections in the following sentences by hyphenating any compound adjectives that require hyphens. Write your answers in the blank provided at the right of each section. If the sentence is correct, write *OK* in the blank line.

1. Use the electric shredder to dispose of these out of date files.

1. _____

2. Please use a sans serif typeface for all headings in this report.

2. _____

3. Most online service providers offer unlimited Internet usage for a monthly flat fee.

3. _____

4. Several delays in yesterday's New York Los Angeles flight caused Mr. Reynolds to be late for the meeting.

4. _____

5. Many of the out of town visitors did not bring enough warm clothing for our cold weather.

5. _____

6. After reading your run of the mill e-mail messages, delete them from your mailbox.

6. _____

7. While working at the computer, maintain an erect position so that you do not become round shouldered.

7. _____

8. Only Florida University students with tickets are to be admitted to the football game.

8. _____

9. Most of these million dollar homes have been on the market for at least six months.

9. _____

10. Begin shutdown procedures on this heavy duty equipment approximately half an hour before closing time.

10. _____

11. For our back to school sale, we will need to order additional notebooks, pens, erasers, and other such stationery supplies.

11. _____

12. You will need to order an additional supply of 12 inch rulers for our sale.

12. _____

13. When your money market account matures, do you wish to have it roll over?

13. _____

14. Encourage television viewers to hurry in to our nearest location to take advantage of our rock bottom prices.

14. _____

15. Someone left a pair of dark rimmed glasses in the reception area.

15. _____

16. Fees for regularly scheduled classes at our college are $46 per unit.

16. _____

17. Cinco de Mayo is a holiday that is celebrated in the United States by many Mexican American people.

17. _____

18. Remind the conference speakers to allow enough time for a question and answer period at the end of their sessions.

18. _____

19. We may need to reduce even further the price of the least desirable lots in this housing tract.

19. _____

20. Many of our callers still do not use push button telephones.

20. _____

21. Stop by sometime soon to see our new line of high quality carpets.

21. _____

22. Ask the technicians to set up the public address system by 9 a.m. Tuesday.

22. _____

23. Locating this information on the Internet should not become an all day task.

23. _____

24. After six months a new employee is eligible to participate in the company's profit sharing plan.

24. _____

25. Present day communications systems—such as e-mail, fax transmission, and texting—enable written messages to be exchanged within minutes.

25. _____

*The answers to this exercise appear in the **Instructor's Manual and Key** for **HOW 13: A Handbook for Office Professionals**, 13th edition.*

Name _____ Date _____

Practice Guide 3

Instructions: Make any necessary corrections in the following sentences by hyphenating any compound adjectives that require hyphens. Write your answers in the blank provided at the right of each sentence. If the sentence is correct, write *OK* in the blank line.

1. Our car loans are set up for 3, 4, 5, and 7 year contracts. _____

2. Floral arrangements we have purchased from Flowers Galore have always been picture perfect. _____

3. Do you have any smaller size note paper? _____

4. When you spend money from the petty cash fund, please provide me with a receipt for the purchases. _____

5. Most of our part time employees are students at the nearby college. _____

6. Our brokerage firm does not handle over the counter securities. _____

7. For Flight 382 all seats in coach class have been sold, but some first class seating is still available. _____

8. Since the downtown area consists of so many one way streets, include a map for each applicant. _____

9. The developers of this shopping mall have applied for an open end mortgage. _____

10. For your convenience our management oriented degree programs are offered online. _____

11. Futuro Software has available a series of computer based accounting programs for small businesses. _____

12. Please purchase from the post office a roll of one hundred 45 cent stamps. _____

13. These independently sponsored Web sites provide career services for job seekers in a wide variety of occupations. _____

14. On the city freeways, you will need to stay within the 65 mile an hour speed limit. _____

15. Our management consulting firm specializes in assisting small and medium size businesses. _____

16. Presently the only job openings we have are part time. _____

17. Financing has been obtained for a number of the new construction projects in the downtown area. _____

18. The speed limit in this residential area is 35 miles an hour. _____

19. His last minute response was too late to be included in the survey results. _____

20. Several of our employees use voice recognition software to prepare all their written documents, including e-mail messages. _____

21. Use only 24 pound laser printer paper in our new color laser printer. _____

22. John always waits until the last minute to submit his reports. _____

23. To finish this construction project, we will need to replenish our supply of 3 inch nails. _____

24. Please prepare this report on 8½ by 11 inch paper. _____

25. Were you able to obtain a take out menu from Weiler's Delicatessen? _____

*The answers to this exercise appear in the **Instructor's Manual and Key** for **HOW 13: A Handbook for Office Professionals**, 13th edition.*

Name _____ Date _____

Practice Guide 4

Instructions: Make any necessary corrections in the following paragraphs. Delete unnecessary hyphens and insert hyphens where they should be placed. Underline your corrections. Place your corrections in the blanks at the right. You should have 20 corrections.

Last week we received several hundred letters from our readers. These letters dealt mostly with the hotly-controversial articles we published on Mexican American citizens in our community. This four week series caused considerable interest. In fact, it resulted in our receiving a record breaking number of responses.

These articles also comprise the highest-income producing series we have published. Circulation rose to a peak-point, one we had not experienced for at least a five year period. Increased circulation was not only in single copy purchases but also in the number of home delivery subscriptions.

The amazingly-large number of responses received from the series was not all one sided. Although some readers may have had a highly-critical response to one part of the article, they often then praised the high quality reporting in another section. Other readers thought the entire series was thought-provoking and well-written. As a whole, our readers praised these well researched and thoroughly documented pieces of writing. Only the highest level newspaper-reporting techniques were used in these articles.

The long term goals of our newspaper should include more such feature articles that deal with the pulse of our community. These articles should rely on factually based reporting that can withstand controversially-provoked criticism.

1. _____

2. _____

3. _____

4. _____

5. _____

6. _____

7. _____

8. _____

9. _____

10. _____

11. _____

12. _____

13. _____

14. _____

15. _____

16. _____

17. _____

18. _____

19. _____

20. _____

*The answers to this exercise appear in the **Instructor's Manual and Key** for **HOW 13: A Handbook for Office Professionals,** 13th edition.*

End-of-Line Divisions (5-5 Through 5-8)

Practice Guide 5

Instructions: Rewrite the following words or word groups in the blanks provided. Use a diagonal line to indicate the *preferable* line-ending divisions for the word or word group. If the word or word group may not be divided or word division should be avoided, write *ND* in the blank provided.

Example: corporation   0. <u>cor / pora / tion</u> _____

1. novelty   1. _____

2. undesirable   2. _____

3. January 14   3. _____

4. 4397 Halstead Street   4. _____

5. stripped   5. _____

6. letter   6. _____

7. Mary N. Gomez   7. _____

8. response   8. _____

9. 25 percent   9. _____

10. Columbus, OH 43210   10. _____

11. readers   11. _____

12. critical   12. _____

13. techniques   13. _____

14. San Francisco   14. _____

15. Agriculture   15. _____

16. Ms. Darlene Jackson   16. _____

17. 3942 East 21st Street

17. _____

18. December 17, 2014

18. _____

19. possible

19. _____

20. connection

20. _____

21. brother-in-law

21. _____

22. thoroughly

22. _____

23. Massachusetts

23. _____

24. self-reliance

24. _____

25. couldn't

25. _____

Check your answers with those given on page 363 before completing the next exercise.

Name _____ Date _____

Practice Guide 6

Instructions: If a line-ending word or word group is divided correctly, write *OK* in the blank at the right. However, if the word or word group is divided incorrectly or the word division shown is not preferred, rewrite the correct answer in the blank. Show all preferred word divisions with a diagonal. If a word or word group may not be divided, write *ND* in the blank. Follow the style shown in the example exercise.

Example: be / ginning   0. ___begin / ning_____

1. pos / itive   1. _____

2. congra / tulations   2. _____

3. Dr. Nicholas / R. Montesano   3. _____

4. careful / ly   4. _____

5. March 10, / 2014   5. _____

6. sup / ply   6. _____

7. 6721 West / 83rd Street   7. _____

8. necess / ary   8. _____

9. ob / jective   9. _____

10. gui / dance   10. _____

11. Norcross, Georgia / 30093   11. _____

12. supervi / sor   12. _____

13. Vir / ginia   13. _____

14. Ms. / Schmidt   14. _____

15. acknow / ledge   15. _____

16. exec / utive   16. _____

17. November / 10   17. _____

18. tent / ative   18. _____

19. 42 / Pontiac Road   19. _____

20. cus / tom   20. _____

21. KRAC- / TV   21. _____

22. brevi / ty   22. _____

23. infor / mation   23. _____

24. 1,350, / 000   24. _____

25. abbrevia / tion   25. _____

The answers to this exercise appear in the **Instructor's Manual and Key** for **HOW 13: A Handbook for Office Professionals**, 13th edition.

Name _____ Date _____

Section 6   Abbreviations and Symbols

Practice Guide 1

Instructions: In the following sentences, underline those words or phrases that *may* or *must be* abbreviated in e-mail messages or business correspondence. Place the correct form of the abbreviated word or phrase in the blank that appears to the right of each sentence. If no word or phrase in a sentence may be abbreviated, write *OK* in the blank at the right.

Example: One of our leading citizens, <u>Mister</u> Richard Montgomery, has consented to donate $1 million for the construction of a new art center.

0. _____ Mr. _____

1. Please book me on a flight to Chicago that will arrive by 2 p.m., Central Standard Time.

1. _____

2. Some of the artifacts in this museum date back to the year 900 before Christ.

2. _____

3. Sarah Nguyen, Chartered Life Underwriter, was promoted to head the Claims Department.

3. _____

4. We have sent Senator Lancaster several e-mails about this problem, but so far we have received no response from his office.

4. _____

5. This show will be broadcast on National Broadcasting Company television next month.

5. _____

6. A copy of these materials should be sent to Doctor Carol Larson Jones.

6. _____

7. Only Professor Thomas Peterson was unable to accept our invitation.

7. _____

8. Please purchase three 2-liter containers of 7UP for the reception.

8. _____

9. The digital camera about which you inquired has been replaced by our Model Number 1683.

9. _____

10. Your order will be sent collect on delivery on Monday.

10. _____

11. The mailing address we have for Ann Kellogg is 1147 West 118th Street.

11. _____

12. When you call our office, ask for Extension 327.

12. _____

13. Our imports from the United Kingdom have declined during the past five years.

13. _____

14. Send these contracts to the client's attorney at 4700 Bell Avenue, Northeast, Portland, Oregon 97206-1054.

14. _____

15. The reception will be given in honor of Brigadier General Retired Foster L. Klein.

15. _____

16. Existing fixtures, carpeting, draperies, and so forth, are included in   16. _____
the sale price of this condominium.

17. The length of all packages is limited to 36 inches.   17. _____

18. Make your check payable to Christopher Rose, Doctor of   18. _____
Medicine.

19. Last week Ralph T. Drengson Senior announced that the company   19. _____
would be moving its headquarters to Albuquerque.

20. Have you already made arrangements to purchase a Hewlett-   20. _____
Packard laptop?

21. I believe Mark J. Benson, Esquire, drew up the majority of these   21. _____
contracts with Atlas Corporation.

22. Our offices close weekdays at 5 post meridiem; on Saturdays they   22. _____
close at 12 noon.

23. Number 456B air-conditioning units are temporarily out of stock;   23. _____
therefore, please notify these customers of the shipping delay.

24. Sharon Williamson, Doctor of Philosophy, has been selected to   24. _____
receive the 2014 Outstanding College Professor of the Year
Award.

25. *Merriam-Webster's Collegiate Dictionary* is also available on a   25. _____
compact disk-read only memory.

Check your answers with those given on page 363 before completing the next exercise.

Name _____ Date _____

Practice Guide 2

Instructions: In the following paragraphs, some words or word groups that should be written in full are abbreviated; in other cases words or word groups that should be abbreviated are written in their entirety. Please make any necessary corrections; underline the word or word group that is expressed *incorrectly*, and write the correct form in one of the blank lines that appears at the right.

Last week Mister Jack Carter notified us that three universities have already invited Gov. Evans to speak at their graduation ceremonies: UCLA, University of Southern California, and UCSB.

The new chancellor of UCLA, Victor Madison, Doctor of Philosophy, and the governor's personal friend, Jeremy Weiss Junior, both extended invitations to Gov. Evans for the UCLA graduation. The ceremony is scheduled for Thurs., June 2, at 4 P.M. Since the governor will leave New York City at 10 A.M., Eastern Standard Time, he should be able to arrive in Los Angeles in time for the graduation ceremony. Therefore, please phone the chancellor's assistant, Dixie Slater, at (213) 555-8282, extension 113, to inform her that the governor will accept the university's invitation for June 2.

The University of Southern California and UCSB have scheduled their graduations for the same day—Fri., June 10. Since the invitation from Prof. James Wrigley arrived first, the governor has agreed to accept the invitation from UCSB. Please write Prof. Wrigley at 800 W. College Dr., Santa Barbara, CA 93107, to let him know that the governor can accept his invitation. Also, please send the governor's regrets to President Daniel Young at the University of Southern California. Explain carefully the circumstances, and indicate that the lieutenant governor would be available to substitute for Gov. Evans.

1. _____

2. _____

3. _____

4. _____

5. _____

6. _____

7. _____

8. _____

9. _____

10. _____

11. _____

12. _____

13. _____

14. _____

15. _____

16. _____

17. _____

18. _____

19. _____

20. _____

*The answers to this exercise appear in the **Instructor's Manual and Key** for **HOW 13: A Handbook for Office Professionals,** 13th edition.*

Name _____ Date _____

Contractions (6-14)

Practice Guide 3

Instructions: Make any necessary corrections in the following sentences. If a contraction is written incorrectly, underline it and place the correct form in the blank at the right of the sentence. If a contraction is written correctly, write *OK* in the blank.

Example: We <u>have'nt</u> received your last payment for May.   0. ____haven't_____

1. It won't be necessary for you to visit our store personally to order   1. _____
   your new Floyd 48-inch high-definition television set.

2. I amn't convinced that our management and the union will reach   2. _____
   agreement on all the contract issues before the 1st of the year.

3. This is'nt the same grade of upholstery fabric I ordered from your   3. _____
   sales representative.

4. Our company doesn't sell its products directly to retail stores.   4. _____

5. Your one of the youngest students in this class.   5. _____

6. Melanie has'nt received an increase in salary for the past two   6. _____
   years.

7. We'll be sure to credit your account for the full amount.   7. _____

8. This movie has not yet been able to recover it's production costs.   8. _____

9. Yes, their available to assist you with the completion of this project.   9. _____

10. Who's in charge of administering our company's medical insurance   10. _____
    program?

Check your answers with those given on page 363.

Section 7 Words Often Confused and Misused

Practice Exercises for Words **A/An** Through **Aisle/Isle**

Practice Guide 1

Instructions: Select the correct word or a form of the word from each set of word confusions to complete the following sentences. Write your choice in the blank.

A/An

1. We have not yet received _____ acknowledgment from Parker Manufacturing as to whether it received our last order.

2. Please ask _____ sales representative from your company to call me.

3. You may wish to discuss this situation with _____ union representative.

4. Kevin will need at least _____ hour to review each file.

5. Before the doctor will see a patient, we must obtain _____ history of the patient's medical conditions and previous treatments.

A lot/Allot/Alot

6. For the past few days, _____ of dust has been coming through the air-conditioning vents on this floor.

7. We are unable to _____ any additional funds for this project.

8. All members of the investment club have agreed to _____ $100 a month for stock purchases.

9. Laura has been spending _____ of time on the Internet doing preliminary research for our survey.

10. How many hours have you _____ for us to complete this project?

A while/Awhile

11. We have not heard from this client for _____.

12. If you read _____ each day, your comprehension and speed should improve.

13. _____ ago I sent you information about our new home security system.

14. Although you have not placed an order with us for _____, we still consider you among our preferred customers.

15. Only by resting _____ each afternoon will you be able to regain your strength.

Accede/Exceed

16. When making decisions, be careful not to _____ your authority.

17. Has management agreed to _____ to the union's requests?

18. If this budget is accepted, it will _____ last year's by more than 10 percent.

19. We cannot _____ to the property manager's request for a 20 percent rent increase.

20. Your commission on this sale may not _____ $200.

Accelerate/Exhilarate

21. If we are to meet the deadline date, we must _____ our progress.

22. There are a number of software programs available that can _____ the processing speed of your computer.

23. The fresh air during an early morning walk will surely _____ you.

24. Accidents at this intersection are caused mainly by drivers _____ down the hill on Fourth Street.

25. The executive staff was _____ by the news that our company stock had risen 9 points during the past week.

Accept/Except

26. Our restaurant does not _____ dinner reservations on weekends.

27. Everyone in our department _____ Aaron has received a new computer for his or her work station.

28. For money market checking accounts, the number of withdrawals are unlimited _____ those made by check.

29. We _____ only cash or major credit cards—VISA, MasterCard, or American Express.

30. Applications for this position will be _____ through June 30.

Access/Excess

31. Because of the floods, all the _____ roads to the city were closed.

32. Building costs for the new offices were in _____ of $16.5 million.

33. Please ship all _____ supplies and materials to our Toledo warehouse.

34. Only the president and executive vice president have _____ to the combination of this safe.

35. All our store locations have easy freeway _____.

Ad/Add

36. How many more salespeople do you plan to _____ to our staff?

37. If you _____ a security system to the building, you will be able to reduce your insurance costs.

38. Placing an _____ in our classified section will allow you to reach more than 52,000 readers.

39. Students may not _____ classes after the second week of the semester.

40. Our last _____ in our local newspaper attracted only a few new customers.

Adapt/Adept/Adopt

41. Do you believe the manager will _____ our new supervisor's policy recommendations?

42. Too many of our employees do not _____ readily to technological advancements.

43. Fortunately, Nicole is _____ at providing rapid and intelligent responses to customer inquiries.

44. Will you be able to _____ this software to operate on our new computers?

45. The instructor's manual, PowerPoint slides, and a computer test bank are all given free of charge to instructors who _____ our textbook.

Addict/Edict

46. Too many of today's youth are computer game _____.

47. The general's _____ was not well received by the other officers.

48. Only a bare majority of the city council members support the mayor's _____.

49. Most of the drug _____ in our clinic are from the local area.

50. Bill manages by _____ rather than by soliciting cooperative participation.

Addition/Edition

51. When will the new _____ of this textbook be available for purchase?

52. We anticipate several new _____ to our staff this year.

53. An _____ to our main dining room has been planned for next year.

54. These artists' prints are available in limited _____ only.

55. Please obtain for me a copy of the morning _____ of *The New York Times*.

Adherence/Adherents

56. _____ to these policies will be strictly enforced.

57. The _____ of his many fans has kept alive the memory of Elvis Presley.

58. Football's many _____ have turned this sport into a multimillion-dollar industry.

59. The governor's _____ were disappointed when he withdrew his name as a contender for the presidential nomination.

60. Your _____ to these regulations is required as long as you occupy this apartment.

Adverse/Averse

61. I am not _____ to experimenting with new ideas and methods to improve communication within our organization.

62. Yesterday's _____ publicity has caused our stock to drop 3 points on the New York Stock Exchange.

63. Our manager appears to be _____ to adopting any suggestions offered by the younger members of the staff.

64. _____ conditions in the building industry have resulted in substantial losses for many subcontractors.

65. The Board of Directors is _____ to expanding our operations at the present time.

Advice/Advise

66. Would you _____ us to contact an attorney for further information?

67. To select the correct courses, you should seek the _____ of a counselor.

68. I appreciate your _____ and will pursue the ideas you shared with me.

69. Upon the _____ of an investment counselor, we have purchased additional shares of CompuTab stock.

70. We _____ you to investigate this company carefully before purchasing any of its stock.

Affect/Effect

71. We have been unable to determine what _____ this advertising campaign has had on sales.

72. Did the unusual summer heat wave _____ your August sales?

73. Do you believe the new manager will _____ many changes in our department?

74. How will this merger with General Computer Systems _____ our present employees?

75. The changeover from a semester system to a quarter system has had no apparent _____ on enrollment at the college.

Aggravate/Irritate

76. If you scratch the infected area as it heals, you will only continue to _____ the surface skin.

77. Do not _____ the situation by making unreasonable demands.

78. Arguing with irate customers will only _____ them further.

79. The defendant continued to _____ the judge with his sarcastic replies.

80. Our president appeared _____ by the board's decision not to expand the company's operations.

Aid/Aide

81. Our representatives are trained to _____ you in selecting insurance policies that will best suit your needs.

82. May we _____ you further by supplying information about our tax-exempt investments?

83. Please contact the general's _____ to obtain more information about enlistment opportunities in the U.S. Army.

84. Each department in our company has been supplied with a fully stocked first-_____ kit.

85. According to the news report, none of the presidential _____ could be reached for questioning.

Aisle/Isle

86. The carpet in the center _____ of the theater needs repair.

87. Please check the fire regulations to determine how much space must be left between the _____.

88. Catalina is an _____ approximately 23 miles from the Pacific coastline at Long Beach.

89. The _____ of Bermuda is a vacationer's paradise, often equated to Hawaii.

90. Before you take that "walk down the _____," be sure to visit our bridal gown showroom.

Check your answers with those given on pages 364–365 before completing the next exercise.

Name _____ Date _____

Reinforcement Guide 1

Instructions: Select one of the words (or a form of the word) shown below to complete each of the following sentences.

A/An	Access/Excess	Adverse/Averse
A lot/Allot/Alot	Ad/Add	Advice/Advise
A while/Awhile	Adapt/Adept/Adopt	Affect/Effect
Accede/Exceed	Addict/Edict	Aggravate/Irritate
Accelerate/Exhilarate	Addition/Edition	Aid/Aide
Accept/Except	Adherence/Adherents	Aisle/Isle

1. On the _____ of his doctor, Mr. Reed requested a three months' leave of absence.

2. According to the last _____ issued by our company president, *no* employee may park in the customer parking lot.

3. We will _____ applications for enrollment for the next academic year only through March 31.

4. In each of our classrooms, we must separate each row of computer stations with a 42-inch _____.

5. Although I am not _____ to working overtime, I would prefer to work only my regularly assigned hours.

6. This firm specializes in conducting seminars that help staff _____ to technological change and other modifications in the work environment.

7. Your continual criticism of company policies has begun to _____ many of your coworkers as well as the department manager.

8. Government _____ programs for the elderly have been curbed substantially during the past few years.

9. Strict _____ to outdated policies and procedures has been a major contributor to the company's present financial difficulties.

10. Student records are protected by law, and only certain authorized individuals may have _____ to their contents.

11. Anyone who makes an appointment with Dr. Martinson can expect to wait _____ before being seen.

12. Large increases in raw material costs will _____ the price of all our products.

13. This construction company specializes in house _____.

14. We have run this _____ in the *Daily Star* for the past three weeks but still have not found a qualified assistant to replace Ms. Chin.

15. Please have _____ union representative contact me as soon as possible.

16. These new personnel practices are certain to have a(n) _____ effect on employee morale.

17. Fortunately, most of our employees are _____ at upgrading their skills as new versions of word processing, spreadsheet, and database programs are released.

18. We wish it were possible to _____ to your request for an increased wage scale, but conditions within the industry forecast a profit decline during the next six months.

19. The new owners of the mall have already begun to _____ a number of changes.

20. Credit card purchases that _____ your account limit will not be approved for payment.

21. We have received _____ of customer complaints from the Orange County area.

22. You may obtain e-mail _____ through any of the Internet service providers listed on the enclosed sheet.

23. These _____ materials must be disposed of properly.

24. All union employees have been granted a 4 percent pay increase _____ those still on probationary status.

25. The Juvenile Division is recommending to the court that the Smiths' petition be accepted and that the Smiths be allowed to _____ the child named in the petition.

*The answers to this exercise appear in the **Instructor's Manual and Key** for **HOW 13: A Handbook for Office Professionals**, 13th edition.*

Practice Exercises for Words *All ready/Already* Through *Appraise/Apprise*

Practice Guide 2

Instructions: Select the correct word or a form of the word from each set of word confusions to complete the following sentences. Write your choice in the blank.

All ready/Already

1. The page proofs for these brochures are _____ to be returned to the printer's.

2. We have _____ received over 50 orders as a result of the new advertising campaign initiated last week.

3. As you may _____ know, our division is being merged with another division in the company.

4. Most of our staff has _____ received training on using the database features of Excel.

5. We were _____ to interview candidates when Mr. Graham informed us that the position has been placed on hold.

All right/Alright

6. Your test answers were _____.

7. For you to begin your vacation on July 1 is _____ with me.

8. To extend your lunch hour 15 minutes every day is not _____.

9. Our accountant agreed that Lisa's classifying the entries as she had done was _____.

10. Unfortunately, the answers in this test key are not _____.

All together/Altogether

11. I believe _____ we can expect 75 participants for this conference.

12. Please gather _____ the written documents we have available regarding this project.

13. We need to work _____ so that we can finish this instruction manual by May 1.

14. _____ we raised $10,400—far from our $15,000 goal—for the hospital's Breast Cancer Treatment Center.

15. This year's holiday sales are _____ lower than last year's.

All ways/Always

16. You have _____ been a prompt-paying customer.

17. Our accountant has _____ notified us of any discrepancies in our accounts.

18. We have tried _____ possible to please you, but you still seem to be dissatisfied with our service.

19. Our employees are _____ paid on the 1st and 15th of each month.

20. Please note that _____ have been explored to expedite the manufacture and delivery of these airplane parts.

Allowed/Aloud

21. No minors under 21 years of age are _____ on the premises.

22. Federal law has not _____ major corporations to form industry monopolies since the last century.

23. Please read _____ to the committee the president's response to our inquiry.

24. The Graduation Office has always _____ students to petition for graduation until April 30 of the graduation year.

25. You are requested not to speak _____ in the Study Room of the library.

Allude/Elude

26. Did the manager of human resources _____ to any possible openings in his department?

27. Mr. Roberts has managed to _____ answering my questions for the past week.

28. In your opening address at our national sales meeting, you may wish to _____ to the projected market increase forecast by our sales analysts.

29. Andrea seems to spend more time _____ work than she would need to accomplish her assigned responsibilities.

30. In our annual report, please _____ to the technological advancements made by our company during the past year.

Almost/Most

31. _____ everyone in our department has been employed by the company for at least five years.

32. _____ managers expect their staff to arrive at work on time.

33. These sales catalogs have already been sent to _____ all our new customers.

34. We anticipated that _____ every airline would have already been booked for this date.

35. I did not realize that we had sold _____ all our stock of Hi-Tech DVD recorders.

Altar/Alter

36. Please do not _____ any dates on this delivery schedule.

37. We manufacture a variety of artifacts for church _____.

38. As a result of the electrical fire, the _____ was badly damaged.

39. If you wish to _____ your travel plans, please contact our agency rather than the airlines or the hotels.

40. Our architect is reluctant to _____ the church plans any further.

Alternate/Alternative

41. Whom have you selected as an _____ delegate to the convention?

42. We have no other _____ but to issue additional stock and offer it for sale to the general public.

43. During the renovation please locate an _____ conference room for our weekly meetings.

44. Please _____ the responsibility for closing the store between Leslie and Dana.

45. Our goal is to offer employees several _____ in selecting a health plan to meet their needs.

Among/Between

46. Please distribute these brochures _____ all our agency managers.

47. There appeared to be major discrepancies _____ the two witnesses' testimonies.

48. The commission is to be divided equally _____ Ann and Phil.

49. We are unable to disclose the information you have requested because it is confidential _____ the client and our agent.

50. You may wish to have the office employees discuss this proposal _____ themselves before they make a decision.

Amount/Number

51. A large _____ of people gathered to learn who had been elected to the Third Council District.

52. During the next three years, we will reduce the _____ of employees in our Springfield plant.

53. Our company recently sold a large _____ of farm properties to independent growers.

54. Please check the _____ of cash our bank has available this holiday weekend for our ATMs.

55. Our store was understaffed to handle adequately the _____ of sales we had yesterday.

Anecdote/Antidote

56. Our manager has many _____ about his previous experiences in dealing with customers.

57. Most speakers begin their presentation with an _____.

58. Is there an _____ for lead poisoning?

59. One of our community service seminars for new mothers discusses emergency procedures and _____ for common household poisons.

60. The entire audience was amused by Ms. Green's series of _____ regarding the recent election.

Annual/Annul

61. The agent was able to _____ the contract because it had been prepared incorrectly.

62. The _____ membership fee for the use of your Money-Bonus card is only $50.

63. Our audit is conducted on an _____ basis.

64. If the Board of Directors chooses to _____ this long-established policy, it may alienate a number of stockholders.

65. Both parties were eager to _____ the marriage.

Anxious/Eager

66. Our manager appears _____ about the forthcoming visit from our director of marketing.

67. I am _____ to see the page proof for our new sales brochure.

68. All the members of our staff are _____ to begin work on the development of this new software version.

69. Many of the nursing students in our graduation class are _____ about taking their state board examinations online through an independent testing service.

70. We are all _____ to learn who was chosen to fill the vacancy on the board of education.

Any one/Anyone

71. Hand a leaflet describing our sale prices to _____ who enters the store.

72. _____ of our salespeople can help you select the refrigerator you will need.

73. Please notify _____ of the instructors in our Computer Center if you plan to drop the course.

74. _____ in our Counseling Department can give you this information.

75. We have not yet received an application from _____ who is qualified for the position.

Section 7, Words Often Confused and Misused

Any time/Anytime

76. If you have _____ next week to schedule a doctor's appointment, please let me know.

77. Please visit our showroom _____ within the next few days to select the upholstery fabric for the furniture you ordered for your reception area.

78. Our auto body shop can repair your car _____ next week.

79. We cannot divert _____ from this project to review new manuscripts.

80. You may call our toll-free number _____ you need technical assistance with one of our software programs.

Any way/Anyway

81. We are not in a position to finance this project, _____.

82. _____ you select to assign these tasks is acceptable to me.

83. We have not yet found _____ to bond these two surfaces permanently.

84. Our supplier cannot in _____ promise a May 1 delivery date.

85. _____, this model printer is no longer available.

Appraise/Apprise

86. Be sure to _____ Ms. Reynolds of any sudden changes in the price of our stock.

87. We have not been _____ of any offers to purchase our company.

88. According to our accountant, the property has been _____ for nearly $112,000 more than the prospective buyers offered.

89. Once you have had an opportunity to _____ the situation, please give us your candid opinion.

90. Have you _____ the parents of their daughter's belligerent behavior in the classroom?

Check your answers with those given on pages 365–366 before completing the next exercise.

Reinforcement Guide 2

Instructions: Select one of the words (or a form of the word) shown below to complete each of the following sentences.

All ready/Already	Almost/Most	Annual/Annul
All right/Alright	Altar/Alter	Anxious/Eager
All together/Altogether	Alternate/Alternative	Any one/Anyone
All ways/Always	Among/Between	Any time/Anytime
Allowed/Aloud	Amount/Number	Any way/Anyway
Allude/Elude	Anecdote/Antidote	Appraise/Apprise

1. We have not yet found _____ to market our products outside the United States.

2. Unfortunately, I do not know a(n) _____ for unmitigated greed and a compelling quest for power.

3. Because of the contract deadline, we have asked _____ everyone on our staff to work overtime next week.

4. Although Mr. Bryce was not selected, our staff was not _____ disappointed in the Board of Director's choice for executive vice president.

5. Please call on us _____ we can be of further service to you.

6. None of us could believe the _____ of errors that appeared in the sales letter written by the new manager.

7. The best way to solve a problem is not _____ readily apparent.

8. If your exchanging desks is _____ with your supervisor, I have no objection.

9. Are you able to recommend _____ for this position?

10. Please distribute these files _____ Peter, Diana, and Chris.

11. Be sure to _____ our company president of any news events that may affect our industry.

12. Ms. Davis was _____ to leave for the airport when she learned that her flight had been canceled because of weather conditions.

13. Although neither party wished to _____ the contract, the court ruled the contract was invalid as written.

14. How many times have you been forced to _____ the plans for opening our new branch office?

15. In your progress report, you may wish to _____ to the difficulties we have experienced because of the recent snowstorms.

16. No children are _____ in the pool area unless accompanied by an adult.

17. Once you have had an opportunity to _____ the situation in our Chicago plant, please call me directly.

18. Companies that continue to dump waste into the harbor will no longer be able to _____ court action.

19. You may choose _____ of the items illustrated in the brochure as your free gift.

20. Please store this equipment in the closet _____ Room 14 and Room 16.

21. Most credit card companies charge an _____ fee to cardholders in addition to interest charges for unpaid balances.

22. After being housed in these temporary quarters for the past six months, everyone is _____ to move into the new offices in the Blackburn Building.

23. Please post a sign in the reading area requesting children and adults not to read _____.

24. If you were making the decision, which _____ would you choose?

25. _____ everyone in our group has agreed to ratify the proposed new union contract.

*The answers to this exercise appear in the **Instructor's Manual and Key** for **HOW 13: A Handbook for Office Professionals**, 13th edition.*

Practice Exercises for Words *As/Like* Through ***Bolder/Boulder***

Practice Guide 3

Instructions: Select the correct word or a form of the word from each set of word confusions to complete the following sentences. Write your choice in the blank.

As/Like

1. Ms. Harris manages the office _____ a conscientious and competent office manager should.

2. We are striving to operate this charity boutique _____ a business.

3. You may be certain that we will deliver this order by July 15, just _____ we promised.

4. Although these sunglasses look _____ ours, they were produced and sold illegally by a manufacturing counterfeiter.

5. _____ I said in yesterday's staff meeting, we must create several innovative new toys to remain competitive in this market.

Ascent/Assent

6. The recent _____ of stock market prices has caused even more trading on the New York Stock Exchange.

7. Do you think the Board of Directors will _____ to the president's plan for expanding our operations?

8. Mr. Brooks' rapid _____ to executive vice president has caused quite a stir among the other young executives.

9. The _____ of the plane to its cruising altitude was hindered by strong headwinds.

10. Will management _____ to the union's request for an additional 1 percent pay increase?

Assistance/Assistants

11. Were you able to obtain any additional financial _____?

12. Please ask the receptionist for _____ in completing these forms.

13. Congress recently provided for additional _____ to the elderly and others on fixed-income programs.

14. Neither of the doctor's _____ could provide the information we need for this report.

15. If you are unable to attend the meeting, please have one of your _____ substitute for you.

Assure/Ensure/Insure

16. Can you _____ that this project will be completed by its deadline date, July 1?

17. You may wish to _____ your property against other losses besides fire.

18. If you can _____ that I will be able to see Dr. Norris, I will make an appointment for that time.

19. We _____ you that these evening dresses will be available in time for holiday purchases.

20. Please allow me to _____ you that we will do all we can to retrieve your stolen goods.

Attendance/Attendants

21. Your poor _____ record was the decisive factor in your dismissal.

22. How many members of the council must be in _____ to make up a quorum?

23. Each of the bride's _____ will carry a bouquet of delicate pink rosebuds.

24. Before accepting each instructor's _____ roster, please ensure that it has been signed.

25. Please ask one of the ambulance _____ to sign the patient release form.

Bad/Badly

26. I feel _____ that we were unable to locate your lost briefcase.

27. The incumbent was defeated _____ by his young, energetic opponent.

28. I did not realize that I had done so _____ on this examination.

29. Why does the air in this office always smell _____?

30. Marie must certainly feel _____ that she did not receive the promotion to assistant sales manager.

Bail/Bale

31. How many _____ of hay did you order for the horses?

32. This defendant is being held without _____.

33. The judge has agreed to set _____ for our client tomorrow.

34. We cannot even begin to estimate how many _____ of wheat were destroyed by the fire.

35. Please tie all these newspapers in _____ for recycling.

Bare/Bear

36. Many successful businesses have emerged from _____ beginnings.

37. I do not know how much longer XYZ Corporation can _____ these exorbitant financial losses.

38. We maintain only the _____ minimum balance in our checking account; other liquid assets are deposited in accounts earning higher interest.

39. The house had been allowed to deteriorate so badly that in many places the _____ wood was exposed.

40. The time allotted for my presentation enabled me to discuss only the _____ findings of the study.

Base/Bass

41. Do you still play the _____ violin in our community orchestra?

42. The _____ of this statue is filled with lead.

43. All the fillings in our candies have a chocolate _____.

44. If these conclusions do not stem from a solid _____ of data, then our sales efforts will be unsuccessful.

45. We are still looking for a _____ voice to join the company "barbershop quartet."

Bazaar/Bizarre

46. Our new television series is based on documented eyewitness accounts of _____, peculiar, and curious events.

47. We manufacture gaming equipment for church _____ and other charity events.

48. Most of the proceeds from our annual _____ are used to provide clothing and toys for underprivileged children.

49. This witness's account of the event is so _____ that scarcely anyone else believes it.

50. Fewer and fewer of our students are focusing on _____ hair styles and clothing trends.

Because of/Due to

51. _____ the recent price increases in gasoline, we must raise our shuttle fares.

52. Many of our employees have been absent _____ the flu epidemic.

53. If you were unable to view our online presentation _____ the citywide power outage, you may wish to view the rebroadcast at 7 p.m. on May 23.

54. _____ the large number of challenges facing the company, our president has decided not to expand its operations internationally.

55. College enrollments have increased _____ recent legislation providing financial assistance to a larger segment of the population.

Berth/Birth

56. We expect the Queen of the Seas to _____ here tomorrow afternoon shortly after 3 p.m.

57. Mrs. Gilmore gave _____ to twin girls at Valley Hills Hospital yesterday.

58. Was the father present during the _____ of this child?

59. All the _____ on this train have already been sold.

60. Only three of the _____ at Island Harbor are presently occupied by cruise ships.

Beside/Besides

61. Who else _____ Don is entitled to a bonus this month?

62. Place one of these new copyholders _____ each computer.

63. Please move the file cabinet _____ the desk in my new office.

64. Several distinguished government officials _____ the mayor were present for the opening session of our convention.

65. You should probably invite other clients _____ those with whom we have had business dealings for more than ten years.

Bi-/Semi-

66. The _____ weekly issues of our local newspaper are published on Thursdays and Sundays.

67. All our employees are paid _____ monthly; checks are issued on the 1st and 15th each month.

68. _____ monthly meetings of our committee are held in February, April, June, August, October, and December.

69. Employment opportunities posted on our company Web site are updated _____ weekly; that is, every other Friday I add new listings and remove those that have been filled.

70. The _____ monthly meetings of the board of education are held on the second and fourth Tuesdays at 2 p.m.

Biannual/Biennial

71. Your _____ royalty checks are issued in March and August.

72. The first of this year's _____ reports to stockholders will be issued in February.

73. _____ elections of officers for our organization are held in even-numbered years.

74. These _____ reports must be submitted to the federal government by January 31 and July 31.

75. Unfortunately, this research digest is published only _____; the next issue will not appear for another year.

Section 7, Words Often Confused and Misused

Bibliography/Biography

76. Be sure to include a _____ at the end of your report.

77. Did you place any Internet references in your _____?

78. The manuscript on your desk is a _____ of Ronald Reagan.

79. Use the format shown in Chapter 12 of *HOW 13* to prepare the entries in your _____.

80. You can probably find a copy of this book in the _____ section of the library.

Billed/Build

81. Have you _____ Ms. Davis for her last order?

82. How many homes has Hodge & Sons been contracted to _____?

83. We plan to _____ our new offices on this site within the next two years.

84. Our plan is to _____ a good relationship with the community before relocating our plant there.

85. Your company has not yet _____ us for the two laptop computers we purchased last January.

Boarder/Border

86. This brochure would be more attractive if you would remove the _____ around the graphic.

87. Did you advertise in the *Daily News* that you had a room available for a _____?

88. At the present time, Oakley House has only 18 _____.

89. You may pick up the shipment at the Texas state _____ on August 2.

90. If you do not plan to frame this photograph, we can place an attractive _____ around it.

Bolder/Boulder

91. Unless we adopt _____ merchandising policies, we will face even greater losses in this tough, competitive market.

92. Traffic was held up for more than two hours because a loose _____ had blocked the tunnel entrance.

93. Our new store manager is somewhat _____ than I thought he would be.

94. You should perhaps be _____ in expressing your concerns to the management team.

95. The foundation for this eighteenth-century house is comprised of _____ from the local countryside that are held together by thin layers of mortar.

Check your answers with those given on pages 367–368 before completing the next exercise.

Name _____ Date _____

Reinforcement Guide 3

Instructions: Select one of the words (or a form of the word) shown below to complete each of the following sentences.

As/Like
Ascent/Ascent
Assistance/Assistants
Assure/Ensure/Ensure
Attendance/Attendants
Bad/Badly
Bail/Bale

Bare/Bear
Base/Bass
Bazaar/Bizarre
Because of/Due to
Berth/Birth
Beside/Besides
Bi-/Semi-

Biannual/Biennial
Bibliography/Biography
Billed/Build
Boarder/Border
Bolder/Boulder

1. Place a fancy _____ around this flyer.

2. Four other dignitaries _____ General Taylor were honored at the banquet.

3. All of us feel _____ that we were unable to finish this construction project by its initial completion date.

4. _____ our receptionist told you, we may sell our products only to companies or individuals with resale licenses.

5. Our _____ conventions are held in odd-numbered years.

6. Please request the feed company to deliver daily an additional _____ of hay.

7. Your account balance has dropped below the _____ minimum to maintain an account free of service charges.

8. This month three of our clients were _____ for services they did not receive.

9. _____ material shortages in the construction industry, building costs have risen beyond normal expectations.

10. The sudden _____ of material costs will effect price increases throughout the automobile industry.

11. Without the _____ of you and your staff, we would have had great difficulty supplying the requested information to the Internal Revenue Service.

12. Unless you can _____ that our order will arrive in time for holiday sales, we are unable to guarantee its acceptance.

13. Please explain to the manager that his _____ at this meeting is of prime importance.

14. The new shopping center will be located at the _____ of the Flintridge Foothills.

15. Within the past few months, the committee has adopted _____ policies regarding the collection of delinquent accounts.

16. All of us who worked long hours on this project feel _____ that another architectural firm was selected to design the community's Performing Arts Center.

17. Before we can take your proposal to the stockholders, the Board of Directors must _____ to the merger.

18. To _____ that each payment has been credited to the proper account, please double-check each entry.

19. One sales representative behaved so _____ at the meeting that the sales manager had to ask him to leave.

20. Dividends on this stock are paid _____, once in January and then again in July.

21. The funds allocated to the department for this year's expenses cover only the_____costs.

22. This cruise line itinerary shows that the ship will _____ for two days in a harbor with access to St. Petersburg.

23. News coverage concerning this _____ incident has been nationwide for the past week.

24. Issues of our _____ weekly campus newspaper are published and distributed to students on Mondays and Thursdays.

25. All references appearing in the footnotes of your report should be cited in the _____.

*The answers to this exercise appear in the **Instructor's Manual and Key** for **HOW 13: A Handbook for Office Professionals**, 13th edition.*

Section 7, Words Often Confused and Misused

Practice Exercises for Words *Born/Borne* Through *Cite/Sight/Site*

Practice Guide 4

Instructions: Select the correct word or a form of the word from each set of word confusions to complete the following sentences. Write your choice in the blank.

Born/Borne

1. According to the doctor's records, the child was _____ with a serious heart defect.

2. Because of poor management decisions, our division has _____ major financial losses for the past two years.

3. This multimillion-dollar industry was _____ scarcely three decades ago.

4. How many children has the patient _____?

5. The plants in this vineyard have not _____ fruit for the past three seasons.

Bouillon/Bullion

6. We are completely out of stock on Hillsdale's _____ cubes.

7. The possession of gold _____ in this country was once illegal.

8. The safe was filled with ingots of gold and silver _____.

9. The addition of chicken _____ instead of boiling water will enhance considerably the flavor of this recipe.

10. Pierre DuBois, our new chef, prefers to serve hearty cream soups instead of _____.

Breach/Breech

11. As the months wore on, the _____ between the two partners grew even wider.

12. The judge had difficulty determining which of the parties had _____ the contract.

13. A crack in the _____ of the gun rendered it useless.

14. Does your client wish to sue ABC Corporation for _____ of contract?

15. Please pack the _____ between the two properties with clean fill dirt.

Bring/Take

16. For each class session be sure to _____ your textbook and your USB drive.

17. Patients often will _____ with them magazines we have in the reception area.

18. If you are required to have your signature verified by a notary public, be sure to _____ with you an official photo identification.

19. When you come to our store, be sure to _____ the pattern for the glass tabletop you wish to have cut.

20. Please _____ all these extra copies of our annual report to the storage room.

Calendar/Colander

21. Plastic _____ are considerably less expensive than the stainless steel ones.

22. Will we be sending new wall _____ for next year to each of our clients?

23. As soon as you check your _____, please let me know if Thursday, April 21, at 2 p.m. will be a convenient time for you to meet with me.

24. Have you received the _____ of events scheduled for the summer months in the Hollywood Bowl?

25. If the holes in the _____ are too large, some of the smaller food particles will fall through.

Callous/Callus

26. Continually remind our medical staff not to become _____ in dealing with the needs of patients.

27. Your _____ attitude toward the children with disabilities forces us to dismiss you as a teacher's aide.

28. My index finger has developed a _____ from using this industrial drill.

29. Police officers soon learn to become _____ to the remarks of irate motorists.

30. The protection of our new Syntho-fiber gardening gloves will keep your hands free from _____.

Can/May

31. You _____ send us your response by replying to this e-mail.

32. Only members of our human resources staff _____ have access to these employee records.

33. Most of our staff members _____ use word processing, spreadsheet, and database software.

34. _____ you provide us with this information by May 1?

35. Of course, you _____ borrow these instructions to set up your accounts receivable program.

Section 7, Words Often Confused and Misused

Canvas/Canvass

36. We are presently out of stock on _____ tents.

37. How many salespeople have been assigned to _____ the Rolling Hills area?

38. Some athletes still prefer to wear _____ tennis shoes rather than leather ones.

39. Several agents in our real estate office have volunteered to _____ the area.

40. If you were to _____ the shopping malls in the area, perhaps you could determine the buying patterns of residents in this community.

Capital/Capitol

41. How much _____ will you need to launch this business?

42. The Department of Education is located in Room 450 of the state _____.

43. Our senior class will visit the state _____ in May to tour the city and its surrounding area.

44. In many countries murder is considered to be a _____ crime.

45. When you visit Washington, DC, be sure to visit the _____ to view Congress in session.

Carat/Caret/Carrot/Karat

46. One of our customers wishes to purchase a 5-_____ blue topaz pendant for her daughter.

47. We carry a few chains in 18-_____ gold, but most of our jewelry is made of 14-_____ gold.

48. When proofreading documents, please use a _____ to indicate where letters or words are to be inserted.

49. The banquet coordinator has requested _____ cake with whipped cream icing to be served for dessert.

50. Many pieces of European jewelry are made with 10-_____ gold.

Cease/Seize

51. Our competitors have been ordered by the courts to _____ their false advertising.

52. When did Lenox _____ manufacturing this crystal pattern?

53. Young executives today must _____ every opportunity to move ahead, even if promotion means relocating to other parts of the country.

54. Was Drake Industries able to _____ control of Litchfield Petroleum Corporation?

55. We must _____ work on this project until after the rainy season.

Ceiling/Sealing

56. When will the work crews finish _____ the wooden floors in our offices?

57. Many investment analysts believe the stock market has reached its _____ for this year.

58. _____ these surfaces with Varathane-3 has kept them from cracking and peeling.

59. Price _____ on many agricultural products have been lifted temporarily.

60. All the walls and _____ in this building need to be repainted.

Censor/Censure

61. Many countries regularly _____ all mail directed outside their borders.

62. Senator Billings was subjected to public _____ once the press disclosed his questionable financial affiliations.

63. The board of education _____ the principal for his negligence in not investigating the numerous parent complaints he received about this hazardous situation.

64. The _____ have barred this film from television viewing.

65. Not all the _____ material had been removed from the script before filming.

Census/Senses

66. Which _____ are being tested by this new procedure?

67. Enrollment _____ figures are reported to the state monthly for each of our classes.

68. The latest _____ reports show that the population of our state has increased 5.7 percent during the past decade.

69. At the present time, the _____ in this retirement home is 12 persons below capacity.

70. When one of the _____ becomes impaired, research has shown that others seem to become keener and compensate somewhat for the loss.

Cent/Scent/Sent

71. Although Mr. Wilson is a millionaire, he acts as if he doesn't have a _____ to his name.

72. Last week you were _____ three copies of the signed contract for your files.

73. We are in the process of testing several new _____ for our Avanté perfume collection.

74. Before completing the arrangements, be sure to inquire if anyone in the wedding party is allergic to the _____ of gardenias.

75. Please do not include _____ amounts in this report; round each figure to the nearest dollar value.

Section 7, Words Often Confused and Misused

Cereal/Serial

76. The _____ numbers of all our equipment have been recorded on individual cards and entered into our computer database.

77. This new breakfast food is made from 100 percent whole grain _____.

78. When advertising our new high-fiber _____, be sure to mention its crunchiness and tasty cinnamon-apple flavor.

79. Our company will not purchase advertising time on daytime _____ television programs.

80. You may upgrade your version of WordProcessor for only $90 by sending us payment and the _____ number of your current program.

Choose/Chose

81. Last year most of our employees _____ to receive their bonuses in stock issues.

82. Please _____ your vacation dates for this year by April 15.

83. The committee will _____ the final Rose Queen contestants by December 1.

84. Although the manager _____ not to select an assistant at this time, she reserved the right to do so at a later date.

85. You may _____ any color shown in this chart for the exterior of your home.

Chord/Cord

86. Wind the electrical _____ loosely around the hair dryer to prolong the life of this product.

87. Piano House's Web site is an excellent source for locating finger settings for any piano _____.

88. Be sure to tape all loose _____ to the floor in setting up the conference rooms.

89. The _____ for connecting the data projector to the computer is missing from the carrying case.

90. Please order three _____ of wood for the fireplace in our mountain restaurant.

Cite/Sight/Site

91. Within the next two weeks, we will select a _____ for our new warehouse facility.

92. Please _____ at least two authorities to substantiate your position.

93. Our travel agency can offer you _____-seeing tours in all parts of the world at reasonable prices.

94. The defendant was also _____ for driving without a license.

95. None of the _____ we have seen so far are suitable for the construction of the entertainment center we have in mind.

Check your answers with those given on pages 368–369 before completing the next exercise.

Name _____ Date _____

Reinforcement Guide 4

Instructions: Select one of the words (or a form of the word) shown below to complete each of the following sentences.

Born/Borne	Canvas/Canvass	Cent/Scent/Sent
Bouillon/Bullion	Capital/Capitol	Cereal/Serial
Breach/Breech	Carat/Caret/Carrot/Karat	Choose/Chose
Bring/Take	Cease/Seize	Chord/Cord
Calendar/Collander	Ceiling/Sealing	Cite/Sight/Site
Callous/Callus	Censor/Censure	
Can/May	Census/Senses	

1. Be sure to record the _____ numbers of all the bonds in this issue before forwarding them to our New York office.

2. If you refuse to _____ these illegal practices, we will be forced to seek an injunction.

3. You _____ call our toll-free number, (800) 555-3783, anytime to obtain information about current interest rates on the accounts we offer.

4. Use a _____ to tie these old newspapers together.

5. Most nonallergenic cosmetics have no discernible _____ whatsoever.

6. Proofreaders and editors use a _____ to indicate where insertions should be placed in a document.

7. When elected officials become _____ and indifferent to the needs of their constituents, they should be replaced.

8. The _____ for the new hospital and medical center has not yet been selected.

9. None of the latest _____ projections support the mayor's claim that business investments in our city have doubled since he has been in office.

10. Our offices are located in Room 450 of the state _____.

11. Within the past few weeks, the _____ between the mayor and several city council members has become apparent to the public.

12. Whom did the Board of Directors _____ to replace our retiring treasurer?

13. Although the governor's personal business activities were not in direct violation of the law, he was _____ by the press for his inability to explain his connection with the Zorga Corporation.

14. How many of our employees have been assigned to _____ the area directly south of Wilshire Boulevard?

15. May I suggest that you select as the first course for the banquet a beef _____.

16. Franchises usually require their participants to invest a substantial amount of _____ before permitting them to operate under their company name.

17. To substantiate your proposal, please _____ to the meeting the names of several companies that have used this plan successfully.

18. At the present time, most of our housing projects are in the outlying areas adjacent to the Florida state _____.

19. After the convention you may wish to view some of the historic _____ in and around Boston.

20. You will need to _____ this movie substantially for television viewing.

21. The parent company, BTP Enterprises, has _____ the losses of its two subsidiaries for the past five years.

22. To ensure that your application will be processed quickly, _____ it in person to the Admissions Office.

23. Send e-mail messages to our Midwestern sales representatives so they can mark their _____ for the regional sales meeting scheduled for January 15–19.

24. Many real estate agents fear that this period of climbing interest rates has not yet reached the _____.

25. As the company continues to purchase new equipment, please label the equipment and record the _____ numbers in our database.

*The answers to this exercise appear in the **Instructor's Manual and Key** for **HOW 13: A Handbook for Office Professionals**, 13th edition.*

Section 7, Words Often Confused and Misused

Name _____ Date _____

Practice Exercises for Words *Close/Clothes/Cloths* Through *Decent/Descent/Dissent*

Practice Guide 5

Instructions: Select the correct word or a form of the word from each set of word confusions to complete the following sentences. Write your choice in the blank.

Close/Clothes/Cloths

1. We plan to _____ out this line of swimsuits at the end of the season.

2. Play Time, Inc., manufactures children's _____ and accessories.

3. Ask the building superintendent's assistant to order an additional supply of dust _____.

4. When you _____ the office at the end of the day, be sure the front door is fastened securely.

5. Several of our _____ racks are broken and need to be replaced.

Coarse/Course

6. You may wish to complete our beginning accounting _____ before taking any other business classes.

7. Before committing themselves to any specific _____ of action, the committee wanted to review more carefully the consultant's recommendations.

8. The texture of this sand is too _____ for use in the manufacture of ceramic tile.

9. Luxury homes and condominiums will be built around this new golf _____.

10. During the _____ of the conversation, neither party discussed the financial commitments that would be necessary from each of them.

Collision/Collusion

11. The two executive officers had been in _____ for several years, embezzling funds steadily from their investors.

12. The impact of the _____ was heard over a block away.

13. Although the state official was suspected of being in _____ with the contract awardee, no one could produce sufficient evidence to substantiate the suspicion.

14. You can see from just observing the manager and his assistant, they are on a definite _____ course.

15. The evidence clearly indicated that the security guard was not in _____ with the bank robbers, as the robbers had indicated.

Command/Commend

16. Please _____ Ms. Harris on her excellent sales performance during this quarter.

17. You are to be _____ for having the foresight to install this computer network when the division was reorganized.

18. To use this software, you must first learn a series of voice _____.

19. The Navy's personnel department has assigned a new officer to _____ this ship.

20. Effective managers will always _____ employees under their supervision for a job well done.

Complement/Compliment

21. You may wish to _____ your tempura shrimp entrée selection with a mixture of stir-fried vegetables.

22. None of the wall decorations in the outer office _____ the rest of the office decor.

23. Please select upholstered chairs to _____ the gray carpeting that will be installed in our offices next week.

24. These calendars will be given to all the conference participants with our _____.

25. Did you remember to _____ all the agents on their outstanding sales performance this month?

Complementary/Complimentary

26. We appreciate your _____ remarks about our products and service.

27. None of the fabrics recommended by the decorator are _____ to the new carpeting.

28. The qualifications possessed by Ms. Lee are certainly _____ to those possessed by other members of our staff.

29. To celebrate the opening of our new La Habra store, we will serve _____ coffee and cookies at all our stores on October 1.

30. In general, student evaluations of Mr. Reed have been quite _____.

Confidant/Confident

31. Mr. Burns has been the senator's _____ for many years.

32. When you feel more _____ about your skills, please return to our Department of Human Resources to take the employment test.

33. I am _____ that we will have more than 100 registrants for this conference.

34. The information was evidently passed on to the press through the president's assistant and _____.

35. Our sales manager feels _____ that her staff members will reach their quotas by the end of the fourth quarter.

Conscience/Conscious

36. In all good _____, I cannot permit you to take this equipment until we have completed all the safety tests.

37. We were not _____ of the new marketing strategies launched by our toughest competitor until last week.

38. Obviously these publishers have little _____ if they are willing to publish such obscene materials.

39. The two entrapped victims were still _____ when the police entered the vault.

40. Patients who elect to undergo LASIK eye surgery are completely _____ during the procedure.

Console/Consul

41. This _____ may be purchased with either an oak or a walnut finish.

42. The organ _____ was damaged by falling ceiling tiles during the hurricane.

43. To receive a refund of the value-added tax, you must have the German _____ witness your affidavit that the goods purchased were brought to the United States.

44. Place this television _____ on the east wall of the family room in our Elegant Living model home.

45. Did you invite the _____ to join us for dinner on May 24?

Continual/Continuous

46. Our receptionist's _____ talking irritates a number of our other staff members.

47. We have been experiencing rainy weather _____ for the past week.

48. Please place this roll of _____-form paper hand towels in the dispenser.

49. The water had run _____ for three days before the gardeners shut it off.

50. Customers are _____ complaining about our service in the southwest area of the city.

Convince/Persuade

51. Were you able to _____ any of the current stockholders to invest additional funds in the company?

52. No matter how hard we tried, we were unable to _____ Aaron to remain with our brokerage firm.

53. Were you able to _____ our manager that networking the computers in our division would increase efficiency and lower costs?

54. Before we move ahead with this project, we must _____ the president of its profitability.

55. How can we _____ you to accompany us on this business trip to Orlando?

Cooperation/Corporation

56. We would appreciate your _____ in distributing the survey to members of your department and ensuring that they are returned.

57. Several managers from our _____ will be attending the technology convention scheduled to be held in Chicago from April 22 through April 24.

58. Only with the _____ of the majority of our employees will this incentive plan be successful.

59. We were able to plan and host this successful trade convention with the _____ and hard work of all our staff.

60. A number of large _____ have expressed an interest in purchasing our office furniture.

Corespondent/Correspondence/Correspondents

61. Who was named as _____ in the divorce case?

62. Would you please direct to my attention all _____ related to this matter.

63. None of our foreign _____ have yet responded with a story from this part of the world.

64. We have received _____ from all over the United States expressing concern over the complexity of the new tax laws.

65. Please have one of the _____ in our Customer Relations Department answer this inquiry.

Corps/Corpse

66. Authorities still have not been able to identify the _____ found last week in the desert near Palm Valley.

67. A _____ of reporters flocked around the winning pitcher as he left the dressing room.

68. A recruitment officer from the U.S. Marine _____ will visit our campus next week.

69. The _____ has already been moved to the downtown morgue.

70. A large _____ of government workers has petitioned the governor to reconsider his stand on proposed wage and salary cuts.

Costumer/Customer

71. Only one _____ who purchased this mattress set requested a refund.

72. Our company prides itself on providing excellent _____ service.

73. Have you hired a _____ for next season's production of *Mamma Mia*?

74. Contact a local _____ to see if any Disney character ensemble is available for the Halloween party.

75. The holiday catalogs have already been mailed to all our charge _____.

Council/Counsel

76. Three members of our city _____ are up for reelection this year.

77. I suggest that you seek _____ from an attorney before taking any further action.

78. The _____ meeting was postponed because a quorum was not present.

79. You should write your city _____ representative directly about the problem.

80. Each staff member _____ at least 12 to 15 students daily.

Credible/Creditable

81. We have received this information from several _____ sources.

82. Your sales record with our company is certainly _____.

83. Mr. Holmes' _____ service record with our organization indicates that he is a likely candidate for promotion.

84. The witness's testimony was hardly _____ in view of the evidence uncovered by the police laboratory.

85. Unless our candidate's campaign promises are viewed by the voting public as _____, he will not have any chance to win this election.

Deceased/Diseased

86. Please notify the family of the _____ victim before releasing his name to the press.

87. The surgeon was able to remove all the _____ tissue without amputating the limb.

88. All the _____ animals must be separated from the herd before they infect the others.

89. What kind of fungicide should we use for these _____ plants?

90. One of the beneficiaries in this will has been _____ for six months.

Decent/Descent/Dissent

91. Most of the people who live in this area are of Irish _____.

92. People in this country are able to earn a _____ wage.

93. _____ among the workers is causing a major problem for our manager.

94. The company's profit picture began its _____ approximately four years ago.

95. Several major stockholders have sensed the _____ between the president and the chairman of the Board of Directors over this issue.

Check your answers with those given on pages 370–371 before completing the next exercise.

Section 7, Words Often Confused and Misused

Reinforcement Guide 5

Instructions: Select one of the words (or a form of the word) shown below to complete each of the following sentences.

Close/Clothes/Cloths	Conscience/Conscious	Corps/Corpse
Coarse/Course	Console/Consul	Costumer/Customer
Collision/Collusion	Continual/Continuous	Council/Counsel
Command/Commend	Convince/Persuade	Credible/Creditable
Complement/Compliment	Cooperation/Corporation	Deceased/Diseased
Complementary/Complimentary	Corespondent/Correspondence/C	Decent/Descent/Dissent
Confidant/Confident	orrespondents	

1. One of the vendors will be serving _____ wine and cheese in the exhibit area from 5 to 7 p.m.

2. If Mr. Smith does not cease his _____ harassment of employees in the Sales Department, we will discontinue our business relationship with him.

3. So far, only three of the _____ members have submitted their reports.

4. Too many customers have complained about the _____ grains in our new bran cereal.

5. At least two government officials were in _____ with the more than 50 individuals collecting welfare payments fraudulently.

6. Ms. Morris has been the president's assistant and _____ for nearly twenty years.

7. If no one else in the _____ is willing to assume this responsibility, I will gladly do so.

8. The Wilson Agency's many contributions to charitable organizations in the community are certainly _____.

9. Be sure to _____ Melanie on the excellent luncheon she arranged for our seminar.

10. Are you _____ of the fact that nearly 10 percent of our employees are absent on a regular basis?

11. Please respond to any incoming _____ within three days of its receipt.

12. The recent _____ of interest rates has stimulated real estate sales in general and the home-buying market in particular.

13. For this specific china pattern, a _____ crystal selection would be either Rosebud or Fontaine.

14. All the shelves in our _____ have mar-proof finishes.

15. Both the defendant and his attorney rushed past the _____ of reporters gathered outside the courtroom door.

16. None of the _____ on these racks are on sale.

17. Be sure that your floral selections _____ the tablecloths and the room decor.

18. The air purifiers in our offices operate _____—24 hours a day, seven days a week.

19. Upon the advice of legal _____, we have decided not to pursue this case any further.

20. Although his reasons for late payment are always _____ and certainly understandable, we cannot waive the late-payment penalty.

21. We must _____ our sales manager to delay these price increases until after the 1st of the year.

22. Unless she remarries, lifetime benefits will continue for the widow of the _____ policyholder.

23. Many of our _____ have requested that we remain open longer hours during the holiday season.

24. From the police report, everyone could easily see that the defendant was responsible for the _____.

25. Growing _____ among several of our staff members is beginning to affect their performance.

*The answers to this exercise appear in the **Instructor's Manual and Key** for **HOW 13: A Handbook for Office Professionals**, 13th edition.*

Name _____ Date _____

Practice Exercises for Words *Defer/Differ* Through *Every Day/Everyday*

Practice Guide 6

Instructions: Select the correct word or a form of the word from each set of word confusions to complete the following sentences. Write your choice in the blank.

Defer/Differ

1. You may _____ payment of this invoice until March 1.

2. Although I _____ on the media we should use, I agree we should increase our advertising efforts.

3. We can no longer _____ calling in these high-interest bonds.

4. All such retirement programs only _____ the payment of taxes until a later date.

5. The candidates seemed to _____ on each issue brought up for discussion.

Deference/Difference

6. We have expanded our business course offerings in _____ to the many requests from the community.

7. I find little _____ between the new edition and the previous edition of this textbook.

8. Would you please explain the _____ between analog and digital signals.

9. Have you noticed any _____ in the quality of custodial services within the past month?

10. Most of our imported food products have been grouped according to the country of origin in _____ to our customers' preferences.

Deprecate/Depreciate

11. Please do not _____ any further management's attempt to introduce new technologies in our office.

12. Under the revised tax laws, investors may still _____ rental properties.

13. The value of some cars _____ more rapidly than the value of others.

14. Employees who continually _____ their coworkers decrease employee morale and increase personnel problems.

15. Property owners are fearful that the proposed airport expansion will _____ property values in this area.

Desert/Dessert

16. This project will bring water to many barren Arizona _____ areas.

17. Do not bring the _____ tray to customers' tables until the entrée dishes have been cleared.

18. Our company specializes in creating, packaging, and marketing low-calorie _____.

19. Pumpkin pie is our most popular _____ item during the Halloween-Thanksgiving holiday season.

20. Many of our retirement centers have been built in _____ areas next to major cities.

Device/Devise

21. Can you _____ a plan to prevent employees from copying for personal use company-purchased software packages?

22. Because of snowstorms in the East, we must _____ an alternate route to Philadelphia.

23. A _____ within this switch reacts to sound and activates the light switch.

24. Did you _____ an alternate plan for marketing these remote controls in case Video Industries refuses our offer?

25. By attaching this security _____ to expensive pieces of clothing, you can reduce your losses from shoplifting.

Dew/Do/Due

26. Payments are _____ by the 15th of each month.

27. The early morning _____ prevents hotel guests from enjoying breakfast on the patio.

28. When _____ you expect the shipment to arrive?

29. The shipment from Hartfield Industries is _____ to arrive within the next three days.

30. You are _____ for your annual physical examination next month.

Die/Dye

31. Mark on the label the _____ lot number of each of these rolls of carpet.

32. If you do not water these young plants daily, they will _____.

33. Workers can easily _____ from the inhalation of these toxic fumes.

34. Do not allow the red _____ to bleed into any other colors in the fabric.

35. These washing machines may not be used to _____ clothing or any other articles.

Disapprove/Disprove

36. Did the zoning commission _____ our proposal?

37. The prosecuting attorney was unable to _____ the witness's testimony.

38. Although we can _____ his alibi, we cannot prove his presence at the scene of the crime.

39. If the insurance company _____ your claim, we will be forced to initiate legal action.

40. The dean will automatically _____ any student petitions that request course waivers for state-mandated requirements.

Disburse/Disperse

41. The crowd began to _____ even before the football game ended.

42. The executor will _____ among the three beneficiaries the remaining articles in the house and the cash resulting from the sale of the house.

43. Dividends for these bonds are _____ biannually on January 1 and July 1.

44. When we entered Cheryl's office, we found papers from the files _____ throughout the room.

45. Payroll checks will no longer be _____ through the Payroll Office; all employees will receive salary payments through direct deposit.

Discreet/Discrete

46. You are to be commended for your _____ handling of these potentially embarrassing circumstances.

47. Mr. Jacob's administrative assistant is always _____ in discussing his availability and calendaring his appointments.

48. CompAmerica needs to assess its market options by investigating a wide range of _____ possibilities.

49. Please be _____ in divulging any further information about our pending acquisition by AMCO Enterprises.

50. We are investigating several _____ plans for financing the proposed construction project.

Disinterested/Uninterested

51. Only _____ parties may serve as witnesses in cases involving traffic accidents.

52. If you are _____ in learning a software program, no amount of instruction will enable you to succeed.

53. Most of the audience acted _____ in what the speaker had to say.

54. You will need two _____ persons to sign this affidavit in the presence of a notary.

55. If clients appear to be _____ in a property, do not attempt to convince them of its potential.

Done/Dun

56. To sell these _____-colored slacks, we will probably need to discount them considerably.

57. You will need to _____ the people on this list to obtain at least a partial payment on their past-due accounts.

58. We have _____ everything we can to persuade these customers to submit their overdue payments.

59. The white sandy beaches portrayed on the travel brochure turned out in reality to be dirty and _____ colored.

60. If you think we should no longer _____ these customers for payment, then I will turn their accounts over to an agency for collection.

E.g./I.e.

61. You may use our service to send shipments overnight within the United States, _____, within the continental United States.

62. Observe e-mail "netiquette" in sending messages over the Internet; _____, ensure your message has a purpose, limit your message length to a screenful of data, and be courteous.

63. To cite references in a research report, use a conventional style; _____, the *Chicago Manual* style, the MLA style, or the APA style.

64. You may purchase from our catalog a variety of accessories to complement your business wardrobe; _____, shoes, purses, scarves, and jewelry.

65. None of these applicants appear to be qualified for the position we advertised; _____, all the applicants are lacking in the skills, knowledge, and/or experience the position requires.

Elicit/Illicit

66. Were you able to _____ any further information from the witnesses?

67. The therapist still has not been able to _____ any verbal responses from the accident victim.

68. The FBI investigated the _____ activities of this company for more than six months before making any arrests.

69. Reporters have been unable to _____ a formal response from any of the company's officials.

70. You certainly cannot expect that such _____ maneuvers will be condoned by the Board of Directors.

Section 7, Words Often Confused and Misused

Eligible/Illegible

71. How many of your students are _____ for graduation at the conclusion of the spring semester?

72. To be _____ for participation in the athletic program, students must maintain a C average.

73. The water damage sustained by the document has made this handwritten will _____.

74. _____ signatures are easier to forge than those written clearly and distinctly.

75. You will become _____ for full benefits after six months' employment with the company.

Emigrate/Immigrate

76. Most of the new residents in our community have _____ from the Far East.

77. How many members of your family have _____ from South America?

78. Several members of our company plan to _____ to Australia to establish an import-export business there.

79. Although most of our employees were born in South Africa, their families originally _____ from England.

80. In what year did you _____ to Canada from Italy?

Eminent/Imminent

81. An _____ Miami physician has recently made major breakthroughs in rehabilitating patients with spinal cord injuries.

82. Were you able to engage an _____ speaker for the opening session of our convention?

83. If these trends continue, a substantial decline in stock market prices is _____.

84. Foreclosure on this apartment complex is _____ unless the owner can raise sufficient capital elsewhere to make the loan payments.

85. The _____ success of this venture lies in the sales staff's ability to convince homeowners that this security device offers low-cost protection.

Envelop/Envelope

86. Please include a self-addressed _____ with your request.

87. An early morning fog often _____ this airport during the winter months and causes delays in scheduled arrivals and departures.

88. Mr. Ross is so _____ in this project that he has neglected his other duties.

89. A layer of pollution usually _____ the area and remains until wind or rain dissipates it.

90. All these _____ have been printed with an incorrect return address.

Every day/Everyday

91. _____ we receive at least one complaint about the new salesperson we hired last month.

92. _____ problems such as this one can be handled easily by one of my assistants.

93. _____ next week, we will receive at least three shipments from Richfield Industries.

94. For your _____ china pattern, you may wish to look at these less expensive selections.

95. Please be sure to sign out _____ after you finish your shift.

Check your answers with those given on pages 371–372 before completing the next exercise.

Section 7, Words Often Confused and Misused

Name _____ Date _____

Reinforcement Guide 6

Instructions: Select one of the words (or a form of the word) shown below to complete each of the following sentences.

Defer/Differ	Disapprove/Disprove	Eligible/Illegible
Deference/Difference	Disburse/Disperse	Emigrate/Immigrate
Deprecate/Depreciate	Discreet/Discrete	Eminent/Imminent
Desert/Dessert	Disinterested/Uninterested	Envelop/Envelope
Device/Devise	Done/Dun	Every day/Everyday
Dew/Do/Due	E.g./I.e.	
Die/Dye	Elicit/Illicit	

1. In _____ to the many requests from our employees with children below school-age, the company will establish a child-care center.

2. Several members of our staff have _____ from the Philippines.

3. If the hospital administrator _____ our budget request for an additional therapist, we will need to reduce our outpatient caseload.

4. Employees who continually _____ their supervisors are usually substandard workers who are unable to adjust to the work environment.

5. We will _____ making a decision on this matter until next week.

6. The _____ threat of further flood damage has caused the area to be evacuated.

7. Did you hire an agency to _____ these flyers throughout the neighborhood?

8. For the board meeting next week, we plan to serve _____ and coffee.

9. Most of the _____ employees have enrolled in the stock-participation program.

10. All the employees stood in shock as they watched the flames _____ the warehouse.

11. The only distasteful part of this job is having to _____ slow-paying customers.

12. As soon as you _____ a new method for handling these payment coupons, please let me know.

13. We will be subjecting all our new products to more stringent testing procedures in _____ to customers' demands for higher-quality, longer-lasting electrical appliances.

14. Our receptionist has been late to work _____ this week.

15. Were you able to _____ from any of our customers any further information about ITV's new operating system?

16. These payroll reports are _____ quarterly and must be submitted on time.

17. According to the decedent's will, his real estate holdings are to be sold and the proceeds _____ to the charities named.

18. When did you _____ to the United States?

19. _____ physicists from all over the world will gather for this convention.

20. Our editor in chief should not let the _____ problems of operating the division occupy the major part of her time.

21. All hair-_____ products on the market are now billed as "hair colorings."

22. During the negotiations both parties were _____ in releasing information to the press.

23. Most of the people who have viewed our video sales presentation for the Landmark Development have appeared _____ in investing in this project.

24. A truck will be in your neighborhood next week, and the Salvation Corps would appreciate receiving your donations; _____, used clothing, furniture, sports equipment, and appliances.

25. Our accountant informed us that we may _____ the cost of these computers over a three-year period.

*The answers to this exercise appear in the **Instructor's Manual and Key** for **HOW 13: A Handbook for Office Professionals**, 13th edition.*

Name _____ Date _____

Practice Exercises for Words *Every one/Everyone* Through *Flaunt/Flout*

Practice Guide 7

Instructions: Select the correct word or a form of the word from each set of word confusions to complete the following sentences. Write your choice in the blank.

Every one/Everyone

1. _____ in our office will be attending the company holiday party.

2. _____ of the oak consoles was sold by the end of the first day of our sale.

3. Please ask _____ to check his or her backpack before entering the student bookstore.

4. Almost _____ in the company has been notified of our plans to move the main plant to Springfield.

5. We have not yet been able to interview _____ of the qualified applicants.

Example/Sample

6. Offer our customers a _____-size vial of our new perfume when they purchase one of our other fragrances.

7. Before the client confirms her selection, she wishes to view a larger _____ of the fabric.

8. All members of our _____ population are from the Chicago area.

9. In our new training manual, be sure to provide ample _____ of screen displays.

10. As an _____ of an employment applicant tracking system, you may wish to describe the procedures used by AmCoast Financial Corporation.

Executioner/Executor

11. Whom has Mr. Benson named as _____ of his will?

12. The _____ was unable to locate several expensive paintings that were known to have been in the estate.

13. In many states the death penalty is carried out by a state _____.

14. The defendant is purported to be an _____ for an organized crime syndicate on the East Coast.

15. Please have the _____ prepare for the court a list of the decedent's assets.

Expand/Expend

16. Do not _____ any additional effort to persuade Ms. Hall to remain with the company.

17. Within the next few months, we will _____ our operations to the Canadian provinces.

18. In revising this textbook, you may wish to _____ its coverage to include a chapter on international correspondence formats and standards.

19. As a result, we can _____ no additional funds for advertising during this quarter.

20. As soon as additional funds are available, we will _____ our offerings in computer applications courses.

Expansive/Expensive

21. _____ wastelands are dominant in this area of the country.

22. The cost of implementing your proposal is more _____ than we had anticipated.

23. Many _____ paintings were damaged by the fire.

24. Only _____ gourmet foods are stocked in this section of the store.

25. The city council has voted to develop an _____ industrial center on all this acreage.

Explicit/Implicit

26. Your _____ directions to the airport were easy to follow.

27. _____ instructions for assembling these toys have been placed on the back panel of each box.

28. The front label states _____, "Keep out of reach of children."

29. You are _____ consenting to these price increases by stating no objections.

30. The fact that you are qualified for the job is _____ in your being offered employment by three major corporations.

Extant/Extent

31. We still have been unable to determine the _____ of the damage caused by the warehouse fire.

32. All our _____ construction projects have been financed fully by American National Bank.

33. Some of the _____ buildings occupied by our company at the turn of the twentieth century have been restored to represent their original architecture.

34. To what _____ do you foresee our involvement in this political campaign?

35. Most of the _____ earliest automobiles are owned by museums.

Facetious/Factious/Fictitious

36. According to the author, all the characters in his new book, *The White House Controversy*, are
_____.

37. Although seemingly _____, Tom's statement bordered on sarcasm.

38. The new manager's _____ disposition can only result in continual dissension.

39. Our declining profit picture during the past year can be attributed directly to three board
members' _____ personalities and their unwillingness to operate as a team.

40. Our manager is well-known for his _____ comments and dry sense of humor.

Facility/Faculty

41. These workshops have been financed by the state chancellor's office for the professional
development of our college _____.

42. You may use this _____ for the professional development workshops.

43. This lot is for _____ parking only.

44. If you wish to use a room in our new _____, please reserve it beforehand by contacting
Julia in the Office of Academic Affairs.

45. The only _____ available on campus for this meeting is the Administrative Conference
Room.

Fair/Fare

46. We can expect to see substantial _____ increases for December on all airlines.

47. The county _____ is held annually during the latter part of September.

48. Our firm has been engaged to ensure a _____ distribution of assets to all the creditors of
record at the time of the bankruptcy.

49. We expect our employees to do more than just a _____ job.

50. How well did you _____ in the speech competition?

Farther/Further

51. If we can assist you any _____, please let us know.

52. Your office is _____ from the airport than mine.

53. Once I have had an opportunity to look into this matter _____, I will contact you again.

54. The _____ you live from campus, the better chance you will have to obtain
on-campus university housing.

55. Had you read _____, you would have seen the paragraph in the contract that grants the
publisher full editing authority.

Feat/Fete

56. The banquet to _____ our retiring football coach will be held on May 22.

57. Such a _____ of daring and courage could have been accomplished by only a few.

58. The _____ accomplished by Rafer Johnson in the 1960 Olympics are still showcased in sports annals.

59. How many people do you expect will attend this _____ to celebrate our company's one hundredth anniversary?

60. After the election the new mayor was _____ by his many supporters and friends.

Fever/Temperature

61. Be sure to record each patient's _____ in his or her chart directly after you read the thermometer.

62. The patient complained of having a _____ for the past three days.

63. Does the patient still have a _____ ?

64. If the child continues to have a _____, take him to the Urgent Care Unit at West Hills Hospital.

65. This patient's _____ has been normal for the past 24 hours.

Fewer/Less

66. Because _____ than 15 students had registered for the class, the dean canceled it.

67. We received _____ responses to this advertisement than we had anticipated.

68. All deposits on our flooring contracts may be no_____ than 50 percent of the total contract price.

69. Only orders containing ten or _____ items may be processed through our fast-service checkout line.

70. _____ than 30 percent of the office building had been renovated by the contract deadline.

Finally/Finely

71. We were _____ able to contact all the sweepstakes winners.

72. These walnut pieces are too coarse to be graded as "_____ chopped."

73. Our _____ trained athletes should perform well in the next Olympics.

74. When we _____ received the information from our central office, it arrived too late to assist us in making a decision.

75. We _____ raised enough capital to purchase the building site on Washington Boulevard.

Section 7, Words Often Confused and Misused

Fiscal/Physical

76. Our company maintains a fitness center on the premises because the executive staff is interested in the _____ well-being of our employees.

77. The accompanying brochure outlines all the _____ benefits you can obtain from using the Schwer ExerBike.

78. Our school district's _____ period begins July 1 and ends June 30.

79. If you do not expend all the funds in your budget by the end of the _____ period, you will lose them.

80. Recent indiscreet investments by our company president have elicited from several board members accusations of _____ irresponsibility.

Flagrant/Fragrant

81. The board of education could not even begin to defend the _____ actions of its newly appointed superintendent.

82. How could the mayor have made such a _____ error?

83. Do not send highly _____ flowers to persons who suffer from allergies.

84. The newspapers were filled with stories of the _____ crimes committed by the hired assassins.

85. Our new line of _____ spices has achieved popularity as gift items for this holiday season.

Flair/Flare

86. Because our office manager has a _____ for color coordination and interior design, she will supervise the refurbishing of our reception area.

87. Your _____ for calming irate customers will prove to be beneficial in your sales career.

88. If Mr. Dodd allows his temper to _____ each time he encounters an adverse situation, he will certainly not be considered for promotion.

89. Be sure to get sufficient rest so that your laryngitis does not _____ up again.

90. _____ skirts are popular again this season.

Flaunt/Flout

91. People who _____ their wealth are usually not well liked by others.

92. American tourists should not _____ foreign customs when visiting other countries.

93. By _____ his attorney's advice, the defendant was sentenced to an even longer term.

94. Any construction workers who _____ the safety rules and procedures on this project will be dismissed immediately.

95. Bob distracts and embarrasses many members of the staff by continually _____ his vices.

Check your answers with those given on pages 373–374 before completing the next exercise.

Name _____ Date _____

Reinforcement Guide 7

Instructions: Select one of the words (or a form of the word) shown below to complete each of the following sentences.

Every one/Everyone
Example/Sample
Executioner/Executor
Expand/Expend
Expansive/Expensive
Explicit/Implicit
Extant/Extent

Facetious/Factious/Fictitious
Facility/Faculty
Fair/Fare
Farther/Further
Feat/Fete
Fever/Temperature
Fewer/Less

Finally/Finely
Fiscal/Physical
Flagrant/Fragrant
Flair/Flare
Flaunt/Flout

1. Please give _____ at the meeting a copy of this report.

2. Any _____ memorabilia belonging to Elvis Presley has already been sold at public auction.

3. All funds raised by this telethon will be donated to _____ cancer research.

4. A large _____ is planned for the benefit of the proposed new hospital wing.

5. The hillside fires, which were thought to be under control yesterday evening, _____ out of control this morning.

6. Any child who continually _____ the school rules will be suspended.

7. The court date for your official appointment as _____ of the estate has been set for August 21.

8. By not objecting to the proposal, the national sales manager gave us her _____ consent to follow through with this new marketing plan.

9. Please telephone our travel agent and request information regarding airline _____ to Atlanta for the week of November 10.

10. Ms. Butler has a _____ for solving problems that users have with our loan-tracking software.

11. If _____ than ten people sign up for the seminar on August 10, we will need to reschedule it after the vacation period.

12. This sales brochure is an excellent _____ of creative and aesthetically pleasing graphic design.

13. _____ deviations from company policy such as these will surely cost the manager his job.

14. To meet the deadline date for this project, our department worked together like a _____ tuned orchestra.

15. If you continue to allow such _____ behavior among the members of your sales staff, we will be forced to hire a new sales manager.

16. Before we can hire any new _____, we must review the projected budget for the next academic year.

17. Please supply us with _____ instructions for cleaning these flat-screen monitors.

18. Minors who present _____ identification are in violation of the law.

19. The speaker's presentation was filled with _____ remarks and humorous stories.

20. Although Don was elated that he had been chosen for the position, he should not have _____ his success in front of others who had applied.

21. Do not _____ any additional time or effort attempting to locate these misplaced files.

22. To accommodate all the buildings in the architect's renderings, a more _____ area than the site offered by your company will be required.

23. When the child was brought to the hospital, her _____ was 103 degrees.

24. During the past _____ period, Hart Industries showed a profit increase of 7 percent.

25. Please use Internet resources to locate the lowest airline _____ from Los Angeles to Minneapolis on April 27.

*The answers to this exercise appear in the **Instructor's Manual and Key** for **HOW 13: A Handbook for Office Professionals**, 13th edition.*

Name _____ Date _____

Practice Exercises for Words *Flew/Flu/Flue* Through *Human/Humane*

Practice Guide 8

Instructions: Select the correct word or a form of the word from each set of word confusions to complete the following sentences. Write your choice in the blank.

Flew/Flu/Flue

1. Please call a service person to repair the chimney _____ in Suite 1420-22.

2. Many of our employees have had the _____ this winter.

3. Please instruct the hotel guests to open the _____ before using the fireplace.

4. The executive staff _____ first-class to New York, but all other company personnel were seated in coach class.

5. Do the residents in this retirement home receive _____ shots each season?

Foreword/Forward

6. Because Ryan Corporation appears to be a _____-looking company, its stock has risen steadily.

7. We are looking _____ to receiving your reply.

8. Have you read the _____ in Mark Lansing's new book?

9. The editor has requested Jonathan Fredericks, president of New York Institute of Science and Technology, to write the _____ for a book of readings on molecular biology and immunology.

10. In most cases the _____ of a book is written by a person other than the author or editor.

Formally/Formerly

11. The committee's selection will be announced _____ on July 14.

12. Ms. Greeley was _____ associated with Stanfield Industries.

13. Yes, we were _____ the primary distributors for Del Monaco Foods on the East Coast.

14. Our new product line will be _____ introduced at the International Computer Show in Chicago on March 25.

15. For this event all ladies and gentlemen must be _____ attired.

Former/Latter

16. Please send a copy of this report to the _____ company president.

17. From among your present and _____ instructors, please list three references.

18. Our inventory must be completed during the _____ part of January.

19. Mr. Thompson's _____ business plan seems to be more realistic than his present one.

20. Both John Dixon, manager of our Toledo branch, and Brett Johnson, manager of our Louisville branch, applied for the position; but Brett, the _____, is more qualified.

Forth/Fourth

21. Amalgamated Enterprises represents the _____ contract we have received this month.

22. Please do not hesitate to set _____ any ideas you may have regarding this proposal.

23. Nearly one _____ of our sales staff has already reached its quota for the year.

24. You may need to reword for clarity the _____ question in this survey instrument.

25. Before we begin writing the grant proposal, we need to set _____ goals and objectives.

Fortunate/Fortuitous

26. Locating the long-lost heirs occurred only through a _____ incident.

27. Toys from this holiday toy drive will be distributed to less-_____ children.

28. Let us hope that we are _____ enough to underbid Lexigraph for this multimillion-dollar contract.

29. Their partner's embezzlement was discovered _____ by an accounting student who was working part-time for the company.

30. If I am _____ enough to obtain a position with your company, I would be willing to relocate.

Good/Well

31. The last group of candidates did very _____ on this promotional examination.

32. Since I did not feel _____ yesterday, I left the office early.

33. If employees do not feel _____ about themselves and their work, they will become disgruntled.

34. At the present time, economic forecasts for our industry look _____.

35. Unfortunately, our basketball team did not do _____ enough in the semifinals to qualify for the finals.

Grate/Great

36. I hope that the new mayor and his staff will meet the _____ expectations of our citizenry.

37. Place a solid cover instead of a _____ over this open shaft.

38. You may wish to _____ all these smaller, unusable pieces into wood shavings.

39. Do his rude manners and loud voice _____ on your nerves too?

40. A number of _____ American leaders have stayed in this hotel during the past century.

Hail/Hale

41. During the storm large pieces of _____ damaged windshields throughout the city.

42. Will I be able to _____ a taxi easily during the afternoon rush hour?

43. The falling _____ melted quickly once it hit the ground.

44. At eighty years of age, the chairman of the board is still _____ and hearty.

45. All along the parade route, the crowd _____ the Rose Queen and her court.

He/Him/Himself

46. Although the choice is only between you and _____, the committee still has not made a decision.

47. We all suspected that the new president would be _____.

48. Bill _____ volunteered to write the report if the other committee members would assist him with editing and proofreading it.

49. The person selected for this top administrative post was not _____.

50. Please ask Marie, Chris, or _____ to assist you with compiling the sales figures for this month.

Healthful/Healthy

51. Daily running is considered by many to be a _____ activity.

52. Physical exercise contributes to a person's well-being and builds a _____ body.

53. Your condition can be improved only by following carefully a _____ diet.

54. Do not overwater your indoor plants if you wish to keep them green and _____.

55. Our manager always strives to keep a _____ spirit of cooperation among the members of her department.

Hear/Here

56. Return the form _____ when you have completed it.

57. Were you _____ when the manager requested us to join her for a brief meeting after the store closes?

58. None of us in the back row were able to _____ the general session speaker.

59. If you _____ of any job openings in this area, please let me know.

60. These tests are administered only _____ in the laboratory.

Her/Herself/She

61. Donna _____ was unsure whether or not she had set the alarm before leaving the store.

62. If Bob or _____ requests this confidential information, please give it to either one of them.

63. As soon as we receive the signed contracts, I will assign either my assistant or _____ to set up the account.

64. The most qualified person for this position is obviously _____.

65. If I were _____, I would request a leave of absence instead of resigning outright.

Hew/Hue

66. We must _____ this giant tree before its roots penetrate the retaining wall.

67. This fabric contains most of the _____ present in a rainbow.

68. Musicians and music fans of every _____ should be attracted to this exhibition.

69. Most of the artwork displayed in the Hillcrest Gallery are _____ from wood or stone.

70. We have not yet been able to locate a silk fabric with the pinkish _____ we need.

Hoard/Horde

71. A _____ of fans gathered around the star as he attempted to leave the stadium.

72. _____ of locusts severely damaged the crops in this region last year.

73. Please request employees not to _____ quantities of office supplies in their desk drawers and file cabinets.

74. Rumors of shortages can cause consumers to _____ goods, which in turn can cause an artificial demand for these products.

75. The officers seized the smugglers' _____ of contraband.

Hoarse/Horse

76. Because the caller had a _____ voice, my assistant had difficulty understanding his question.

77. Mr. Lyons' voice became _____ from lecturing over the continuous hum of the wall air conditioners.

78. John shouted himself _____ at the football game.

79. All the properties in this canyon are zoned to permit _____.

80. Does Dr. Miller's veterinary clinic treat _____ as well as dogs and cats?

Hole/Whole

81. Our doughnut-_____ sales are almost one third of our regular doughnut sales.

82. Honey Baked Hams are sold only _____ or in halves.

83. We will not make any decisions until we have heard the _____ story.

84. Tenants who drill _____ in the walls will be responsible for the cost of patching and repainting the walls when they move.

85. The _____ conference will be devoted to developing research methods and reporting findings.

Holy/Wholly

86. I am not _____ convinced that the proposed new building should receive priority as we plan the renovation of our campus.

87. A number of _____ relics were destroyed in the fire.

88. All members of the committee _____ support your idea.

89. The new stock issue was purchased _____ by small investors.

90. Although you may not _____ agree with our decision, I hope you understand the reasons for it.

Human/Humane

91. This diagram illustrates the flow of blood through the _____ heart.

92. These new mannequins look almost _____.

93. If you are interested in adopting a pet, visit the Web site of the _____ society in your state.

94. Our editor has requested us to submit more _____-interest stories for the Sunday edition.

95. The American prison system advocates the _____ treatment of inmates.

Check your answers with those given on pages 374–375 before completing the next exercise.

Name _____ Date _____

Reinforcement Guide 8

Instructions: Select one of the words (or a form of the word) shown below to complete each of the following sentences.

Flew/Flu/Flue   Grate/Great   Hoard/Horde
Foreword/Forward   Hail/Hale   Hoarse/Horse
Formally/Formerly   He/Him/Himself   Hole/Whole
Former/Latter   Healthful/Healthy   Holy/Wholly
Forth/Fourth   Hear/Here   Human/Humane
Fortunate/Fortuitous   Her/Herself/She
Good/Well   Hew/Hue

1. Our company was _____ a subsidiary of Walton Industries.

2. Many people today still _____ large sums of cash instead of depositing them in savings accounts.

3. The winner of our monthly sales contest was _____, David Larson.

4. The prosecution's surprise witness seemed to come _____ from nowhere.

5. Some of the crops were damaged by the recent unseasonable _____ storm.

6. Once we receive the _____ shipment, we will send you full payment for Invoice 874659H.

7. Only through a _____ occurrence did we discover that one of our salespersons was selling competitive products while representing our line.

8. This student does not read _____ enough to work at grade level.

9. Because the _____ had inadvertently been closed, smoke from the fireplace filled the restaurant and set off the fire alarm.

10. Based on the outcome of the vote, we can only assume that the board was not _____ convinced that our proposal is the solution to this problem.

11. Mary requested the respondents to return the questionnaire to _____.

12. Mark down all our fireplace _____ 40 percent for this weekend sale.

13. As soon as we _____ from the lender, we will notify you.

14. Our society has dedicated itself to alleviating starvation and _____ suffering throughout the world.

15. Most of the stones used to build this home were _____ from giant rocks in the adjacent mountain area.

16. The foundation sponsors programs to promote the _____ treatment of children throughout the world.

17. The crowd _____ the athletes as they made their way to the center of the coliseum.

18. Be sure to read the _____ before you begin reading *Business Etiquette Around the Globe*.

19. Most of our high school students do _____ on college entrance examinations.

20. As I left the court, a _____ of reporters surrounded me.

21. The Northridge Chamber of Commerce will honor its _____ presidents at the next meeting.

22. After a two-week treatment at the Livingston Health Spa, you will leave feeling _____ and hearty.

23. Eat _____ foods and engage in daily exercise to maintain your well-being.

24. Although my voice is still somewhat _____, I will do my best to deliver an interesting presentation at tomorrow's session.

25. Was your coughing and runny nose accompanied by the _____?

*The answers to this exercise appear in the **Instructor's Manual and Key** for **HOW 13: A Handbook for Office Professionals**, 13th edition.*

Section 7, Words Often Confused and Misused

Practice Exercises for Words *Hypercritical/Hypocritical* Through *Lessee/Lesser/Lessor*

Practice Guide 9

Instructions: Select the correct word or a form of the word from each set of word confusions to complete the following sentences. Write your choice in the blank.

Hypercritical/Hypocritical

1. _____ and demanding supervisors generally experience a high degree of personnel turnover in their units.

2. Your inflexible and _____ view of new technologies will certainly cost you your job.

3. The press labeled this "would-be" council member _____ after citing several glaring inconsistencies in speeches to different community groups.

4. In my estimation the Board of Directors was _____ of the president's reorganization plan.

5. Too many politicians are _____; they tell the voters what they want to hear before the election but do as they please after the election.

I/Me/Myself

6. You may submit your reports to either Jan or _____.

7. It was _____ who conducted the in-service training program last month.

8. David, Lisa, and _____ are responsible for conducting this survey of consumer preferences.

9. Please ask the branch managers to fill out and return these questionnaires to Ms. Reynolds or _____.

10. The only person in our unit who has access to these files is _____.

Ideal/Idle/Idol

11. Our receptionist appears to have too much _____ time.

12. In just three years, this pitcher has become a baseball _____ and earned millions of dollars.

13. The site on the corner of Fourth Street and Jefferson Avenue is an _____ location for our proposed new restaurant.

14. The server has already lain _____ for nearly six hours, so we have been unable to access any information on the network.

15. Although none of these solutions is _____, we must select one temporarily.

Imply/Infer

16. Silence on the part of coworkers or subordinates does not necessarily _____ consent.

17. I did not mean to _____ that your statement was incorrect.

18. May we _____ from the consultant's report that our present distribution system needs to be modernized?

19. We _____ from the vice president's bulletin that the company would be downsizing our division within the next two months.

20. The newspaper article _____ that several computer software companies would be making significant announcements this month.

In behalf of/On behalf of

21. This plaque is being presented to the president of the Des Moines Chamber of Commerce _____ its members.

22. At the banquet Ms. Wells presented four scholarships _____ Midtown Industries.

23. Would you please speak to the dean of academic affairs _____ this student?

24. _____ Lismore Cosmetics, I am pleased to enclose a check to support your research program in skin abnormalities and disease.

25. The attorney requested to speak to the judge privately _____ his client.

Incidence/Incidents

26. Have you reported any of these _____ to the police?

27. We have yet to encounter any _____ requiring us to use this feature of your software.

28. Because such an _____ would be highly unlikely in our industry, your proposal does not relate to our circumstances.

29. All the _____ you describe occurred without my knowledge or the knowledge of any other member of the administrative staff.

30. Too few _____ require our using teleconferencing for us to invest in our own facility.

Incite/Insight

31. Perhaps the incoming president of our homeowners' association will _____ more members to participate actively in our organization.

32. A small group of agitators _____ the union members to strike.

33. The Board of Directors is looking for a chief executive officer with _____ and experience in human relations.

34. Without any _____ into the internal workings of this company, I cannot predict how successful it might become.

35. Do your political science courses _____ students to become more politically active?

Section 7, Words Often Confused and Misused

Indigenous/Indigent/Indignant

36. Although pineapples are not _____ to Hawaii, for nearly a century pineapple production was one of Hawaii's major agricultural industries.

37. Mr. Simon, whose parents were _____ farmworkers, has risen to become one of America's financial giants.

38. _____ accused of crimes in this state may secure the services of a public defender.

39. Your _____ attitude seems unjustified in this situation.

40. This kind of generosity and concern is _____ of her personality and character.

Ingenious/Ingenuous

41. _____ ideas such as this one come only once in a lifetime.

42. According to the news reports, the _____ eighth-grader was able to invade the computer files of many major corporations throughout the state.

43. Our _____ receptionist would never be suspicious of anything our clients tell her.

44. This makeshift car door opener formed from a wire coat hanger is an _____ device.

45. The defendant seemed to give an _____ account of his acts, concealing nothing.

Interstate/Intrastate

46. Since our grocery store chain is _____, we are subject only to Utah statutes.

47. Our _____ activities are primarily among Texas, Oklahoma, and New Mexico.

48. Commercial trucks traveling _____ must be licensed by all states in which their companies have offices.

49. The federal government regulates _____ commerce.

50. Our licensing program does not have reciprocity with any other state; therefore, you may practice _____ only.

Irregardless/Regardless

51. We must have these contracts prepared by tomorrow afternoon, _____!

52. _____ of your company's current circumstances, would you reemploy this candidate if you had the opportunity to do so?

53. These outdoor sporting events will be held _____ of the weather forecasts projecting rain for the weekend.

54. Steve has permitted customers to purchase cars on credit _____ of their poor credit rating.

55. We will ship the Freestone Company order by Friday _____ of whether or not we have received prepayment.

Its/It's

56. If _____ too late for us to purchase tickets for the August 12 performance, please see if you can obtain tickets for August 19 or August 26.

57. We have been forced to close our Westchester branch temporarily because _____ new location is not yet ready for occupancy.

58. The building has been closed down by the fire department because _____ unsafe for occupancy.

59. The union has requested all _____ members to approve the new contract.

60. When will the chamber of commerce have _____ annual holiday party for needy children?

Later/Latter

61. All the electrical work in this housing tract must be completed by the _____ part of April.

62. Unfortunately, we are unable to schedule a _____ appointment for you on October 20.

63. Is this class offered at a _____ time also?

64. Her _____ design for the building facade is more creative and appealing.

65. Neither of his proposals was accepted by the committee, although the _____ one showed more promise.

Lay/Lie

66. Please request the patient to _____ down on the examination table.

67. Our computer system has _____ idle for nearly 24 hours.

68. The victim had _____ in his car for more than two hours before the highway patrol discovered the wreckage in the gully beside the highway.

69. Why have these files been _____ on my desk for the past week?

70. The new shopping center _____ at the base of the Verdugo Foothills.

Lead/Led

71. Process Harman Manufacturing's order for 12 dozen No. 4384 _____ casings this afternoon.

72. All crystal sold in the United States must be labeled clearly with the amount of _____ content.

73. Sandra has _____ in new car sales for the past three consecutive months.

74. The firefighter _____ the three children to safety before the flames fully enveloped the house.

75. At yesterday's session Dr. Hansen _____ the discussion on the impact the Internet has had on the digital generation.

Section 7, Words Often Confused and Misused

Lean/Lien

76. Our restaurant serves only _____ meats and fresh vegetables.

77. I believe the Board of Directors _____ toward divesting the company of all its technology stocks.

78. Several subcontractors have already placed _____ against the property.

79. Do not _____ the folding chairs against the newly painted walls.

80. After satisfying the _____ against the property, the former owners will receive $10,085 upon the close of escrow.

Leased/Least

81. We have received at _____ 30 applications for this open position.

82. The _____ we can do for our displaced employees is to offer them retraining for existing jobs within the company or six months' severance pay.

83. Our company uses only _____ trucks and automobiles.

84. All our _____ properties are insured through Mutual Insurance Company of America.

85. We have _____ these offices for more than ten years.

Lend/Loan

86. We have sufficient collateral to obtain a _____ for $1.5 million.

87. If the bank will not _____ us these additional funds, we will be forced to curtail our expansion.

88. Would you be able to _____ me a few minutes of your time tomorrow to go over last week's receipts?

89. The balloon payment on this _____ is due in six months.

90. None of the financial institutions we contacted would _____ us the funds for this housing development.

Lessee/Lesser/Lessor

91. Your monthly rental checks should be made payable to TRC Management Associates, the agent for the _____.

92. You, as the _____, are responsible for any damages to the property caused by you, your family members or friends, or any other person you willingly admit to the property.

93. Because the _____ wishes to convert these apartments to condominiums, he is not renewing any leases.

94. If you elect to receive the _____ amount, the annuity payments will continue for an additional five years.

95. Until I have had an opportunity to investigate the situation further, I cannot decide which issue is of _____ importance.

Check your answers with those given on pages 376–377 before completing the next exercise.

Name _____ Date _____

Reinforcement Guide 9

Instructions: Select one of the words (or a form of the word) shown below to complete each of the following sentences.

Hypercritical/Hypocritical   Indigenous/Indigent/Indignant   Lead/Led
I/Me/Myself   Ingenious/Ingenuous   Lean/Lien
Ideal/Idle/Idol   Interstate/Intrastate   Leased/Least
Imply/Infer   Irregardless/Regardless   Lend/Loan
In behalf of/On behalf of   It's/Its   Lessee/Lesser/Lessor
Incidence/Incidents   Later/Latter
Incite/Insight   Lay/Lie

1. Before occupying the premises, the _____ must sign the lease and give us a cashier's check to cover the first and last months' rent, a security deposit, and a nonrefundable cleaning fee.

2. If you need to _____ down, please use the cot in the employees' lounge.

3. Do not be deceived by his mild mannerisms and _____ smile.

4. Which financial institution has agreed to _____ the Petersons sufficient funds to purchase the home on Monogram Avenue?

5. Because she is consistently _____ of everyone else's efforts, other members of the staff avoid working with her.

6. Although both plans for financing this building project seem sound, the accountant's _____ one will probably be accepted by the board.

7. I did not intend to _____ that your products were inferior to those of your competitor.

8. If you will return the completed application to either Ms. Davis or_____, we will process it without any further delays.

9. We have already _____ all the office space in this building, even before it has been completed.

10. The council canceled _____ next meeting, which was scheduled for December 23.

11. These rallies are designed to _____ college students to take a more active role in politics and elections.

12. Politicians are often accused of being _____when they do not fulfill their campaign promises.

13. To avoid having a _____ placed against your property, you must pay these subcontractors' charges.

14. If you plan to operate _____ only, you need not comply with these federal regulations.

15. In the future please file a written report for any _____ of this nature, even ones that do not appear to have resulted in injury.

16. Most of these cacti are _____ to Palm Springs and the surrounding desert areas.

17. For this holiday season, our bank is soliciting canned goods and toys for _____ families.

18. Your administrative assistant appears to have too much _____ time on his hands.

19. Our _____ research staff has made another breakthrough in miniaturizing the components for our digital video cameras.

20. If you travel _____ by truck or car, you may not transport fruit, vegetables, or plants across many state lines.

21. We have no other choice but to _____ from the number of complaint letters we have received that the service provided by your branch office needs to be improved.

22. Our company credit union _____ money at interest rates lower than those charged by other financial organizations.

23. At the closing session, Ms. Harris will present the William S. Hartnell award _____ Western Publishing Company.

24. _____ of the stated guarantee, what has been your experience with A&A Computers' service center?

25. Drinking consistently from crystal with a high _____ content can prove hazardous to your health.

*The answers to this exercise appear in the **Instructor's Manual and Key** for **HOW 13: A Handbook for Office Professionals**, 13th edition.*

Name _____ Date _____

Practice Exercises for Words *Lessen/Lesson* Through *Ordinance/Ordnance*

Practice Guide 10

Instructions: Select the correct word or a form of the word from each set of word confusions to complete the following sentences. Write your choice in the blank.

Lessen/Lesson

1. Unless we _____ our efforts in this declining market, we will continue to suffer substantial losses.

2. The federal government has _____ its control in this area and permitted state governments to assume jurisdiction.

3. Next week's _____ will cover importing spreadsheet and database files into word processing files.

4. Perhaps we should _____ our commitment in those areas that produce long-term results and focus temporarily on achieving some necessary short-term goals.

5. We learned our _____ when we hired someone without first checking thoroughly her references.

Levee/Levy

6. There are _____ in many places along the lower Mississippi River.

7. This tax _____ will pay for local school improvements.

8. Every government must _____ taxes to pay its expenses.

9. During the summer season, many tourists use this _____ to access our resort by boat.

10. Unpaid tax _____ against these properties have resulted in foreclosure.

Liable/Libel/Likely

11. If you do not repair the large potholes in the parking lot, you will be _____ for any damages resulting from this hazardous condition.

12. Unless a parcel is insured, the U.S. Postal Service is not _____ for the loss of or damage to any package mailed.

13. If your evidence is not conclusive, this statement about the mayor could be construed as _____.

14. Be sure to avoid making any _____ statements in your article.

15. If you do not purchase your airline ticket by the end of April, you are _____ not to get a reservation.

Lightening/Lightning

16. What _____ agent is used in these hair-coloring products?

17. By _____ our laptop computers, we were able to gain an additional 10 percent of the market share.

18. Remind the lifeguards to prohibit swimmers from entering the pools during the summer thunder and _____ storms.

19. Several plans for _____ airport congestion are presently under consideration by the city council.

20. Metal rods are often fixed on buildings to protect them from _____.

Local/Locale

21. _____ residents are protesting the construction of this youth detention center in their community.

22. The _____ we had originally selected for our self-storage site subsequently proved to be unsuitable.

23. Can you suggest a _____ for our West Coast distribution center?

24. Which television channel in our area provides the best _____ news coverage?

25. If you are interested in learning about our _____ government, you should attend a city council meeting.

Loose/Lose

26. When did you _____ your briefcase?

27. Please call our building maintenance service to have this _____ door handle repaired.

28. If we _____ this contract, our company will suffer a substantial loss of income.

29. If these _____ tiles are not repaired immediately, someone may fall and suffer a serious injury.

30. We cannot afford to _____ the confidence of our customers.

Magnate/Magnet

31. In navigating your boat, be sure that no _____ is nearby to distort the compass readings.

32. A Texas oil _____ has purchased this ranch and the surrounding acreage.

33. Although his father was a railroad _____, he was unable to achieve any kind of success with the family fortune.

34. The carnival was like a _____, attracting children and their parents from miles around.

35. Many television performers have risen to stardom because of their _____ personalities.

Section 7, Words Often Confused and Misused

Main/Mane

36. Our _____ office is located in New York City.

37. One of our _____ concerns centers around the ability of this vendor to meet our delivery schedule.

38. The trainer grabbed the lion by its _____.

39. The _____ event is scheduled to begin at 9 p.m.

40. After the race the winning jockey stroked the horse's _____.

Manner/Manor

41. I am not sure whether or not we should proceed in this _____.

42. Many nineteenth-century European _____ have been converted into hotels or tourist sights.

43. The opening scene of this movie takes place in a French _____ located in the outskirts of Paris around the turn of the nineteenth century.

44. Perhaps we should find a more economical _____ to package the dental floss replacements for our new product, Reach.

45. His arrogant _____ has caused us to lose several valuable clients.

Marital/Marshal/Martial

46. May we request applicants to indicate their _____ status on an employment application?

47. Each year the dean of the college acts as _____ of the graduation procession and directs the lineup for the conferring of degrees.

48. High school bands in the Veterans Day parade commemorated the sacrifices of veterans throughout the country with _____ music.

49. A U.S. _____ is an officer of a federal court and has duties similar to those of a sheriff.

50. Do the current income tax laws permit a _____ deduction for a married couple filing jointly?

May be/Maybe

51. You _____ eligible for additional benefits upon retirement.

52. _____ you will be eligible for additional benefits upon retirement.

53. If you are unable to pick up this airport shipment by 5 p.m. on Wednesday, _____ United Airfreight will deliver it to your store.

54. As an investor in tax-free municipal bonds, you _____ interested in this new issue that has just become available.

55. This information _____ available on the Internet.

Medal/Meddle

56. Do not _____ in the personal lives of your staff members.

57. How many gold-_____ winners did the United States have in the last Olympics?

58. The _____ is silver and bears on the obverse an effigy of the Queen.

59. One academic department should not _____ in the internal affairs of another.

60. Corey is known to _____ frequently in other people's affairs.

Miner/Minor

61. Because the beneficiary is still a _____, the court must appoint a conservator.

62. We cannot deal with such _____ matters at this time.

63. Frank had been a coal _____ in Pennsylvania before he moved to Arizona.

64. In this state _____ may not enter into legal contracts.

65. Correct the major deficiencies in this report before you deal with the _____ errors.

Mode/Mood

66. Our supervisor always appears to be in a good _____.

67. The automobile, comparatively speaking, is a slow _____ of transportation in this fast-paced business world.

68. The vice president explained in his usual solemn _____ the critical situation the company is presently facing.

69. Natural hair styles became the _____ in the late 1990s.

70. When you are in the _____ to reorganize the files, please let me know.

Moral/Morale

71. Employee _____ has risen under the leadership of Neil Marcus, the new department manager.

72. The football team's _____ was low after its defeat.

73. Our company supports the _____ responsibility of not producing products that may be harmful to the health or well-being of society.

74. This speaker's topics all deal with _____ issues.

75. According to recent research results, companies that sponsor profit sharing plans have greater productivity and higher employee _____ than those companies that do not.

Section 7, Words Often Confused and Misused

Morning/Mourning

76. Because of the dense fog, all early _____ flights have been delayed.

77. We serve complimentary coffee to our customers every _____ from 8 a.m. until 11 a.m.

78. The nation went into _____ upon the news of the terrorists' attacks on September 11, 2001.

79. My most productive hours are those in the early _____.

80. Please do not disturb the family with business matters while they are in _____.

Naval/Navel

81. Two students from this year's graduating class have received appointments to the _____ Academy.

82. This surgery will leave you with a 3-inch scar directly below the _____.

83. We purchase all our _____ oranges from distributors in Florida.

84. The senator is a graduate of Harvard and a former _____ officer.

85. Our business depends entirely upon _____ contracts.

Ordinance/Ordnance

86. A local _____ prohibits excessive noise after 10 p.m.

87. Most large cities have _____ that control the use of smog-producing fuels.

88. The army has planned to move its _____ warehouse from Seal Beach to Oceanside.

89. Which officer is in charge of _____ procurement?

90. Fines for the violation of local traffic _____ range from $75 to $585.

Check your answers with those given on pages 377–378 before completing the next exercise.

Name _____ Date _____

Reinforcement Guide 10

Instructions: Select one of the words (or a form of the word) shown below to complete each of the following sentences.

Lessen/Lesson	Magnate/Magnet	Miner/Minor
Levee/Levy	Main/Mane	Mode/Mood
Liable/Libel/Likely	Manner/Manor	Moral/Morale
Lightening/Lightning	Marital/Marshal/Martial	Morning/Mourning
Local/Locale	May be/Maybe	Naval/Navel
Loose/Lose	Medal/Meddle	Ordinance/Ordnance

1. News of our new employee benefits program has certainly boosted employee _____.

2. Unless you can substantiate these allegations with concrete evidence, your statements could be construed as _____.

3. This _____ was selected as our next convention site because of its accessibility.

4. The family has closed the business for three days during this _____ period.

5. We _____ interested in computerizing our payroll system, so please call me for a demonstration of your software.

6. If you _____ any items while on campus, please check with the Campus Police Department.

7. The fire on the _____ base destroyed nearly $2 million in supplies and equipment.

8. Enclosed is a list of the police officers in our precinct who have received a _____ for bravery beyond the call of duty.

9. Hilton was a hotel _____ of an earlier era.

10. Because the sale and the use of fireworks without a license are prohibited by a city _____, individuals may not purchase or use them for private Independence Day celebrations.

11. Although a seemingly _____ consideration, our all-day complimentary cookie-and-coffee service attracts many customers.

12. The lion's _____ had become tangled in the bars of the cage.

13. This additional 0.01 percent _____ on real property will remain in effect for three years.

14. Our primary _____ for shipping furniture to our dealers is via surface carriers.

15. This beautiful _____ has been in the Winchester family for more than two centuries.

16. _____ and thunder storms are forecast for the next two days.

17. You cannot expect Johnson Industries to pay $23 million for a company and then not _____ in its internal operations.

18. Please have a _____ deliver the summons to the defendant.

19. These specialized high-quality _____ schools are designed to draw children from all parts of the city.

20. Hydro-Clor bleach may be used for safely _____ all dull, gray-looking white fabrics.

21. Our attorney believes that the company is _____ for the plaintiff's medical expenses and lost income for the past six years.

22. When assisting customers with their purchases, you should always project a cheerful _____.

23. Our counseling staff specializes in assisting couples with their _____ problems.

24. The client's _____ source of income is from a trust fund set up by his deceased parents.

25. Copies of our new procedures manual are being assembled in _____-leaf binders.

*The answers to this exercise appear in the **Instructor's Manual and Key** for **HOW 13: A Handbook for Office Professionals**, 13th edition.*

Practice Exercises for Words *Overdo/Overdue* Through *Pray/Prey*

Practice Guide 11

Instructions: Select the correct word or a form of the word from each set of word confusions to complete the following sentences. Write your choice in the blank.

Overdo/Overdue

1. This invoice is already 60 days _____.

2. If you _____ the comedy scenes in this production, you will lose your audience.

3. Two of our chefs seem to _____ the meats and vegetables.

4. His plane is already three hours _____.

5. Do not ignore making an appointment for your _____ annual physical examination.

Pair/Pare/Pear

6. Did the chef _____ the apples before putting them in the salad?

7. The landscape design includes several Oriental _____ trees.

8. During the sale one customer purchased 17 _____ of shoes.

9. We have been directed to _____ all expenses by 10 percent during the next quarter.

10. Pictures of the bridal _____ appeared in yesterday's newspaper.

Partition/Petition

11. How many registered voters signed the _____?

12. In our new offices, a _____ separates each work station.

13. When will the executor _____ the court for approval to distribute the remaining assets of the estate?

14. We plan to renovate the second floor and _____ it into four medical suites.

15. Please have the client file a naturalization _____ as the first step toward obtaining United States citizenship.

Passed/Past

16. Based on this company's _____ performance, we cannot rely on it to complete a job according to schedule.

17. Why has Chris continually been _____ up for promotion?

18. In the _____ we have always closed our offices the Friday after Thanksgiving.

19. Has this information been _____ on to all our employees?

20. As a _____ award winner, you are invited to attend each annual banquet as a guest of the foundation.

Patience/Patients

21. Be sure to notify all our _____ of our new address and telephone number.

22. You will need to exhibit more _____ in dealing with clients and potential investors.

23. During this flu season, the waiting room has been filled from early morning until late afternoon with _____.

24. All new _____ must complete this medical information form before seeing the doctor.

25. An effective supervisor must show _____ and understanding in dealing with employees' temporary personal problems.

Peace/Piece

26. If you are interested in becoming a _____ officer, our counseling office can provide you with information about this career.

27. These offices have been leased by a new world _____ organization.

28. The _____ of land upon which ATV Industries bid consists of 77 acres.

29. Most of the properties in this area are second homes owned by city dwellers who enjoy the _____ and quiet of the countryside.

30. This manufacturer's china sets all contain 144 _____.

Peak/Peek

31. What has been this year's _____ selling price for this stock?

32. This well-educated, ambitious young lawyer has yet to reach the _____ of her career.

33. In July the unemployment rate reached its _____ for the year.

34. Children often stop to _____ into the window of our candy store.

35. Place the answer sheet to this placement examination out of sight so that students cannot inadvertently _____ at it.

Peal/Peel

36. At the first _____ of thunder, be sure to stop the construction crew and begin transporting the workers and equipment back to the service facility.

37. The backers knew their play was a success as _____ of laughter resounded throughout the theater.

38. Ask the chef to _____ the tomatoes before cutting them into any salads.

39. The church bells of the magnificent cathedral in Cologne _____ forth their message of Christmas joy.

40. Please inform the landlord that the paint on the outside of our office building is _____.

Section 7, Words Often Confused and Misused

Peer/Pier

41. If you must _____ closely to read newspapers and magazines, you should have an optometrist check your eyes.

42. Advancement in academic rank at this university is determined solely by a committee of one's _____.

43. Our new restaurant, Sea Harbor, will be located overlooking the harbor at the end of the Santa Maria _____.

44. Many of the younger children _____ at Santa Claus awhile before mustering up enough courage to approach him.

45. No night fishing is permitted on the _____.

Persecute/Prosecute

46. What steps have you taken to prohibit coworkers from continuing to _____ Ms. Smith?

47. People living in this region are _____ by small stinging insects during July and August.

48. Has the state decided whether or not it will _____ your client?

49. Because this student is unwilling to read her textbook, she continually _____ our instructional aides with persistent requests for assistance.

50. Drunken drivers will be _____ to the fullest extent of the law.

Personal/Personnel

51. Most of our _____ have been employed by the company for more than five years.

52. These benefits are for full-time _____ only.

53. Employees' cell phone use during working hours should be limited to _____ emergencies.

54. If you wish to view your _____ file, please contact the director of human resources.

55. The former tenant still needs to remove his _____ possessions from this furnished apartment.

Perspective/Prospective

56. To increase sales, we must broaden our market _____.

57. Please have a member of our sales staff visit each of these _____ clients personally.

58. All _____ employees must submit a letter of application and a scannable résumé.

59. To be a successful leader, one must be able to view issues in their proper _____.

60. His limited _____ of opportunities in foreign markets has held up our entry into the international marketplace.

Peruse/Pursue

61. If Capital Investment Company does not _____ a different course, it will continue to lose more of its client base.

62. Much of the e-mail I receive may be left unread or just _____.

63. You may wish to _____ the final draft of this report before it is distributed to the other committee members.

64. Our Web site is devoted to assisting individuals who wish to _____ a career in accounting.

65. The first step in financial planning is deciding which goals to _____.

Plaintiff/Plaintive

66. Who is the _____ in this case?

67. The _____ were unable to provide sufficient evidence to substantiate their case.

68. The _____ testimony of the witness seemingly stirred the jury.

69. Has the attorney for the _____ filed the case?

70. This particular songwriter is best known for his _____ lyrics.

Pole/Poll

71. Evidently a car crashed into and damaged this light _____.

72. A _____ of our students indicated that the majority preferred morning classes instead of afternoon classes.

73. Underground utilities free populated areas from unsightly telephone and electric _____.

74. Have you _____ all the residents on this street to determine whether or not they favor the installation of speed bumps to slow down through traffic?

75. In 2012 were the exit _____ able to forecast the outcome of the presidential election?

Populace/Populous

76. So far we have polled the _____ of three Midwestern communities.

77. Less _____ areas such as Greenview and Bellhaven have been slow in attracting large retail chains to serve their communities.

78. Is New York the most _____ state in the United States?

79. In your opinion, which of these two candidates will have greater appeal to the general _____?

80. The _____ in this region is increasing at the rate of 4.5 percent annually.

Section 7, Words Often Confused and Misused

Pore/Pour

81. Our new cleansing formula removes excess oil buildup from your _____ while keeping your skin soft and moist.

82. We will just have to _____ over this problem until we find a solution.

83. The company cannot continue to _____ money into subsidiaries that fail to show reasonable earnings.

84. As the three-day weekend began, holiday travelers by the thousands _____ out of the city.

85. We spent nearly three hours _____ over past invoices to locate the source of the discrepancy.

Pray/Prey

86. Inexperienced investors often fall _____ to land investment schemes.

87. After each service the minister asks the congregation to _____ in silence for 30 seconds before leaving the church.

88. In public schools teachers may not require children to _____.

89. Each year more and more people are _____ to this dreaded disease.

90. Small struggling companies are often _____ to large powerful conglomerates.

Check your answers with those given on pages 379–380 before completing the next exercise.

Reinforcement Guide 11

Instructions: Select one of the words (or a form of the word) shown below to complete each of the following sentences.

Overdo/Overdue	Peak/Peek	Peruse/Pursue
Pair/Pare/Pear	Peal/Peel	Plaintiff/Plaintive
Partition/Petition	Peer/Pier	Pole/Poll
Passed/Past	Persecute/Prosecute	Populace/Populous
Patience/Patients	Personal/Personnel	Pore/Pour
Peace/Piece	Perspective/Prospective	Pray/Prey

1. A _____ of our employees revealed that almost 30 percent would be willing to work overtime during the inventory period.

2. If he continues to _____ the smaller children in the class, Tom will be suspended from school.

3. To function successfully as a manager, you will need to develop more _____ in dealing with your fellow employees.

4. Do not allow yourself to fall _____ to any of his investment schemes.

5. This applicant's _____ voice and mannerisms are unsuitable for the receptionist position we have open.

6. Do not allow anyone to _____ over your shoulder as you tally the daily receipts.

7. We have been audited by the Internal Revenue Service for the _____ three years.

8. If you continue to _____ over these books in such poor lighting, you will certainly damage your eyesight.

9. You must evaluate all these sudden sales increases in their proper _____.

10. The hourly _____ of our grandfather clocks often turns away potential purchasers.

11. Residents on our street signed a _____ requesting the city council to approve funds for repaving our street.

12. Franchises for Burger Haven are available only in the less _____ cities; the other franchises have already been sold.

13. Most of our _____ are highly trained chemists or engineers.

14. Until we receive this _____ of information, the entire project remains at a standstill.

15. Please _____ at least $3,000 from this budget.

16. Our firm represents the _____ in this case.

17. We cannot afford to _____ resources into a project that has so little promise of a substantial return.

18. During the remodeling of our offices, the _____ between the two conference rooms will be removed.

19. Two _____ clients wish to discuss their investment portfolios with you.

20. The _____ of this city has remained stable between the 2000 census and the 2010 census.

21. You should take an alternate route to the airport during _____ traffic hours.

22. This federal grant will permit him to _____ further his study of spinal cord regeneration.

23. Our company has just _____ through a difficult transition resulting from decreased government defense contracts.

24. Many of the _____ admitted to our hospital are insured by health maintenance organizations (HMOs).

25. Applications for employment are not permitted to solicit _____ information such as age, gender, marital status, religious preference, or ethnicity.

*The answers to this exercise appear in the **Instructor's Manual and Key** for **HOW 13: A Handbook for Office Professionals**, 13ᵗʰ edition.*

Name _____ Date _____

Practice Exercises for Words *Precede/Proceed* Through *Scene/Seen*

Practice Guide 12

Instructions: Select the correct word or a form of the word from each set of word confusions to complete the following sentences. Write your choice in the blank.

Precede/Proceed

1. The committee has decided to _____ in the usual manner with this case.

2. Please note that in a business letter the reference initials should _____ an enclosure notation, if one is necessary.

3. You may wish to _____ the demonstration with a brief overview of the capabilities of this color laser printer.

4. Bill Harris _____ Jill Newcomb as president of our local chamber of commerce.

5. We will be unable to _____ with this project until early spring.

Precedence/Precedents

6. We have agreed to give _____ to all requests from the governor's office.

7. This project takes _____ over all other projects handled by our office.

8. There were no _____ for our firm's venturing into sales and production outside the United States.

9. Last year's fund-raising banquet set a _____ for sponsoring this event annually.

10. In the army a general takes _____ over a captain.

Presence/Presents

11. All these _____ must be wrapped for the holiday party.

12. This subpoena requires your _____ in court on October 23.

13. Everyone in the courtroom was amazed at the calm _____ of the witness as the district attorney continued to fire questions at him.

14. Did you purchase _____ for the administrative assistants in our office?

15. The _____ of the auditors disrupted our office routine for nearly a week.

Principal/Principle

16. Our _____ branch in your city is located on the corner of Fifth Avenue and Main Street.

17. Saving a regular amount from each paycheck serves as a major _____ for many people.

18. If you wish to discuss this situation with the high school _____, please call her office for an appointment.

19. Bringing the issue out into the open was not only a matter of _____ but also a matter of good politics.

20. How much of the _____ remains unpaid after this year's payments?

Propose/Purpose

21. How do you _____ we rectify this deficit?

22. The _____ of this survey is to assess the effectiveness of our Internet advertising.

23. After sitting and listening for more than an hour, I still could not determine the _____ of the meeting.

24. Residents in the area have already begun to oppose the _____ freeway extension.

25. May I _____ that we investigate further the suitability of this site for a new branch before we make an offer on the property.

Quiet/Quite

26. These clients wish to purchase a home in a _____ residential neighborhood.

27. We were _____ disappointed when the contract was awarded to another company.

28. I am _____ sure you recognize the importance of turning in these reports on time.

29. Many executives contend that they are able to get more work done in the _____ of their homes than they are in their busy offices.

30. These charges are so serious that you should be _____ sure they are valid before you proceed.

Raise/Raze/Rise

31. How much did interest rates _____ this week?

32. The city council had approved the petition to _____ this old building until a committee proved it was a historical site.

33. Last week the legislature voted to _____ the state sales tax ½ percent.

34. This stock _____ 16 points before it suffered any decline.

35. The old church was _____, and a new one was built in its place.

Section 7, Words Often Confused and Misused

Rational/Rationale

36. There must certainly be a _____ explanation why Ethan has not responded to our e-mail messages.

37. The _____ for a networked environment in our offices is as compelling as it was when a system was proposed two years ago.

38. Finding a _____ solution to this problem seems nearly impossible since so many people are providing me with conflicting information.

39. In this report the president explains thoroughly the _____ for establishing a company-sponsored child-care center for employees' preschool children.

40. Effective leaders continue to make _____ decisions, even when faced with controversial situations.

Real/Really

41. We are _____ pleased that you will be joining our firm as a financial analyst.

42. All the consultant's suggestions have been _____ helpful in setting up our training center.

43. Working with you on this proposal has been a _____ pleasure for me.

44. Does Carnation use imitation or _____ chocolate chips in its ice cream?

45. If you are _____ concerned about the integrity of this company, perhaps you should take your business to another vendor.

Reality/Realty

46. Have you dealt with this _____ company in the past?

47. The _____ of the situation is that the company's merger with Allied Mutual has left more than a thousand people unemployed.

48. After your _____ agent contacted me, I notified the buyers that you had accepted their offer.

49. From the beginning I doubted the _____ of what he had reportedly seen.

50. The company owns more than $190 million worth of _____ in the Chicago downtown area.

Receipt/Recipe

51. Please note that your canceled check is your _____.

52. Many people claim to have the _____ for See's famous fudge.

53. Is there a book that publishes _____ from famous restaurants throughout the world?

54. Save this _____ for income tax purposes.

55. Be sure to obtain _____ for all your expenses so that you will be reimbursed adequately.

Regime/Regimen/Regiment

56. Ms. Bailey's daily _____ includes a 5-mile walk before breakfast.

57. Within the next three months, your _____ will be deployed to a location out of the country.

58. Powerful _____ ruled by intimidation and terror continue to be a threat to free nations.

59. Professional athletes are expected to maintain a strict exercise _____, during both season and off-season play.

60. By following Alo-Derm's recommended _____, your skin will look younger within just 30 days and continue to retain its elasticity and youthful appearance.

Residence/Residents

61. _____ from the community have signed a petition to halt the airport expansion.

62. If you are interested in selling your _____, please contact me for an appraisal.

63. Please list the address of your current _____ on this form; do not list a post office box address.

64. How many _____ live in this retirement community?

65. As the hurricane approached the coastal region, all _____ were requested to evacuate the area.

Respectably/Respectfully/Respectively

66. If your client does not address the court _____, he will be fined for contempt.

67. John, Lisa, and Karen are our senior employees; they have been with the company eight, seven, and five years, _____.

68. We insist that the nursing staff in our convalescent facility treat the patients _____.

69. Although she was a poor, struggling widow, Mrs. Smith raised her five children _____.

70. This month's first- and second-prize winners were Ann Freeman and Carl Irwin, _____.

Ring/Wring

71. Do not _____ this garment while it is wet.

72. If the doorbell does not _____, just knock on the door.

73. Whenever I hold meetings in my office and the telephone _____, I permit calls to defer to the message center.

74. If you _____ out this bathing suit after swimming, it will lose its shape.

75. With his smooth line and promise of higher returns, this fraudulent broker could _____ money from almost anyone.

Role/Roll

76. Congratulations upon your making the Dean's Honor _____ this semester.

77. Our senator played a major _____ in getting this piece of legislation through Congress.

78. Please have someone _____ down the sunscreens each day by two o'clock to protect diners from the sun's ocean glare.

79. Who played the _____ of Dolly in the senior class's production of *Hello, Dolly*?

80. All instructors should have their _____ sheets for their opening class sessions.

Rote/Wrote

81. Who _____ this report for the Board of Directors?

82. Most children know the alphabet by _____ before entering elementary school.

83. The author of this play _____ the script while serving in the U.S. Navy.

84. Administrative assistants should know by _____ the two-letter postal designations for all states and territories of the United States.

85. How much _____ script learning is required of television actors and personalities?

Rout/Route

86. What _____ should we take from the office to reach your home?

87. The police were summoned when the concert turned into a _____.

88. The flight _____ from Los Angeles to Indianapolis requires a stopover in Chicago—with a possible change of planes.

89. The home football team _____ its opponent by a score of 40 to 7.

90. Most mail _____ in this section of the city permit mail carriers to use electric carts.

Scene/Seen

91. We have not yet _____ any results from this advertising campaign.

92. The opening _____ of the play is in 1929 on Wall Street.

93. If a customer begins to create a _____, politely invite him or her into your office.

94. How many times has the patient _____ Dr. Moyer?

95. I have not yet _____ the final draft of the contract.

Check your answers with those given on pages 380–381 before completing the next exercise.

Reinforcement Guide 12

Instructions: Select one of the words (or a form of the word) shown below to complete each of the following sentences.

Precede/Proceed	Rational/Rationale	Respectably/Respectfully/
Precedence/Precedents	Real/Really	Respectively
Presence/Presents	Reality/Realty	Ring/Wring
Principal/Principle	Receipt/Recipe	Role/Roll
Propose/Purpose	Regime/Regimen/	Rote/Wrote
Quiet/Quite	Regiment	Rout/Route
Raise/Raze/Rise	Residence/Residents	Scene/Seen

1. The bridesmaids—Sue Smith, Beverly Brown, and Mary Moore—require dress sizes 6, 10, and 8, _____.

2. We were _____ disappointed to learn that our company president has accepted a position with another firm.

3. Many people still follow the _____ of never doing business with friends or relatives.

4. The committee has been given the responsibility to develop a _____ for allocating new and replacement equipment funds to the various departments within our organization.

5. What _____ will our company play in the development and construction of the proposed new shopping center?

6. The listing _____ company has served this area for nearly 25 years.

7. When should we _____ this project to the city council?

8. We cannot _____ with this project until we obtain final approval from the federal government.

9. Most of these third-grade children already know the multiplication tables *one* through *ten* by _____.

10. You must show your _____ to exchange or return this merchandise.

11. Our Aerobotics' diet and exercise _____ provides you with a healthful and consistent weight-loss program.

12. Mailing this contract by 5 p.m. today takes _____ over any of our other responsibilities.

13. Unfortunately, the character part for which you have been cast appears only in the opening _____.

14. All the _____ were requested to evacuate the hotel during the emergency.

15. The builder plans to _____ the present house and construct a multimillion-dollar home in its place.

16. The only way you can ensure the _____ of this witness is to issue him a subpoena.

17. Your monthly statement shows your payment breakdown in terms of _____ and interest.

18. Our company has no written policy or _____ regarding a married couple working in the same department.

19. The home team's defeat soon became a _____.

20. Whenever interest rates _____ considerably, the construction industry suffers.

21. Warn purchasers not to _____ out this garment after washing.

22. Before you begin to write a letter, be sure you have clearly in mind its _____.

23. The Chart House restaurant shares its famous blue cheese dressing _____ with those customers who request it.

24. Did you _____ John Corbin as president of the chamber of commerce?

25. Your _____ for this online purchase will be e-mailed to the account you provided when you made your purchase.

*The answers to this exercise appear in the **Instructor's Manual and Key** for **HOW 13: A Handbook for Office Professional**, 13th edition.*

Practice Exercises for Words *Set/Sit* Through ***Than/Then***

Practice Guide 13

Instructions: Select the correct word or a form of the word from each set of word confusions to complete the following sentences. Write your choice in the blank.

Set/Sit

1. Please _____ these boxes on the counter in my office.

2. Do not allow patients to _____ any longer than five minutes in the reception area before recognizing their presence.

3. We _____ in the reception area for nearly two hours before the doctor would see us.

4. Who has been _____ these dirty coffee cups on the sink instead of placing them in the dishwasher?

5. The client has been _____ here for nearly an hour.

Sew/So/Sow

6. How often do you _____ these fields?

7. Our manager was _____ pleased with Alicia's work that he offered her a permanent position.

8. Most of the farms in this area are _____ with wheat.

9. Someone in our Alterations Department will be able to _____ the emblems on these shirts by Friday afternoon.

10. Who supplies the thread for our _____ classes?

Shall/Will

11. The corporation _____ not assume any liabilities over $5,000 not authorized specifically by the Board of Directors.

12. I _____ contact you as soon as the merchandise arrives.

13. If you are interested in viewing this property personally, we _____ be pleased to schedule an appointment.

14. Our agency _____ be responsible for screening prospective employees and furnishing information about their qualifications.

15. I _____ send you this information by the end of the week.

Shear/Sheer

16. This fabric is too _____ for the draperies in the outer office.

17. The purchase of this electric collator was a _____ waste of money.

18. On all these garments, the fabric has been _____ too close to the seams.

19. From the top of the wall, there is a _____ drop of 100 feet to the sidewalk below.

20. Extreme force on the scissor handles can _____ the rivet holding the blades together.

Shone/Shown

21. The sun has not _____ for the past week in this resort area.

22. Have you _____ these plans to our new architect?

23. All these new fashions are scheduled to be _____ next month.

24. The outside lights have _____ continuously for the past week.

25. His headlights _____ only briefly before they flickered out.

Should/Would

26. If the owner is still interested in selling the property, we _____ like to make an offer.

27. I _____ have the information you requested within the next week.

28. When _____ I file these papers with the court?

29. If you _____ like any additional information about our products or services, please call or e-mail me.

30. We _____ still be able to obtain additional shipments of these silk prints.

Soar/Sore

31. Prices of raw materials in our industry have continued to _____.

32. Our new medication relieves pain from _____ and aching muscles.

33. Our hopes _____ when we learned that the contract had not yet been awarded.

34. A _____ skyscraper will replace the building on the corner of Broadway and Seventh Street.

35. You should consult your physician about your _____ leg.

Sole/Soul

36. Our trademark is embossed on the _____ of every shoe we manufacture.

37. The _____ deterrent to our accepting this offer is the short time allowed for fulfilling the contract.

38. This artist puts her _____ into her work.

39. Please do not breathe a word to a _____ about this possible merger.

40. At present my _____ responsibility is to prepare a grant proposal for our agency.

Section 7, Words Often Confused and Misused

Some/Somewhat

41. Although we were _____ disappointed with your performance on the last construction job, we have decided to accept your bid for the current project.

42. We will need to make _____ further modifications in the architect's plans.

43. If you wish _____ legal counsel, please contact our attorney.

44. These wood carvings are _____ more expensive than I had anticipated.

45. A mystery novel loses _____ of its suspense when read a second time.

Some time/Sometime/Sometimes

46. Please call our office _____ next week for an appointment.

47. Our new building should be completed _____ next month.

48. We sent you this information _____ ago.

49. _____ we receive requests for information about our competitor's products.

50. We have been working on this project for _____.

Staid/Stayed

51. During the holiday season, most of the stores in this mall _____ open until 10 p.m.

52. Successful salespeople usually do not have _____ personalities.

53. Have you ever _____ at the Regency Hotel?

54. In the opening scene of the movie, Grant Evans portrays a _____, boring university professor.

55. If you had _____ a while longer, you would have met the new company president.

Stationary/Stationery

56. Our new _____ will be printed on ivory-colored paper.

57. The _____ supplies are stored in the closet next to Ms. Dillon's desk.

58. All the wall units are _____ fixtures in these offices.

59. The hands on this office wall clock have remained _____ since the onset of daylight saving time.

60. Interest rates have remained relatively _____ during the past month.

Statue/Stature/Statute

61. Our store specializes in clothing for men with above-average _____.

62. The architectural design suggested that a _____ be the focal point of the courtyard.

63. _____ in this state prohibit gambling.

64. Nearly every city has at least one _____ of a famous personality.

65. Bill Gates, cofounder of Microsoft and noted philanthropist, is regarded as a man of _____ by millions of Americans.

Straight/Strait

66. If you have a complaint, please take it _____ to the manager.

67. The ship caught fire at the entrance to the _____.

68. To qualify for this job, you must be able to sew a _____ seam.

69. The _____ of Gibraltar connects the Mediterranean Sea and the Atlantic Ocean.

70. The sheet feeder on our new printer does not feed the paper in _____.

Suit/Suite

71. Please reserve a _____ of rooms at the Hotel Grande for the medical convention.

72. Your _____ will be returned from our Alterations Department by Thursday afternoon.

73. Will you be able to deliver this customer's bedroom _____ by November 15?

74. This living room _____ and several others will be placed on sale next weekend.

75. A _____ was filed yesterday by Midtown Linen Supply against our company.

Sure/Surely

76. You can _____ count on our financial support for this charity event.

77. If I may be of any additional assistance, please be _____ to e-mail me.

78. We can _____ use some additional help to meet the deadline date for this project.

79. Our manager _____ must not have understood fully the circumstances; otherwise, he would have refunded the full purchase price to the customer.

80. Are you _____ the alarm was set when you left the office?

Tare/Tear/Tier

81. The _____ of this shipment is 1,380 pounds.

82. During the reception only one _____ of the wedding cake was eaten.

83. You may repair this _____ in the envelope with transparent tape.

84. Please record the _____ on each bill of lading.

85. For the June 14 ball game, the company has reserved a block of seats on the second _____ of the stadium.

Than/Then

86. You have more seniority _____ anyone else in the department.

87. The deadline date for submitting this grant proposal is earlier _____ we had anticipated.

88. Once we receive your expense report and receipts, we can _____ issue your reimbursement check.

89. As soon as escrow closes, you may _____ begin moving your possessions onto the property.

90. Certificates of deposit earn interest at a higher rate _____ money market accounts.

Check your answers with those given on pages 382–383 before completing the next exercise.

Name _____ Date _____

Reinforcement Guide 13

Instructions: Select one of the words (or a form of the word) shown below to complete each of the following sentences.

Set/Sit	Sole/Soul	Straight/Strait
Sew/So/Sow	Some/Somewhat	Suit/Suite
Shall/Will	Some time/Sometime/	Sure/Surely
Shear/Sheer	Sometimes	Tare/Tear/Tier
Shone/Shown	Staid/Stayed	Than/Then
Should/Would	Stationary/Stationery	
Soar/Sore	Statue/Stature/Statute	

1. The state legislature has enacted a _____ regulating the sale of firearms within the state.

2. I believe the owner's assessment of the value of this property is _____ exaggerated.

3. The lighthouse beacon _____ through the heavy New England fog.

4. Please _____ these figurines in the display case.

5. The Panama Canal is a _____ that connects the Atlantic and Pacific Oceans.

6. Our company plans _____ in the future to build a branch office on this site.

7. I _____ appreciate your filling out and returning the enclosed forms as soon as possible.

8. Our factory _____ garments on a contract basis for well-known clothing designers.

9. Our offices will be relocated to a _____ on the third floor.

10. This applicant's personality is too _____ for him to be successful in the position of national sales manager.

11. Real estate prices continue to _____ as we enter a new year.

12. As soon as we receive your completed loan application, we _____ begin processing your loan.

13. The flight delay in Chicago held us up longer _____ we had originally anticipated.

14. Please send your requests for all _____ supplies to me.

15. There was hardly a _____ in the store at what is normally a prime shopping time.

16. In _____ desperation, the company executives decided to recall our Model 50 automatic garage door opener.

17. These _____ cabinets need to be refinished in light oak to match the remainder of the office decor.

18. We were fortunate to obtain a person of Judge Hill's _____ to deliver the graduation address.

19. My _____ concern regarding this loan centers around the applicant's ability to meet the monthly payments based upon the income shown in the application.

20. Is the _____ of the shipment shown on the invoice as well as the bill of lading?

21. This new computer chip will be ready for shipment to computer manufacturers _____ next month.

22. Since the security guard has lost the key, we will need to _____ the lock off this gate.

23. AloRub will soothe your _____ and aching muscles with only a single application.

24. Which artist did the city council commission for the _____ to be placed at the entrance of the municipal court building?

25. Our tailor will complete the alterations on your _____ by the end of next week, Friday, April 3.

*The answers to this exercise appear in the **Instructor's Manual and Key** for **HOW 13: A Handbook for Office Professionals**, 13th edition*

Name _____ Date _____

Practice Exercises for Words *That/Which* Through *Your/You're*

Practice Guide 14

Instructions: Select the correct word or a form of the word from each set of word confusions to complete the following sentences. Write your choice in the blank.

That/Which

1. The textbook _____ you requested is no longer in print.

2. Milton Industries, _____ is located in Albany, is our sole source of supply for these metal bolts.

3. Your July payment, _____ we received yesterday, was $20 less than the amount stipulated in the contract.

4. One of the dining room sets _____ you shipped us arrived in damaged condition.

5. Any garments _____ are left over 30 days at Hillcrest Cleaners are subject to being sold to recover cleaning costs.

Their/There/They're

6. If _____ unable to make any further payments, we must repossess the car.

7. Will you be able to meet me _____ at 2 p.m.?

8. We will provide you with samples of this new wood flooring as soon as _____ available.

9. None of _____ charges for the past three months have been paid.

10. Do you have _____ current address and telephone number?

Theirs/There's

11. _____ still ample opportunity for young men and women to be successful in our industry.

12. If _____ no competitive advantage to upgrading our software immediately, let's wait until we find it necessary to do so.

13. All these clip art images on CDs are _____.

14. As long as _____ a 10 percent profit margin on these glassware items, we will continue to manufacture them.

15. Since these reference books are _____, please treat them carefully.

Them/They

16. Were the individuals who requested this information _____?

17. Either we or _____ will represent the company at this conference.

18. The last two people to leave the room were _____.

19. If I were either one of _____, I would consult an attorney before taking any further action.

20. As soon as _____ arrive, I will begin the meeting.

Threw/Through/Thru

21. My assistant _____ out all these outdated files last week.

22. Only _____ your efforts and hard work were we able to obtain this contract.

23. This sale runs _____ Friday, November 21.

24. Who _____ all these papers on the floor?

25. To drive _____ the city took us nearly two hours.

To/Too/Two

26. This office is entirely _____ cold during the morning hours.

27. We _____ are in the process of assessing the effectiveness of our Internet ads and our presence on Facebook.

28. Your clients did not seem _____ interested in purchasing the property.

29. If you wish _____ bid on the contract, please submit your formal offer by June 30.

30. _____ many of our clients have complained about the poor service in this branch office.

Tortuous/Torturous

31. Grading these lengthy, complicated accounting examinations is always a _____ experience for most of our staff.

32. This _____ mountain road is too treacherous for us to drive during the snow season.

33. Movie watching should be an enjoyable, not a _____, experience.

34. The patient's _____ reasoning prompted the doctor to order a series of psychological examinations.

35. Executives responsible for downsizing their companies have found this process to be a _____ task.

Toward/Towards

36. Every day we move closer _____ our goal as the donations continue to arrive from all parts of the country.

37. About 50 percent of the rooms in our hotel have large patios or windows facing _____ the ocean.

38. Everyone in our unit agreed to contribute $20 _____ Ms. Stone's retirement gift.

39. To reach our office, continue driving north _____ the mountains.

40. We are working _____ achieving an Internet connection for all student workstations in our school.

Us/We

41. The judgment against the building contractor was divided equally among the Johnsons, the Coxes, and _____.

42. If you were _____, would you purchase this hillside property?

43. The paralegals and _____ legal assistants have agreed to rotate this responsibility among ourselves.

44. The manager took the visiting dignitaries and _____ on a tour of the plant.

45. The persons in charge of the project are _____, Don and I.

Vain/Van/Vane/Vein

46. Because she appears to be so _____, other employees have difficulty working with her.

47. The weather _____ on the old cottage blew off during the storm.

48. Our new line of Ford _____ will be on display next week.

49. I tried in _____ for a week to reach him by telephone and e-mail.

50. The customer complained about a large _____ of gristle in his meat.

Vary/Very

51. We were _____ pleased with the results of the survey.

52. If the writer would learn to _____ his sentence structure, his writing style would be more interesting.

53. Each month the sales in this district _____ considerably.

54. A number of us are _____ interested in taking this cruise through the Panama Canal.

55. Our office routine does not _____ much from day to day.

Vice/Vise

56. The handle on this _____ is stuck.

57. Unfortunately, lying is one of this prison inmate's many _____.

58. Gossiping about the _____ of your fellow workers can only lead to dissension.

59. Every time I see Detective Burns, he has a cigar _____ between his teeth.

60. Child abuse is a _____ that must be eradicated among parents in our civilized society.

Waive/Wave

61. Be sure to _____ to the crowds along the parade route.

62. If you sign this form, you will _____ your rights to sue for malpractice.

63. Too many people think they can buy anything just by _____ money in front of other people.

64. The lawyer _____ his privilege to cross-examine the witness.

65. The announcement caused a _____ of enthusiasm among the hospital staff.

Waiver/Waver

66. Please ask the department chair to sign this course _____.

67. If you _____ from this position, you will surely receive criticism from your political supporters.

68. Our choice _____ between Springfield and Peoria for the location of our next branch office.

69. If your client will sign this _____, we will settle this case for $150,000.

70. As the child hit the showcase, the expensive figurine _____ and then toppled and broke on the shelf.

Weather/Whether

71. Please place the daily _____ reports on my desk as soon as you receive them.

72. We have not yet decided _____ or not we will invest in this shopping mall.

73. Have you decided _____ to reinvest these funds or withdraw them?

74. We cannot resume work on the outside of the hotel until the _____ becomes warmer.

75. I do not believe our company will be able to _____ another financial crisis such as the last one.

Section 7, Words Often Confused and Misused

Who/Whom

76. Our manager is a person _____ deals fairly with each employee.

77. I do not know to _____ this letter should be addressed.

78. _____ should I contact for an interview?

79. _____ is in charge of customer relations?

80. The only applicant _____ we have not yet interviewed is Sharon Blake.

Who's/Whose

81. Do you know _____ scheduled to work in my place tomorrow evening?

82. When you learn _____ briefcase was left in the conference room, please notify him or her.

83. Please let me know _____ rent has not yet been paid this month.

84. If you know of anyone _____ interested in renting this apartment, please let the manager know.

85. The person _____ first on the promotion list has an excellent chance of being placed.

Your/You're

86. If _____ interested in applying for this position, please let us know.

87. As soon as we receive _____ verification of employment, we will approve the loan.

88. Please print _____ name legibly under the signature line.

89. Because _____ one of our valued customers, you are invited to attend a special showing of Avant Fashions on Friday, April 3.

90. _____ certainly welcome to visit our showroom anytime to see personally the beauty and luxury of the new Sarona.

Check your answers with those given on pages 383-384 before completing the next exercise.

Name _____ Date _____

Reinforcement Guide 14

Instructions: Select one of the words (or a form of the word) shown below to complete each of the following sentences.

That/Which   Tortuous/Torturous   Waive/Wave
Their/There/They're   Toward/Towards   Waiver/Waver
Theirs/There's   Us/We   Weather/Whether
Them/They   Vain/Van/Vane/Vein   Who/Whom
Threw/Through/Thru   Vary/Very   Who's/Whose
To/Too/Two   Vice/Vise   Your/You're

1. We do not know yet _____ we will be able to obtain the necessary financing to construct the new hospital wing.

2. Although many of our beauty consultants are quite _____, clients still seek their advice and services.

3. If we were _____, we would not have entered into a contract with this particular construction firm.

4. Families of the accident victims waited in _____ silence for news about the condition of their loved ones.

5. Do you know _____ we can employ to update our payroll system?

6. Although the firefighters' work schedules _____ from month to month, they are made available to each employee three months before taking effect.

7. We will be in these temporary offices from December 1 _____ the end of March.

8. You are eligible to receive discount coupons for several major hotel chains _____.

9. Do you know _____ responsible for approving these budget requests?

10. If you wish, you may _____ your rights to a trial by jury.

11. Because the bank is usually _____ crowded at the noon hour, I delay making our deposits until early afternoon.

12. Our closest branch office, _____ is located at 15150 Camelback Road, would be pleased to open an account for you.

13. When _____ ready to refurnish your home, please visit our showroom.

14. The witness did not _____ once during his testimony as he was cross-examined by the defendant's attorney.

15. The manager never consults _____ employees for information or advice on customer preferences.

16. Unless you hear from me to the contrary, we will meet with the other college presidents and _____ administrative staffs on September 1.

17. The orders for those customers _____ merchandise has not yet been shipped are arranged by date in the Orders Pending file.

18. Please have the claimant sign this _____ before you disburse the settlement check.

19. If these adverse _____ conditions continue, the contractors will not be able to complete the office building in time for June occupancy.

20. The patient is complaining that the large _____ in her right leg are causing pain.

21. _____ has been too little time allocated for us to work on this project.

22. Some of the tourists have complained that the course of the river is too _____, and they have had difficulty maneuvering our houseboats.

23. What is the president's attitude _____ increased medical benefits for our employees?

24. When visiting the Florida Everglades, beware of alligators and their _____-like jaws.

25. Dawn Perry is the candidate _____ I believe will be appointed to head the Traffic Enforcement Department.

*The answers to this exercise appear in the **Instructor's Manual and Key** for **HOW 13: A Handbook for Office Professionals**, 13th edition.*

Section 7, Words Often Confused and Misused

Name _____ Date _____

Additional Practice Exercises for *Affect/Effect*

Practice Guide 15, Part A

Instructions: Use a form of *affect* or *effect* to complete the following sentences.

1. What _____ do you believe this unstable stock market will have on the economy?

2. Our recent price increase is too small to _____ our sales substantially.

3. The continual rains will surely _____ adversely the completion of our new housing tract.

4. The new management has been slow in _____ any major policy changes.

5. Yesterday's announcement about our company's new PZAZZ computer had a startling _____ on the price of our stock.

6. The president's decision to reduce staff at our Burbank plant will _____ approximately 200 workers.

7. Pressure groups have been lobbying to _____ legislation that will provide prekindergarten public education to all children.

8. We are still unable to determine the _____ these new tax laws will have on our firm.

9. How can you possibly _____ additional savings when the cost of raw materials continues to rise?

10. Has the laboratory been able to determine whether this new medication has any side _____?

11. Unfortunately, Mr. Dunn's personal problems are beginning to _____ his job performance.

12. Overexposure to sunlight can _____ the quality of your photographs.

13. You can achieve this _____ only by following these step-by-step instructions.

14. This month *The Journal of Psychology* will feature several articles on _____ behavioral changes in emotionally disturbed children.

15. We have yet to determine the full _____ this merger will have on our employees.

Check your answers with those given on page 384 before completing the next exercise.

Instructions: Use a form of *affect* or *effect* to complete the following sentences.

1. Did the research findings reveal that this medication will have an adverse _____ on adults over thirty?

2. Excessive rains this winter will surely _____ the completion date of our new office building.

3. What _____ will the president's speech have on stock prices?

4. The rise in the number of insurance claims in this area will _____ an increase in premium rates.

5. How were your insurance rates _____ by the recent car accident?

6. DVD players continue to have a stimulating _____ on the revival of old movies.

7. Our new supervisor has _____ several changes in the department.

8. Over 30 percent of our employees will be _____ by the impending strike.

9. How can we possibly _____ reductions in our manufacturing costs when material and labor costs continue to rise?

10. The major _____ of this economic proposal may not be felt until 2015.

11. Please determine what _____ replacing our desktop computers with laptops will have on the productivity of our staff.

12. None of our clients have been _____ by the recent strike in the steel industry.

13. Long-term _____ such as these are not easily predicted.

14. Consumer furniture purchases continue to be _____ by new home construction and full employment.

15. Vigorous protests by citizens' groups may _____ federal legislation to prohibit the sale of identification cards by mail.

16. Have you been able to determine what _____, if any, this advertising campaign has had on sales?

17. The number of air-conditioning ducts installed with each system _____ the efficiency of the unit and the costs of operation.

18. Further investments in this company could have a substantial _____ in minimizing our losses for the current fiscal year.

19. Recent federal legislation will _____ several important changes in our accounting procedures.

20. Significant temperature changes in the work environment _____ the efficiency of our personnel.

*The answers to this exercise appear in the **Instructor's Manual and Key** for **HOW 13: A Handbook for Office Professionals**, 13th edition.*

Section 7, Words Often Confused and Misused

Name _____ Date _____

Reinforcement Guide 15

Instructions: Use a form of *affect* or *effect* to complete the following paragraphs. Write your answers in the blank at the right.

We have not yet been able to determine what (1)_____ our new

pricing policy will have on sales. With the present sales volume, we can only

predict that unless our manager, Mr. Jones, can (2)_____ significant

cost reductions, this pricing policy will result in declining profits. If, on the

other hand, the (3)_____ of our present sales campaign increases our

sales volume, then we can expect the new pricing policy to be successful. In

summary, sales volume and costs will (4)_____ directly the new

pricing structure initiated by Mr. Jones.

During the next quarter, we will be able to analyze the overall

(5)_____ of the new policy and how it has (6)_____ our profit

picture. Before Mr. Jones is permitted to (7)_____ any additional

changes, though, the Board of Directors must review carefully how any new

recommendations will (8)_____ our entire operation in light of the

potential problems that may exist with our new pricing policy. Too many

unprecedented policy decisions could (9)_____ adversely the price of

our stock, and we might encounter difficulty in (10)_____ changes to

restore the price to its normal high level.

1. _____

2. _____

3. _____

4. _____

5. _____

6. _____

7. _____

8. _____

9. _____

10. _____

*The answers to this exercise appear in the **Instructor's Manual and Key** for **HOW 13: A Handbook for Office Professionals**, 13th edition.*

Name _____ Date _____

Cumulative Practice Guide 1

Part A

Instructions: Select the correct alternative from the words shown in parentheses. Write your answer in the blank at the right.

1. Did you know that Mr. Sooyun is (a/an) authority on rare coins?   1. _____

2. We are not permitted to (accept/except) second-party checks.   2. _____

3. Will you be able to (adapt/adept/adopt) this recorder to operate on 110-volt electricity?   3. _____

4. I recommend that you follow the (advice/advise) of our tax consultant.   4. _____

5. The strike should not (affect/effect) our sales volume immediately.   5. _____

6. All the homes in this development have (all ready/already) been sold.   6. _____

7. The research team was (all together/altogether) disappointed in the results of the survey.   7. _____

8. No matter how hard he tried, Mr. Abrams was unable to (allude/elude) the persistent sales representative.   8. _____

9. (Almost/Most) everyone in our office has contributed to the social fund.   9. _____

10. Please divide the remaining supplies (among/ between) the three offices on the second floor.   10. _____

11. You may offer this DVD on a free one-week loan basis to (any one/anyone) who requests it.   11. _____

12. May we have your check for $100, (as/like) you promised.   12. _____

13. Can the seller (assure/ensure/insure) that the present tenants will vacate the building by May 1?   13. _____

14. He has been treated very (bad/badly) by some of his colleagues.   14. _____

15. Dividends are paid (biannually/biennially) on this stock— once in March and again in September.   15. _____

16. Ex-Senator Rifkin must vacate his office in the (capital/capitol) by the first of next week.   16. _____

17. Who will be in charge of selecting the (cite/sight/site) for our new warehouse?   17. _____

18. The new painting in the reception area (complements/ compliments) the carpeting, draperies, and furnishings.

18. _____

19. His (continual/continuous) complaining makes him a difficult person with whom to deal.

19. _____

20. Only one person was absent from the (council/ counsel) meeting.

20. _____

21. All the board members were concerned about the apparent (decent/descent/dissent) among the executive officers.

21. _____

22. The speaker continued to (deprecate/depreciate) the young candidate in the eyes of the public.

22. _____

23. Did Ms. McKearin (device/devise) this new method for crating eggs?

23. _____

24. Your contract is (dew/do/due) for review on the 15th.

24. _____

25. Our South Bend factory has been known to (disburse/ disperse) pollutants into the surrounding area.

25. _____

Check your answers with those given on page 385 before completing the following exercise.

Part B
Instructions: Select the correct alternative from the words shown in parentheses. Write your answer in the blank at the right.

1. How many responses was this ad able to (elicit/illicit)?

1. _____

2. Do you know why the Valerios (emigrated/ immigrated) from the United States?

2. _____

3. Several of our investors feel that the collapse of small banks is (eminent/imminent).

3. _____

4. At least ten people have called (every day/everyday) since the ad appeared last Thursday.

4. _____

5. Please ask (every one/everyone) to sign his or her time card each Friday.

5. _____

6. We have asked the district attorney to investigate these charges (farther/further).

6. _____

7. Our express lines will accommodate customers with 12 or (fewer/less) items.

7. _____

8. Did you know that our sales manager was (formally/ formerly) with the Atlas Corporation?

8. _____

9. You did very (good/well) on the last examination.

9. _____

10. The recent publicity has caused people to (hoard/horde) aluminum foil.

10. _____

11. Please send copies of this report to Paul and (I/me/myself).

11. _____

Section 7, Words Often Confused and Misused

12. I did not mean to (imply/infer) that you were not doing your job properly.

12. _____

13. Mrs. Melhorn, our company president, reminds us frequently of her (indigenous/indigent/indignant) beginnings.

13. _____

14. Once we expand our operations to Virginia and Delaware, we will be subject to all laws governing (interstate/intrastate) commerce.

14. _____

15. The company must expand (its/it's) sales force by January 1.

15. _____

16. Please ask Ms. Feldman to (lay/lie) down.

16. _____

17. Unfortunately, Ron is (liable/libel) for the debts incurred by his partner.

17. _____

18. The belt on this wheelchair motor appears to be too (loose/lose).

18. _____

19. Many of our customers find Mr. Brown's (marital/marshal/martial) manner offensive.

19. _____

20. (May be/Maybe) one of our consultants can help you solve this problem.

20. _____

21. There has definitely been a decline in employee (moral/morale) since the new executive group took over the operations.

21. _____

22. Caution our viewers not to (overdo/overdue) this exercise program.

22. _____

23. Three years have (passed/past) since I was transferred to the East Coast.

23. _____

24. I admire your (patience/patients) in dealing with all these production problems.

24. _____

25. This is not the first time the manager has been charged with (persecuting/prosecuting) one of his employees.

25. _____

Check your answers with those given on page 385 before completing the next exercise.

Part C

Instructions: Select the correct alternative from the words shown in parentheses. Write your answer in the blank at the right.

1. On this application you are not required to disclose any (personal/personnel) information.

1. _____

2. Be sure to send copies of this brochure to all (perspective/prospective) clients.

2. _____

3. You must obtain Ms. Goto's approval before you (proceed/precede) any further with this research.

3. _____

4. All accounts marked with a star must be given (precedence/precedents).

4. _____

5. If I felt he were a person of (principal/principle), I would gladly enter into this agreement.

5. _____

6. This office needs peace and (quiet/quite) for a few days.

6. _____

7. Do you expect the price of gold to (raise/rise) within the next few weeks?

7. _____

8. Our personnel manager is (real/really) impressed with the qualifications of these applicants.

8. _____

9. Contact at least three (reality/realty) firms for an appraisal of this property.

9. _____

10. Did you obtain a (receipt/recipe) for your October payment?

10. _____

11. Mr. Webb (respectfully/respectively) requested the governor to review his petition.

11. _____

12. What (route/rout) will the truck take from El Paso to Chicago?

12. _____

13. Please (set/sit) the heavy packages on the counter.

13. _____

14. Whom have you employed to (sew/so/sow) the costumes for our grand opening?

14. _____

15. I have never before seen a customer with such (shear/sheer) gall.

15. _____

16. If we receive your order (some time/sometime/sometimes) this week, we can guarantee delivery in the continental United States before Christmas.

16. _____

17. Only three inside walls on this floor are (stationary/stationery).

17. _____

18. The (statue/stature/statute) of this art object is too great for the museum patio.

18. _____

19. Your travel agent is (sure/surely) pleased with the arrangements he was able to make for you.

19. _____

20. At present we have more orders for this electronic game (than/then) we have inventory in our warehouse.

20. _____

21. Before we can make any recommendations, we must study (their/there/they're) proposal more fully.

21. _____

Section 7, Words Often Confused and Misused

22. Dr. Mendoza takes (to/too/two) personally the problems of her patients.

22. _____

23. Many of us believe the zoning commission will (waiver/waver) once it is confronted with the citizens' demands.

23. _____

24. All employees have been instructed not to disclose (weather/whether) our stock will go public.

24. _____

25. (Your/You're) one of the leading contenders for this position.

25. _____

Check your answers with those given on page 385 before completing the following exercise.

Name _____ Date _____

Cumulative Practice Guide 2

Instructions: In the following letter, select the correct words from the word confusions shown in brackets. Write your answers in the numbered blanks at the right.

Dear Mr. Newsome:

(1)[Your, You're] request to finance your plumbing and hardware supply expansion has been tentatively approved. When we receive your (2)[explicit, implicit] written statement that you will (3)[accede, exceed] to our request to place as additional collateral your newly acquired plant (4)[cite, sight, site], we will be able to initiate the formal paperwork.

Please excuse our delay in answering your request; we were (5)[formally, formerly] under the impression that you were also seeking financing elsewhere to (6)[ensure, insure] sufficient (7)[capital, capitol] for your business. As you know, we are (8)[principal, principle] lenders only and do not provide secondary financing.

The opinions of (9)[every one, everyone] on our loan committee were (10)[all together, altogether] favorable, and the members agreed to approve the loan tentatively. (11)[Their, There, They're] only concern was that the amount requested is in (12)[access, excess] of the present (13)[appraised, apprised] value of your business. Consequently, we are requesting the additional collateral before we (14)[precede, proceed] any (15)[farther, further] with this loan.

Speaking for the entire loan committee, I can (16)[assure, ensure, insure] you that we will (17)[dew, do, due] everything possible to assist you with your financing needs. We (18)[to, too, two] are interested in the growth and development of this community and wish to encourage (19)[perspective, prospective] investors.

Please contact me as soon as possible to arrange a meeting to tie up the (20)[loose, lose] ends. We should not (21)[defer, differ] getting the paperwork under way any longer. Any afternoon next week will be (22)[all right, alright] with me; the sooner we have this meeting, the sooner we will be able to (23)[disburse, disperse] your funds.

1. _____

2. _____

3. _____

4. _____

5. _____

6. _____

7. _____

8. _____

9. _____

10. _____

11. _____

12. _____

13. _____

14. _____

15. _____

16. _____

17. _____

18. _____

19. _____

20. _____

21. _____

22. _____

23. _____

I look forward to hearing from you and appreciate that you (24)[choose, chose] our bank to obtain your (25)[capital, capitol] funding.

24. _____

25. _____

Sincerely yours,

*The answers to this exercise appear in the **Instructor Manual and Key** for **HOW 13: A Handbook for Office Professionals**, 13th edition.*

Name _____ Date _____

Cumulative Practice Guide 3

Instructions: Select the correct words from the word confusions shown in brackets in the following memorandum. Write your answers in the numbered blanks at the right.

TO: Karen Williams, Director of [1][Personal, Personnel]

FROM: Gary Morgan, Executive Vice President

SUBJECT: THE [2][AFFECT, EFFECT] OF RECRUITMENT, SELECTION, AND IN-SERVICE TRAINING ON OVERALL PLANT OPERATIONS

    I wish to [3][complement, compliment] you on the excellent job you did in recruiting and hiring [4][personal, personnel] for our new plant that opened last year. You are to be [5][commanded, commended] for adding such a large number of new employees during such a short time period.

    Our production and sales this year will [6][accede, exceed] last year's by 30 percent. Much of this increase is [7][dew, due, do] to your [8][continual, continuous] efforts to hire and train well-qualified people.

    Last year when we set a [9][precedence, precedent] in the industry by staffing an entire plant with predominantly new employees, I was concerned [10][weather, whether] or not this action would adversely [11][affect, effect] our production. However, my concern was [12][shear, sheer] nonsense. The people you have hired are more qualified, efficient, and dependable [13][than, then] I had expected. I wish to congratulate you [14][formally, formerly] on your progressive personnel practices.

    May I also indicate that I agree in [15][principal, principle] with the extensive in-service training program you have initiated. We have [16][all ready, already] promoted a number of people from within the company, and this policy of internal promotion has certainly helped

1. _____

2. _____

3. _____

4. _____

5. _____

6. _____

7. _____

8. _____

9. _____

10. _____

11. _____

12. _____

13. _____

14. _____

15. _____

16. _____

17. _____

the (17)[moral, morale] of all (18)[who, whom] work here. Although the cost of this in-service program is relatively (19)[expansive, expensive], it appears to be worth the investment. Other members of the executive staff (20)[appraise, apprise] this program in the same manner.

Your contributions and innovative ideas have (21)[allowed, aloud] us to plan for the future with a (22)[confidant, confident] outlook. We will keep you informed of our (23)[coarse, course] of action so that we may continue to rely on your (24)[assistance, assistants] to (25)[assure, ensure, insure] our continued success.

18. _____

19. _____

20. _____

21. _____

22. _____

23. _____

24. _____

25. _____

*The answers to this exercise appear in the **Instructor's Manual and Key** for **HOW 13: A Handbook for Office Professionals**, 13th edition.*

Name _____ Score _____

Testing Your Understanding

Part 1 (2 points each)

Instructions: Read the following sentences carefully for meaning. If a word has been used incorrectly, underline it. Then write the correct word in the blank at the right. If a sentence is correct, write *OK* in the blank.

1. At the present time, I am adverse to accepting any additional responsibilities.

1. _____

2. Our clients' annual income exceeds the minimum requirement for this home by $18,450.

2. _____

3. Upon the advise of our accountant, we have decided not to invest in this property.

3. _____

4. Large increases in materials costs have affected price increases in nearly all our products.

4. _____

5. A large amount of stockholders have protested our proposal to merge with ICA Corporation.

5. _____

6. Although we cannot ensure that these condominiums will be ready for occupancy on October 1, we are promising purchasers this date.

6. _____

7. Our company has born these financial burdens since 2010.

7. _____

8. The state game licensing bureau is located in Room 480 of the California State Capital.

8. _____

9. This manual explains how to sight sources and prepare footnotes for term papers and reports.

9. _____

10. To receive your complementary copy, just fill out and return the enclosed postcard.

10. _____

11. A number of credible investment firms are endorsing our new stock issue.

11. _____

12. You may wish to seek counsel from your attorney before making a decision on this issue.

12. _____

13. Companies that continue to disburse pollutants into the environment will be fined heavily.

13. _____

14. Not everyone is familiar with the works of the imminent English playwright Shakespeare.

14. _____

15. Most of the employees in our organization have immigrated from Mexico and Central America.

15. _____

16. Almost everyday during the past month we have received a complaint about the service in our Denver office.

16. _____

17. What effect has this advertising campaign had on sales?

17. _____

18. The police in this area are attempting to stop the elicit sale of drugs.

18. _____

19. Every one in the company should receive this new information on employee medical and retirement benefits.

19. _____

20. Do you foresee any substantial decent in interest rates within the next three months?

20. _____

21. At yesterday's meeting the board disproved the plan to purchase these desert properties.

21. _____

22. Although many people depreciate the commercialism of Christmas, they still join the millions of holiday shoppers.

22. _____

23. Personalized invitations to special sales tend to elicit a greater response than nonpersonalized ones.

23. _____

24. The stories being sent by these foreign correspondents seem hardly creditable.

24. _____

25. Our new file clerk is continuously misplacing or misfiling important documents.

25. _____

Section 7, Words Often Confused and Misused

26. Buckingham Palace is among London's most famous tourist sites.

26. _____

27. These two textbooks compliment each other; what one touches upon lightly, the other delves into heavily.

27. _____

28. The local newspaper censored one of the city council members for falsifying records regarding his campaign contributors.

28. _____

29. All these Italian chains are made of 18-carat gold.

29. _____

30. How many people have you hired to canvas neighborhoods in the vicinities of our three offices?

30. _____

31. You may obtain this information from any one of my assistants.

31. _____

32. If you wish to invest any additional capitol in this project, please let me know.

32. _____

33. Who beside you in the office has been able to get tickets to the opening game of the World Series?

33. _____

34. I feel badly that we are unable to offer you a position at the present time.

34. _____

35. I have learned to pack only the bare necessities for my business trips.

35. _____

36. Anytime you are interested in learning more about real estate investments, just give me a call at (626) 555-7439.

36. _____

37. Have you appraised anyone in the Madison branch office of the change in your plans?

37. _____

38. Like I stated in my July 16 e-mail, we will continue to honor the 25 percent discount on all our products in the FS-200 series through July 31.

38. _____

39. The rapid assent of interest rates during the past three months has curtailed the home-buying market considerably.

39. _____

40. Between all of us, we should be able to devise a plan to solve this problem.

40. _____

41. Most everyone on our staff has attended at least one of your computer seminars.

41. _____

42. We have not determined all together the projected final cost of this construction project.

42. _____

43. The cause of cancer continues to allude all medical researchers.

43. _____

44. Due to recent escalations in the cost of steel and lumber, we have been forced to increase our prices by 10 percent.

44. _____

45. Fluctuations in oil prices effect consumer automobile purchasing patterns.

45. _____

46. Unless you adopt readily to change, you will have difficulty working for such a progressive, forward-looking company like Amgen.

46. _____

47. We are unable to except these expired coupons.

47. _____

48. You will need a court order to obtain excess to these files.

48. _____

49. You may wish to seek advice from your accountant before selling these properties.

49. _____

50. What kind of affect, if any, will the retail clerks' strike have on our industry?

50. _____

*The answers to this exercise appear in the **Instructor's Manual and Key** for **HOW 13: A Handbook for Office Professionals**, 13th edition.*

Section 7, Words Often Confused and Misused

Name _____ Score _____

Part 2 (2 points each)

Instructions: Read the following sentences carefully for meaning. If a word has been used incorrectly, underline it. Then write the correct word in the blank at the right. If a sentence is correct, write *OK* in the blank.

1. Unless you give implicit instructions to our administrative assistant, the project may not be done as you expected.

   1. _____

2. Most of our extant projects have been financed by Washington Federal Bank.

   2. _____

3. Less people than we had anticipated responded to our newspaper advertisement for this job opening.

   3. _____

4. If you were me, would you accept this position?

   4. _____

5. Trees from which we obtain this kind of lumber are indigent to the Northwest.

   5. _____

6. These books have lain on the shelves for years without anyone even opening them.

   6. _____

7. We are not libel for any damage caused by the trucking company.

   7. _____

8. If you are interested in purchasing additional computers, we maybe able to obtain them for you at discount prices.

   8. _____

9. A local ordnance prohibits gambling within the city limits.

   9. _____

10. If this manager continues to prosecute individual members in his department, they will certainly file a grievance against him.

    10. _____

11. How many hours did our assistants pore over books in the law library before finding these legal precedents?

    11. _____

12. Our principle stockholder has expressed opposition to our acquiring additional properties in this area.

    12. _____

13. Before constructing any type of building on this property, we will need to raise the existing structures.

    13. _____

14. The founder of our company played a major roll in the development of our city.

    14. _____

15. We may sometime in the future be able to use your services.　　15. _____

16. When did the state legislature enact this stature?　　16. _____

17. All customers who purchase our products online will receive　　17. _____
    there receipts by e-mail.

18. Only the department chair may waive this requirement.　　18. _____

19. During the past decade, persons involved in realty sales have　　19. _____
    been forced to whether periods of high interest rates that have
    resulted in market slowdowns.

20. Since you are located further from the airport than I, I will pick　　20. _____
    up the shipment.

21. As long as you continue to flaunt authority and proper work　　21. _____
    ethics, you will have difficulty holding a job.

22. You did good on this examination.　　22. _____

23. A hoard of reporters surrounded the rock star as he stepped　　23. _____
    from his limousine.

24. Did the vice president infer that our manager had been　　24. _____
    replaced because our office has shown a declining sales
    record?

25. During the past two years, the company has reached it's sales　　25. _____
    quotas six of the eight quarters.

26. If the bank will loan us the money, we will be able to enlarge　　26. _____
    our restaurant.

27. Please have the marshal serve this witness with a subpoena.　　27. _____

Section 7, Words Often Confused and Misused

28. We would appreciate your sending us a check to bring your overdo account up-to-date.

28. _____

29. Please refer any perspective clients to me personally.

29. _____

30. A pole of our employees revealed that the majority prefer receiving stock options and benefit programs over salary increases.

30. _____

31. Which of these requests should receive precedence?

31. _____

32. We are real enthusiastic about the possibility of Thornton Industries acquiring our company.

32. _____

33. Rote learning does not come easily to most people.

33. _____

34. Hurricane-like winds sheered the roofs off three houses in this Florida neighborhood.

34. _____

35. Our new stationary has been ordered and should arrive within the next week.

35. _____

36. At the present time, we have more employees in this branch office then we need.

36. _____

37. There are to many students enrolled in this class.

37. _____

38. No matter how intimidating the opposition may be, do not waiver if you feel your position is correct.

38. _____

39. We called a consultant who we had met in Atlanta.

39. _____

40. If your interested in these kinds of investment opportunities, please give me a call.

40. _____

41. This lot is for facility parking only.

41. _____

42. Because this sales territory includes California, Oregon, Washington, Nevada, and Arizona, my job involves considerable intrastate travel.

42. _____

43. Our goal is to establish branch offices in the most populace areas of the state.

43. _____

44. Most of the residence in this convalescent home are in need   44. _____
    of constant care and supervision.

45. Since all our floor models will be placed on sale this weekend,   45. _____
    you may wish to select a bedroom suit at that time.

46. If home prices continue to sore, fewer and fewer people will   46. _____
    be able to purchase single-family dwellings in our city.

47. Our personnel manager could not overlook such a fragrant   47. _____
    violation of company policy.

48. Students from almost every cultural hew attend our college.   48. _____

49. Such an ingenious plan should surely give us a competitive   49. _____
    advantage in marketing our new digital video cameras.

50. Please have someone from our maintenance staff repair this   50. _____
    lose door plate before one of our clients trips and falls.

*The answers to this exercise appear in the **Instructor's Manual and Key** for **HOW 13: A Handbook for Office Professionals**, 13th edition.*

Section 7, Words Often Confused and Misused

Name _____ Date _____

Section 8 Elements of Writing Style

Planning the Message (8-17)

Practice Guide 1

Instructions: Analyze each of the case situations described below. Determine if the purpose of the intended message is to (1) inform, (2) persuade, or (3) convey negative news. After analyzing each case, write inform, persuade, or convey negative news in the blank at the right. Select the one that best describes the strategy to be used to achieve the purpose and anticipated outcome of the written message.

1. You are the chair of the Work Environment Committee in your company, Mutual Insurance Company. You need to call a meeting of the committee to discuss several recent issues that have arisen. What approach would you use to write an e-mail message to other members of the committee?

   1. _____

2. Your supervisor—the marketing manager of Porto Foods, a wholesale food distributor—has asked you to e-mail all the salespeople in the division. You are to remind them that their first-quarter expense account reports are due no later than April 3.

   2. _____

3. As marketing manager of Franny Faye Cosmetics, you receive a letter from a retail customer requesting to purchase your new product, Miracle Acne Recover Mask, directly from your company. You do not sell directly to the public; your products are sold only through major department stores. What strategy would you use to answer this retail customer?

   3. _____

4. You are the administrative assistant to the sales manager of Crafton Toys, a major toy manufacturer. Crafton's busiest months are from August through October, as the company prepares for the holiday season. A close relative is being married in Hawaii on September 20 and expects you to attend the wedding. You would like to take a week's vacation during that time, but employees are discouraged from taking any time off during this busy three-month period. What approach would you use for a message to your supervisor, the sales manager, requesting to take vacation time to attend the wedding?

   4. _____

5. As a customer service representative for Dalton Communication Systems, you are asked to respond to a customer who has returned a Dalton radio he purchased more than 20 years ago. The radio has stopped working, and he wishes to have it repaired. Parts, however, are no longer available for this model. What strategy should you use to write this message?

   5. _____

6. You represent All-Star Catering, a popular catering company in your local area. A prospective customer telephoned to request pricing for several of the menus she saw on your Web site. You will need to fax her the information she requested. How will you assess the purpose of the fax transmittal message that accompanies the pricing information?

6. _____

7. As an editor for Sawyer Publishing Company, you have evaluated a new software program for preparing book indexes. It is far superior to any other such program on the market and could save many hours in the preparation of indexes for the books your company publishes. This new software is expensive, but you believe its savings will more than offset its costs. What approach should you take to write this message?

7. _____

8. You are the assistant manager of a local health club, Invest-in-Yourself. The health club sells six-month and annual memberships. Refunds are made only within the first 30 days, that is, if clients are not satisfied with your facilities and services. Clients have unlimited use of the club's facilities during their membership period. A client purchased a six-month membership and used the facilities regularly for four months; for the past two months she has not used your facilities and wishes a refund for the unused two months. What kind of message would you send to this client?

8. _____

9. As an assistant in the Procurement Department of McDowell Aircraft Company, you ordered 24 laser printer cartridges from an online source. The company shipped the wrong cartridges. You must now write an e-mail message to request information on how to return the wrong cartridges and receive the cartridges you ordered. How would you design this message based on its purpose and anticipated outcome?

9. _____

10. As office manager for Mission Hills Medical Clinic, a group of doctors, you need to ensure that patients' medical histories are updated annually. Instead of having patients complete their health history in the office before their appointment, you mail them forms beforehand with a covering letter that requests them to bring the updated forms to your office at the time of their visit. What approach would you use in the form letter that accompanies the forms?

10. _____

Check your answers with those given on page 386 before completing the following exercise.

Name _____ Date _____

Using Words Effectively (8-1 Through 8-6)

Practice Guide 2

Instructions: Improve the following sentences by substituting a simpler word or a modern word for the underlined word, phrase, or expression. Write your correction in the blank at the right.

1. Do not <u>divulge to</u> anyone that the company plans to expand its operations into Eastern Europe.

1. _____

2. A number of our employees have second jobs to <u>augment</u> their income.

2. _____

3. What can we do to <u>facilitate</u> your transition from our former management software to our new one?

3. _____

4. The <u>abundant number of</u> responses we have received from our clients favor receiving our newsletter by e-mail.

4. _____

5. What steps can be taken to <u>alleviate</u> the patient's constant pain?

5. _____

6. <u>As a result</u> of recent accidents in the plant, we are discontinuing all student tours.

6. _____

7. We have not yet been able to obtain a decision <u>in the matter of</u> this customer's refund request.

7. _____

8. <u>In the event that</u> you need additional assistance, please let me know.

8. _____

9. The college has placed a hold on your records <u>until such time as</u> the outstanding fees have been paid.

9. _____

10. Your check <u>in the amount of</u> $150.21 has been returned by the bank because of insufficient funds.

10. _____

11. Enclosed <u>you will find</u> two copies of the signed contract.

11. _____

12. <u>Would you kindly</u> return this form by May 10 so that your escrow can close on May 25.

12. _____

13. Kym is a <u>stewardess</u> on one of the private jets owned by Allied Electronics.

13. _____

14. Did you report this incident to a <u>policeman</u>?

14. _____

15. Please provide a copy of your banquet menu to the <u>headwaiter</u>.

15. _____

Check your answers with those given on page 386 before completing the following exercise.

Name _____ Date _____

Practice Guide 3

Part A

Instructions: Improve the following sentences by using specific nouns and adjectives. Make up necessary dates, names, and other details. Be sure to provide specifics for what? when? where? Rewrite the sentence in the blank line below the sentence.

1. The next meeting of the Sales Department is scheduled for next week.

   _____

2. Are funds available for me to attend a convention next month?

   _____

3. Please let us know at your earliest convenience when you will have available the estate records.

   _____

4. You will need to complete the enclosed forms and return them to us before your Caribbean cruise.

   _____

5. For your room reservations from July 21 to 23, please let us know the kind of room you need.

   _____

Part B

Instructions: Improve the following sentences by using synonyms to replace colorless adjectives and repeated words. Rewrite the following sentences, and replace any underlined words with a synonym that conveys the same meaning but adds interest and/or variety to the sentence.

6. Tony designed a <u>nice</u> brochure to advertise our new Buena Vista timeshares.

   _____

7. We had a <u>good</u> turnout for the investment seminar held last week at the Montrose Hotel.

   _____

8. Our manager plans to have a <u>big</u> display at the trade show in Chicago next month.

   _____

9. Trends in the furniture business are related directly to trends in the housing <u>business</u>.

   _____

10. Although our firm continually seeks to recruit lawyers, we also have openings in our <u>firm</u> for qualified support personnel.

   _____

Check your answers with those given on page 386 before completing the following exercise.

Name _____ Date _____

Creating Sentences (8-7 Through 8-10)

Practice Guide 4

Part A
Instructions: The following paragraph contains only simple sentences. Rewrite the paragraph to combine some of the simple sentences into compound sentences so that the paragraph will read more smoothly.

We have established a new toy manufacturing business. We are interested in developing a Web site. The Web site should showcase our products. It should invite visitors to purchase directly from our site. Visitors may hesitate to purchase from a small business Web site. All credit card information for online purchases will be protected through a secure site. Can you assist us in developing such a Web site? Should we, on the other hand, consult another service?

_____

_____

_____

_____

_____

_____

Check your answers with those given on page 387 before completing the following exercise.

Part B
Instructions: The following paragraph contains only simple sentences. Rewrite the paragraph to combine some of the simple sentences into either a complex sentence or a compound sentence so that the paragraph will read more smoothly.

Please send me your expense report by April 1. It is due in our district office by April 3. Copies of receipts are not acceptable for reimbursement. Include all the original receipts with your report. The district office will issue your reimbursement check. Sales representatives must submit their expense reports by April 1 to receive payment this month. Missing the deadline date will result in your reimbursement check being issued next month.

_____

_____

_____

_____

_____

_____

Check your answers with those given on page 387 before completing the following exercise.

Part C

Instructions: The following paragraph contains only simple sentences. Rewrite the paragraph to combine some of the simple sentences into either a complex sentence or a compound sentence so that the paragraph will read more smoothly. Use your knowledge of sentence construction to provide any additional words to improve the paragraph.

We have an opening for a tax accountant in our Accounting Department. More than 50 people have applied for the position. None of the applicants are qualified for the position we have available. We have advertised this position in newspapers throughout the area. This source does not seem to target our desired audience. We have also contacted several employment agencies in our area. They, too, have been unable to recommend qualified candidates. We have posted this job opening on several Internet career center sites. None of the postings on the career center sites have produced a qualified applicant. Do you have any suggestions for recruiting qualified candidates? Please let me know.

_____

_____

_____

_____

_____

_____

_____

_____

_____

Check your answers with those given on page 387 before completing the following exercise.

Name _____ Date _____

Varying Your Sentence Beginnings (8-7)

Practice Guide 5

Instructions: To add interest to your writing style, begin your sentences with a variety of grammatical constructions. Alternate using nouns, pronouns, verbs, adjectives, adverbs, prepositions, and conjunctions to begin your sentences. Practice beginning sentences with the various parts of speech by completing the following sentences. Conclude your sentence with the appropriate punctuation mark.

1. Noun as the subject of a sentence

   Students _____

2. Noun as the subject of a sentence

   Andy _____

3. Noun as the subject of a sentence

   Swimming _____

4. Pronoun as the subject of a sentence

   We _____

5. Pronoun as the subject of a sentence

   They _____

6. Indefinite pronoun as the subject of a sentence

   Who _____

7. Infinitive

   To display _____

8. Verb that is used to command or suggest

   Send _____

9. Verb that is used to command or suggest

   Request _____

10. Article that acts as a modifier

    The _____

11. Adjective that describes

    Large _____

12. Adjective that tells *which one*

Kelsey's _____

13. Adjective that tells *how many*

Four _____

14. Adverb that relates to a following verb

Please _____

15. Adverb that relates to a following verb

Carefully _____

16. Adverb that relates to a following verb

Suddenly _____

17. Adverb that provides transition

Nevertheless _____

18. Preposition used to begin an introductory phrase

In _____

19. Preposition used to begin an introductory phrase

Through _____

20. Preposition used to begin an introductory phrase

Within _____

21. Conjunction used to begin an introductory clause

If _____

22. Conjunction used to begin an introductory clause

Whenever _____

23. Conjunction used to begin an introductory clause

Although _____

24. Conjunctions used to correlate ideas

Either (. . . or) _____

25. Conjunctions used to correlate ideas

Not only (. . . but also) _____

*The answers to this exercise appear in the **Instructor's Manual and Key** for **HOW 13: A Handbook for Office Professionals,** 13th edition.*

Varying Your Sentence Beginnings

Using the Active and the Passive Voice (8-8)

Practice Guide 6

Part A
Instructions: Most sentences are written in the active voice because the active voice is more emphatic and interesting than the passive voice. Some ideas, however, are better expressed in the passive voice, especially those that blame or convey negative ideas. Practice changing the following sentences from the active voice to the passive voice to lessen their impact.

1. Jamie shipped the order to the wrong customer.

    _____

2. We hired someone else for the administrative assistant position.

    _____

3. Last night Jack left the back door to the bakery unlocked.

    _____

4. The board decided not to offer the contract to Phillips Construction Company.

    _____

5. Unfortunately, our vice president inadvertently leaked the story to the press.

    _____

6. Professor Jones is deducting 10 points from the score on papers that are turned in late.

    _____

7. Since the bank returned your check because of insufficient funds, we have held up your order.

    _____

8. For the past two months, you have not sent a payment on your account.

    _____

9. The dean has not approved your petition to waive the prerequisite for this class.

    _____

10. Because you are three months behind in your payments, our Credit Department has closed your account.

    _____

*The answers to this exercise appear in the **Instructor's Manual and Key** for **HOW 13: A Handbook for Office Professionals**, 13th edition.*

Part B

Instructions: Because the active voice is more emphatic and interesting, use it to convey positive and important ideas. Practice changing the following sentences from the passive voice to the active voice. Supply any needed information to ensure that the subject is performing the action.

1. Your request to transfer to the Dallas office has been approved.

   _____

2. Your scholarship check for $1,000 was mailed this morning.

   _____

3. The new printers you requested for your department have been ordered.

   _____

4. A corrected copy of your statement has been mailed.

   _____

5. Your name has been placed on the Dean's Honor Roll.

   _____

6. Sales goals have already been reached by three of our representatives.

   _____

7. Your application for a charge account at Savco has been approved.

   _____

8. The landscaping contract was awarded to your company at yesterday's board meeting.

   _____

9. A 3 percent salary increase has been approved for all employees in our unit, effective July 1.

   _____

10. The home-loan application for the Watsons has been approved by our loan committee.

   _____

*The answers to this exercise appear in the **Instructor's Manual and Key** for **HOW 13: A Handbook for Office Professionals**, 13th edition.*

Name _____ Date _____

Emphasizing and Deemphasizing Ideas (8-9)

Practice Guide 7

Part A
Instructions: Assume you are the manager of the Information Technology Department at Flagstaff Cruises, a major cruise line. The president has just authorized your department to purchase 30 workstations with Intel Core i7 processors—top-of-the-line computers. These computers will have an access speed up to 3.8 GHz, 16 GB of memory, and two built-in 750 GB hard drives. The computers are to be installed at stations occupied by administrative professionals who use high-end software to complete their tasks. You have identified individuals throughout the organization who would benefit from using these new computers—and who would welcome a new computer at their workstation. You will need to write an e-mail message conveying the news of this purchase and the availability of these computers. Based on this scenario, practice using the following methods for emphasizing an idea.

1. Place the idea in a simple sentence (company to purchase workstations).

   _____

2. Use the active voice to emphasize an idea (person will receive a new workstation).

   _____

3. Confine the idea to a one-sentence paragraph (company to purchase workstations and person will receive one of them).

   _____

   _____

4. Use direct address to tie in the idea with the reader's name (person will receive a new workstation).

   _____

   _____

5. Place the idea at the beginning or at the end of the paragraph (person will receive a new workstation at beginning of paragraph).

   _____

   _____

   _____

   _____

   _____

*The answers to this exercise appear in the **Instructor's Manual and Key** for **HOW 13: A Handbook for Office Professionals**, 13th Edition.*

Part B

Instructions: Assume you are the supervisor of Plant Facilities at Wilton Manufacturing Company. The company is in the process of resurfacing the employee parking lot. One half of the parking lot will be resurfaced on Saturday, June 7, but will not be available for use until Thursday, June 12. The other half of the parking lot will be resurfaced on Saturday, June 14; it will be available for use on Thursday, June 19. During this process half the employees will need to park their vehicles on the streets surrounding the company's facilities. You are to decide which half of the employees will park on the street from June 9 through June 11 and which half will park on the street from June 16 through June 18. Then, you will need to write a memo conveying the news of this inconvenience. Based on this scenario, practice using the following methods for deemphasizing ideas.

1. Use the passive voice to convey the negative idea of parking on the street.

   _____

   _____

2. Phrase positively what you have done to cut down on the time the employee parking lot will be unusable (resurfacing only one half of the area at a time and beginning work on Saturdays).

   _____

   _____

3. Use the subjunctive mood to explain why employees must park on the street during the repaving process (no additional facilities are available on the company site).

   _____

   _____

4. Camouflage the negative idea in a complex sentence (employees will need to park on the street for only three days).

   _____

   _____

5. Locate the negative idea in the middle of a paragraph (parking on the street during the repaving process).

   _____

   _____

   _____

   _____

*The answers to this exercise appear in the **Instructor's Manual and Key** for **HOW 13: A Handbook for Office Professionals**, 13th edition.*

Emphasizing and Deemphasizing Ideas

Name _____ Date _____

Balancing Ideas Through Parallel Structure (8-9)

Practice Guide 8

Part A
Instructions: Sentences have parallel structure when matching ideas are expressed similarly. Similar ideas in the following sentences are connected by coordinating conjunctions (*and, but, or,* or *nor*). Edit the following sentences for errors in parallel structure; write your correction in the blank line below the sentence. If a sentence is expressed correctly, write *OK* in the blank line.

1. Please complete the application form *and* then you should mail it in the enclosed envelope.

   _____

2. The major responsibility of our receptionist is to greet prospective clients *and* answering the telephone.

   _____

3. Should we update our employee workstations by adding memory to the existing computers *or* purchase new computers?

   _____

   _____

4. After discussing the issue at length, the committee voted to build a new warehouse *but* is rescheduling the opening of a new retail outlet.

   _____

   _____

5. To prepare for the meeting, we are in the process of obtaining a caterer, soliciting items for the agenda, *and* have to print the invitations.

   _____

   _____

6. To continue an employee benefits package, the company will need to initiate an employer/employee contribution plan *or* beginning July 1 reduce the benefits to match the current funding level.

   _____

   _____

*The answers to this exercise appear in the **Instructor's Manual and Key** for **HOW 13: A Handbook for Office Professionals**, 13th edition.*

Part B

Instructions: Sentences have parallel structure when matching ideas are expressed similarly. Similar ideas in the following sentences are connected by correlative conjunctions (*both . . . and, either . . . or, neither . . . nor*, or *not only . . . but also*). Edit the following sentences for errors in parallel structure; write your correction in the blank line below the sentence. If a sentence is expressed correctly, write *OK* in the blank line.

1. *Both* our sales manager *and* our advertising manager resigned last week.

    _____

2. According to the contract, *either* you must select another health-care provider *or* forfeit your opportunity to make a choice.

    _____

    _____

3. The attorney *neither* offered an equitable settlement *nor* an alternative to the original offer.

    _____

4. The Science Lecture Series is *not only* open to students and staff of the college *but also* to residents of the community.

    _____

    _____

5. If you wish *both* to place your Union Bank savings account *and* your A. G. Edwards stock account in the trust, please sign the enclosed forms.

    _____

    _____

6. By December 5 you will need *either* to decide whether you wish to withdraw the funds from your money market account *or* reinvest them.

    _____

    _____

7. The manager allowed *neither* a refund for the purchase *nor* a store credit for the purchase price.

    _____

8. Our supervisor *not only* recommended purchasing new desks *but also* she recommended purchasing new chairs for six workstations in our area.

    _____

    _____

*The answers to this exercise appear in the **Instructor's Manual and Key** for **HOW 13: A Handbook for Office Professionals**, 13th edition.*

Section 9 Spelling, Proofreading, and Editing

Proofreading (9-10 Through 9-12)

Practice Guide 1

Instructions: Proofread the sentences in Column B by checking them against the ones in Column A. Use proofreaders' marks to make the necessary corrections in Column B.

Column A	*Column B*
1. We are in the process of planning fund-raising activities for the college's proposed building program.	1. We are in the process of planning fund raising activities for the colleges proposed build program.
2. Since the exterminators must tent the building, all tenants will be required to vacate their apartments from August 3 through August 5.	2. Since the exterminators must tent the building all tenant will be required to vacate there apartments from August 3 thru August 6.
3. Perhaps we should engage a freelance photographer to obtain professional pictures for the sales brochure of our new Willow Brook Development.	3. Perhaps, we should engage a free lance photographer to obtain professional picture for the sales brochure of our new Willowbrook development.
4. During this three-day Memorial Day sale, you can save up to 50 percent on regular items that have been reduced temporarily only for this sale.	4. During this 3-day Memorial day sale, you can save up to 50% on regular items that have been reduced temporarily for this sale.

5. For job listings visit the Web site of *Monster Healthcare* at http://healthcare.monster.com; this online career center posts résumés and lists job opportunities in a wide range of health-related occupations throughout the United States.

5. For job listings, visit the web sight of *Monster Healthcare* at http://healthcare.monster.com, this on line career center posts résumés and lists job opportunities a wide range of health related occupations throughout the U.S.

6. New keys will be issued for the parking gates to all employee parking lots.

6. New keys will be issued for all parking gate to the employee's parking lots.

7. Before entering the premises, all visitors must stop at the kiosk to obtain a permit from the security guard.

7. Before entering the premises visitors must stop at the kiosk to obtain a permit from the security guard

8. Plan to register early for this conference; after November 2 registration fees will be $195.

8. Plan to register early for this conference, after November 2nd, registration fees for this conference will be $195 .00.

9. You are among our preferred customers, and we are pleased to invite you to this special by-invitation-only sale.

9. You are among our preferred customers and we are pleased to invite you to this by invitation only sale.

10. We cannot accept any out-of-state or third-party checks; therefore, you will need to find another means for making this payment.

10. We can not except out-of-state or third party checks, therefore, you will need to find another means of making payment.

Check your answers with those given on page 388 before completing the following exercise.

Name _____ Date _____

Practice Guide 2

Instructions: Proofread the sentences in Column B by checking them against the ones in Column A. Use proofreaders' marks to make the necessary corrections in Column B.

Column A	Column B
1. If you will fax me your contact information, including your e-mail address, I will let you know the dates of the convention as soon as the executive board determines them.	1. If you will fax me your contact information including your e-mail address I will let you know the date of the convention as soon the executive board determines it.
2. Will you be able to attend the luncheon that has been scheduled for Thursday, September 20, at 12 noon?	2. Will you be able to attend the luncheon which has been scheduled for Thursday, September 20th, at 12 Noon.
3. CliniShare has been able to serve most of our patients' needs for medical equipment, medical supplies, and nursing care.	3. Clini Share have been able to serve most of our patient's needs for medical equipment, medical supplies and nursing care.
4. Ms. Deborah Marton has been appointed manager of the Accounting Department; she will assume this position on July 1.	4. Ms. Deborah Martin has been appointed Manager of the Accounting department: she will assume this position July 1.
5. According to the posted sign, "Vehicles not displaying a valid parking permit will be towed away at owner's expense."	5. According to the sign posted, "Vehicles not displaying a valid parking permit will be towed away at owners' expense".
6. Stocks, corporate bonds, mutual funds, unit trusts, government bonds, tax-free municipal bonds, and precious metals—all these investment opportunities are available through T. R. Noble.	6. Stocks, corporate bonds, mutual funds, unit trusts, government bonds, tax free municipal bonds and precious metals-all of these investment opportunities are available through T.R. Noble.

7. For reservations for the nights of April 19 and 20 at the Park Regency Hotel in Atlanta, your confirmation number is JRK1892.

7. For reservations for the nights April 19 and 20 at the Park Regency hotel in Atlanta your confirmation number is JRk1892.

8. Copies of the agenda, last year's minutes, a list of advisory committee members, a campus map, and a parking permit are enclosed.

8. Copies of the agenda, last years minutes, a list of advisory committee members, a campus map and a parking permit is enclosed.

9. Do you foresee that these changes will affect our ability to market this high-end software to home computer users?

9. Do you foresee that these changes will effect our ability to market this high end software to home-computer users.

10. All these grant proposals must be submitted to the appropriate offices in Washington, DC, by March 31, or they will not be funded.

10. All of these grant proposals must be submitted to the appropriate office in Washington D C by March 31, or they will not be be funded.

Check your answers with those given on page 389 before completing the following exercise.

Proofreading

Name _____ Date _____

Practice Guide 3

Instructions: Edit the following letter for errors in grammar and punctuation. Use proofreaders' marks to show your corrections.

Dear Mr. Elliott:

Let me take this opportunity to thank you for doing business with M.T. Stein & Co. Inc. Your confidence and patronage is truly appreciated.

You are the most important ingredient to our success. We are committed to doing everything we can to give you the best service in the fields of tax free municipal bonds, mutual funds, unit trusts, United States government obligations, corporate bonds, and precious metals.

Often I avoid showing particular products to a client because I assume that they may not be interested. On the other hand, however, they may very well be. In an effort to provide more prompt and comprehensive service to my valued clients like you, Mr. Elliott, I am conducting a survey to obtain a better understanding of your investment needs. Therefore, would you please fill out the enclosed questionnaire and return it in the enclosed envelope.

Your response would be greatly appreciated in my continuing efforts to better serve you.

Sincerely yours,

*The answers to this exercise appear in the **Instructor's Manual and Key** for **HOW 13: A Handbook for Office Professionals**, 13th edition.*

Name _____ Date _____

Practice Guide 4

Instructions: Edit the following letter for errors in grammar and punctuation. Use proofreaders' marks to show your corrections.

Dear Ms. Nye:

I think you will agree that the potential for saving hundreds of dollars a year on your auto insurance is an opportunity you can not afford to miss. That is why I am urging you to take advantage of this excellent offer.

As part of this program you will receive the following

- Real savings

- Convenience

- First rate service and dependability

Saving however, is not the whole story. With Nationwide Insurances superior reputation, you will feel confident that you selected a company with stability and integrity. Nationwide Insurance has been in business since 1926, and is the fourth largest auto insurer in the United states. They are rated A+ (Superior) by A.M. Best, the leading independent analyst of insurance companies.

Call now for your free no obligation rate quote. To find out how much you can save with Nationwide Insurance just call toll-free (800) 555-3465, extension 827. Be assured there are no high pressure sales tactics. You are under no obligation whatsoever but if you like the quote you can arrange to apply for your coverage right away.

Sincerely,

*The answers to this exercise appear in the **Instructor's Manual and Key** for **HOW 13: A Handbook for Office Professionals**, 13th edition.*

Part 3

Section 1   Address Format and Forms of Address

Address Format (10-1 Through 10-11)

Practice Guide 1

Instructions: For each of the following exercises, format the inside address and furnish an appropriate salutation.

Example: Man within a company	**Inside address**
John R. Dillon, Manager, Production Department, Ellis Decor and Designs, 13500 E. Base Line Rd., Columbus, IN 47203-9652	Mr. John R. Dillon, Manager Production Department Ellis Decor and Designs 13500 East Base Line Road Columbus, IN 47203-9652
	Salutation
	Dear Mr. Dillon:

1. Individual woman

    Lisa Williams, 2853 Elliott Ave., Apt. 17, Medford, OR 97501-1258

1. **Inside address**

    Salutation

2. Individual man

    Allen Mercer, 2823 Manzano St. NE, Albuquerque, NM 87110

2. **Inside address**

    Salutation

3. Woman within a company

    Alicia Robertson, Sales Manager, Young America Designs, Inc., 580 Freeman Ave., Suite 300, Kansas City, MO 66101-2204

3. **Inside address**

    Salutation

4. Company

AmerGeneral Insurance Company, Claims
Department, National Trust Bank Building,
Suite 450, 700 Curtis St., Hartford CT
06106-1354

4. **Inside address**

Salutation

5. Company

Atlantic Wrought Iron Works, 800 N.
Lincoln Ave., P.O. Box 447, Pittsburgh, PA
15233-3768

5. **Inside address**

Salutation

6. Individual, gender unknown

Terry Thompson, 1 Nash St. E., Wilson,
NC 27893-2741

6. **Inside address**

Salutation

7. Individual, married woman

Andrea Mathewson, 1230 W. 14 Ave.,
Anchorage, AK 99501-1064

7. **Inside address**

Salutation

Address Format

8. Individual (gender unknown) within a company

Tran Nguyen, Manager, Hawaiian Imports, Inc., 1778 Ala Moana Blvd., Honolulu, HI 96815-4922

8. **Inside address**

Salutation

---

9. Man within a company (foreign address)

Rafael Marqués, Subdirector, Hotel Zoraida Garden, Avenida de Venezuela, 04740, Roquetas de Mar, España (Spain)

9. **Inside address**

Salutation

---

10. Man within a company

Sid Leavitt, Plant Manager, GDC Manufacturing Corp., 8100 Thom Blvd., Las Vegas, NV 89131-3612

10. **Inside address**

Salutation

---

11. Individual woman

Marlene Begosian, 13233 4th Ave. SW, Seattle, WA 98146-1165

11. **Inside address**

Salutation

---

12. Married woman within a company

Carolyn Yeager, Management Consultant,
Brooks, Kline & Stewart, Barnhardt
Financial Center, Suite 200, 400
Columbus Ave., Boston, MA 02116-3868

12. **Inside address**

Salutation

---

13. Individual man

Kenneth Killian, 4751 NW 24 St., Unit
105, Oklahoma City, OK 73127-6213

13. **Inside address**

Salutation

---

14. Woman within a company (foreign
address)

Maureen L. Parry, Managing Director,
Eaton Bankers & Trust Ltd., 55 Hornby
Ave., Whetstone, London N22, England

14. **Inside address**

Salutation

---

15. Department within a company

Department of Human Resources,
Advanced Powder Coating, 1487 S. 110th
E., Salt Lake City, UT 84105-2423

15. **Inside address**

Salutation

---

*The answers to this exercise appear in the **Instructor's Manual and Key** for **HOW 13: A Handbook for Office Professionals**, 13th edition.*

Address Format

Forms of Address (10-9, 10-11 Through 10-14)

Practice Guide 2

Instructions: For each of the following exercises, format the inside address and furnish an appropriate salutation.

Example: Married couple

Michelle and David Allen, 2775 N. 38 St., Boise, ID 83703-4815

Inside address

Mr. and Mrs. David Allen
2775 North 38th Street
Boise, Idaho 83703-4815

Salutation

Dear Mr. and Mrs. Allen:

---

1. Physician

Sharon Thomas, Facey Medical Clinic, 2113 E. Martin Luther King Jr. Blvd., Austin, TX 78702-1357

1. **Inside address**

Salutation

---

2. Lawyer

William Armstrong, Doyle, Menning & Gemmingen, Rochester Towers, Suites 800-850, 1050 Fairfax Ave., Birmingham, AL 35214-5488

2. **Inside address**

Salutation

---

3. Professor (with doctor's degree)

Patricia Atkinson, Department of Business and Economics, Livingston Technical University, 2400 University Ave., Griffin, GA 30223-1000

3. **Inside address**

Salutation

---

4. Service person, lieutenant, United States Navy

   Jack Clemens, USS Dwight D. Eisenhower, CV 69 FPO AE, Norfolk, Virginia 09532-2830

4. **Inside address**

   Salutation

---

5. Dean of a college

   Lonnie S. Beacon, Academic Affairs, Whitmore College, 220 St. John St., Portland, ME 04102

5. **Inside address**

   Salutation

---

6. Two or more men

   John Buenzli and Robert Carroll, Buenzli & Carroll Auto Imports, 6950 Raymond Ave., Charleston, SC 29406-2103

6. **Inside address**

   Salutation

---

7. Two or more women

   Dorothy Colbert and Eleanor Griffith, Inspection Coordinators, Burlington Woolen Mills, 100 Booth St., Burlington, VT 05401-2210

7. **Inside address**

   Salutation

---

8. United States representative for your state (names available on the Internet at www.house.gov).

   Locate name and address on the Internet site.

8. **Inside address**

   Salutation

---

9. President of the United States

   Full name of current president, The President, The White House, 1600 Pennsylvania Ave. NW, Washington, DC 20500

9. **Inside address**

   Salutation

---

10. United States senator for your state (names available on the Internet at www.senate.gov)

    Locate name and address on the Internet site.

10. **Inside address**

    Salutation

---

11. Governor of your state (name available on the Internet at www.nga.org/governors)

    Locate name and address on the Internet site.

11. **Inside address**

    Salutation

---

12. Jewish clergy

    David Cohen, Chabad of Phoenix, 3570 W. Glendale Ave., Phoenix, AZ 85021

12. **Inside address**

    Salutation

---

13. Catholic bishop

   Vernon E. Meehan, St. John Baptist de la
   Salle, 7001 Fair Oaks Ave., Dallas, TX
   75231-6032

13. **Inside address**

   Salutation

---

14. Protestant minister

   Christopher Flanagan, Hillcrest
   Presbyterian Church, 1151 Thornton Rd.,
   Bangor, ME 04401-3866

14. **Inside address**

   Salutation

---

15. Undetermined individual or group

   No name

15. **Inside address**

   Salutation

The answers to this exercise appear in the **Instructor's Manual and Key** for **HOW 13: A Handbook for Office Professionals**, 13th edition.

Name _____ Date _____

Section 2   E-Mail Messages, Business Letters, and Memorandums

E-Mail Messaging (11-1 Through 11-5)

Practice Guide 1

Instructions: A number of Web sites offer free Internet e-mail accounts. These e-mail accounts differ from those offered by Internet service providers in that messages are stored on the host computer of that Web site. In addition, the user need not access the Internet e-mail account through a specific provider; the user may access the Internet e-mail account through any online connection.

For this exercise you will establish a free Internet e-mail account with Google Gmail, Yahoo! Mail, or Windows Live (Microsoft Hotmail). Not only are these accounts free to anyone worldwide who has an Internet connection but also they may be accessed from any computer anywhere that is connected to the Internet. You may, then, communicate with classmates, college friends, relatives, and persons worldwide—from any connected computer.

Gmail, Yahoo! Mail, and Microsoft Hotmail permit the transfer of word processing, spreadsheet, presentation, and database files. For example, documents prepared in Microsoft Word, Microsoft Excel, and PowerPoint may be downloaded (from anywhere) and opened in the program in which they were created. Downloaded files may be transferred to disk or printed for reference.

Photographs and other images may be attached to a message. Images may appear at the bottom of the message but will also be shown as a link to download. Photographs and other images may be downloaded and saved to disk the same as other files.

Free Internet mail permits users to store from 2 GB of messages and attachments to an unlimited number of messages and attachments for each log-in name, depending upon the service. Because messages are stored on computers owned by the respective providers, messages may be retrieved, reread, or deleted from any computer as long as it is connected to the Internet. Of course, messages from any Internet mail provider may be sent to the mailbox of any e-mail address, regardless of the Internet service provider.

Option 1

Use the following procedures to establish your free Gmail account:

1. Access Google at www.google.com.

2. Click the *Gmail* link that appears at the top left side of the Google home page.

3. At the next screen, click *Create an Account* that appears in the upper right corner of the screen.

New to Gmail?   **CREATE AN ACCOUNT**

4. Complete the registration form that appears on the next screen.

5. Keep a record of your screen name, password, security question, and answer to your security question.

Write your screen name here: _____

Write your password here: _____

Write your security question here: _____

Write your answer here: _____

Option 2

Use the following procedures to establish your free Yahoo! Mail account:

1. Access Yahoo! at www.yahoo.com.

2. Click the *Sign Up* link that appears at the top right side of the YAHOO! home page.

3. Fill out the form that appears on the following screen.

4. Keep a record of your screen name, password, security question, and answer to your security question.

Write your screen name here: _____

Write your password here: _____

Write your security question here: _____

Write your answer here: _____

Option 3

Use the following procedures to establish him your free Windows Live (Hotmail) account:

1. Access www.windowslive.com from your Internet browser.

2. At the lower left side of the page, click *Sign Up*.

Don't have a Windows Live ID? **Sign up**

One Windows Live ID gets you into **Hotmail**, **Messenger**, **Xbox LIVE** — and other Microsoft services.

3. At the next screen, complete the registration form.

4. Keep a record of your screen name, password, security question, and answer to your security question.

Write your screen name here: _____

Write your password here: _____

Write your security question here: _____

Write your answer here: _____

Practice Guide 2

Instructions: Access the new Internet e-mail account that you established in Practice Guide 1. Click the icon that permits you to send a new message and brings up the message composition template. Send an e-mail message to your instructor that includes the following:

1. An opening greeting that includes the name of your instructor.

2. An introductory paragraph that contains any information you wish to share with your instructor about yourself.

3. Two or three paragraphs describing your educational goals and/or your career goals.

4. A friendly closing.

5. A signature line (your first and your last name).

*The answers to this exercise appear in the **Instructor's Manual and Key** for **HOW 13: A Handbook for Office Professionals**, 13th edition.*

Formatting Business Letters and Memorandums (11-6 Through 11-27 and 11-37 Through 11-39)

Practice Guide 3

Instructions: Each of the exercise instructions provided below corresponds with a business letter or memorandum exercise in Part 2, Section 2 (pages 47–88), of this workbook. These business letters and memorandums reinforce the principles of punctuation contained in *HOW 13*. Use your word processing program to prepare the documents according to the instructions provided for each Reinforcement Letter, and supply the proper punctuation as you prepare the document. Use correct formats for business letters and memorandums, and balance all business letters vertically. Unless stated otherwise, use the current date.

1. **Comma Placement, Series, Reinforcement Letter 1 (page 50)**

   Memorandum format

   Addressed to John Cole, Manager, Research Department

   Written by Rory Silva, Senior Partner

   Subject: Research Procedures for New Cases

2. **Comma Placement, Parenthetical, Reinforcement Letter 2 (page 52)**

   Memorandum format

   Addressed to David Post, Vice President, Sales

   Written by Anne Kelly, President

   Subject: Opening of New Branch Offices

3. **Comma Placement, Direct Address, Reinforcement Letter 3 (page 54)**

   Modified block format, blocked paragraphs, mixed punctuation

   Delivery notation—express mail

   Addressed to Mrs. June Smith, 3624 West 59th Place, Los Angeles, California 90043-1753

   Written by Valley Department Store, Joyce Arntson, Manager

4. **Comma Placement, Appositives, Reinforcement Letter 4 (page 56)**

   Full block format, open punctuation

   Addressed to Mr. Eric L. Ray, Sales Manager, Fairmont Publishing Company, Inc., 4900 Avenue of the Americas, New York, New York 10026-3020

   Subject: New Title, *Writing Résumés That Get Jobs*

   Written by Donald R. Hirschell, Editor in Chief, Business and Economics

   Copies to be sent to Edward Sharp, Advertising Department, and Lisa Tsutsui, Editorial Department

5. **Comma Placement, Dates and Time Zones, Reinforcement Letter 5 (page 58)**

   Modified block format, blocked paragraphs, mixed punctuation

   Addressed to Mr. Charles Baker, Manager, Holiday Hotels, 700 South Royer Street, Colorado Springs, Colorado 80903-2076

   Written by V. Ann Freeman, President

   Postscript: I hope you will be able to join us in Chicago.

6. **Comma Placement, Addresses, Reinforcement Letter 6 (page 60)**

   Full block format, open punctuation

   Addressed to Reader's Literary Digest, 2300 North Knoxville Street, Peoria, Illinois 61604-4201

   Attention: Subscription Department

   Subject: Christmas Gift Subscriptions

   Written by Joan M. David, MD

7. **Comma Placement, Coordinating Conjunctions, Reinforcement Letter 7 (page 62)**

   Full block format, open punctuation

   Addressed to Mr. Edward Harris, Manager, Eagle Office Supplies, 7884 48th Avenue, NE, Seattle, Washington 98115-3031

   Subject: New Branches Scheduled for Tacoma, Indianapolis, and Tampa

   Written by James T. Brown, Sales Manager

8. **Comma Placement, Independent Adjectives, Reinforcement Letter 8 (page 64)**

   Modified block format, indented paragraphs, mixed punctuation

   Confidential notation

   Addressed to Mr. William Winters, Senior Partner, Winters, Hagle & Braun, 1700 Summit Street, Sioux City, Iowa 51105-1433

   Written by Adela Garcia, Manager, Department of Human Resources

9. **Comma Placement, Introductory Clauses, Reinforcement Letter 9 (page 66)**

   Memorandum format

   Addressed to Henry Small, Vice President, Finance

   Written by Don Togo, Manager, Sales Department

   Subject: Networking of Computer Stations

   Copy to be sent to Jean Meredith, Office Manager

10. **Comma Placement, Introductory Phrases, Reinforcement Letter 10 (page 68)**

Memorandum format

Addressed to Karen Hill, Office Manager

Written by Donna Anderson, Vice President, Operations

Subject: New Procedures for Handling Routine Correspondence

11. **Comma Placement, Nonrestrictive Phrases and Clauses, Reinforcement Letter 11 (page 70)**

Modified block format, blocked paragraphs, mixed punctuation

Addressed to Mr. Howard Little, 2847 Roscomare Avenue, Orlando, Florida 32806-1894

Written by Pioneer Insurance Company, Gary Morrison, General Agent

12. **Comma Placement, Contrasting/Contingent Expressions and Omitted Words, Reinforcement Letter 12 (page 72)**

Full block format, open punctuation

Addressee notation—fax confirmation

Addressed to Ms. Alice Stadthaus, Buyer, Broude's Department Store, 1900 Russell Cave Road, Lexington, Kentucky 40511-3012

Subject: Your Order No. 87392T

Written by Jean Chung, Manager, Sales Department

13. **Comma Placement, Clarity, Reinforcement Letter 13 (page 74)**

Memorandum format

Addressed to John Allen, National Sales Manager

Written by Roberta Alvarez, Southern Regional Sales Manager

Subject: January Sales Conference

14. **Comma Placement, Short Quotations, Reinforcement Letter 14 (page 76)**

Modified block format, blocked paragraphs, mixed punctuation

Delivery notation—certified mail

Addressed to Mr. Conrad B. Ryan, Owner, Ryan's Stationers, Inc., 735 Punahou Street, Honolulu, Hawaii 96826-1430

Written by Janet Horne, Manager, Credit Department

15. **Semicolon Placement, No Conjunction, Reinforcement Letter 15 (page 78)**

Memorandum format

Addressed to Carol Smith, President

Written by George Borg, Vice President, Marketing

Subject: Incentive Commission Plan

16. **Semicolon Placement, With Conjunction, Reinforcement Letter 16 (page 80)**

    Modified block format, indented paragraphs, mixed punctuation

    Delivery notation—certified mail—return receipt requested

    Addressed to Mr. Curtis L. Mason, House of Fabrics, 4556 Detroit Road, Cleveland, Ohio 44102-7343

    Written by Crest Button and Sash, Helen Sellman, Credit Manager

    Copy to the Corrigan Collection Agency

    Postscript: We hope you choose to protect your credit rating!

17. **Semicolon Placement, With Transitional Expressions, Reinforcement Letter 17 (page 82)**

    Memorandum format

    Addressed to Kristin Harris, Regional Sales Manager

    Written by Ross Byrd, National Sales Manager

    Subject: Sales Decline in the Boston Area

    Copy to be sent to Lynn Reed, Sales Supervisor

18. **Semicolon Placement, Series and Enumerations, Reinforcement Letter 18 (page 84)**

    Full block letter, mixed punctuation

    Addressed to Mr. Jason Williams, President, National Association of Plant Managers, Ludlow Manufacturing Company, Inc., 1550 West Liberty Avenue, Pittsburgh, Pennsylvania 15226-3448

    Written by Keri L. Clark, Executive Director

19. **Colon Placement, Formally Enumerated or Listed Items and Explanatory Sentences, Reinforcement Letter 19 (page 86)**

    Modified block format, blocked paragraphs, mixed punctuation

    Date letter January 9, 2014

    Addressed to Mrs. Dianne Farmer, Manager, Mid-Valley Office Equipment Company, 3412 South Mountain Avenue, Tucson, Arizona 85713-3398

    Subject: Your Order 873962 dated January 5, 2014

    Written by Kevin Mulcahy, Sales Manager

20. **Dash Placement—Parenthetical Elements, Appositives, and Summaries, Reinforcement Letter 20 (page 88)**

    Memorandum format

    Addressed to Susan Brady, Vice President, Real Estate and Development

    Written by Cory Armon, Executive Vice President

    Subject: Closing of Branch Offices

    Copies to be sent to Gail Davis, Chris Ellis, and Tony Garcia

*The answers to this exercise appear in the **Instructor's Manual and Key** for **HOW 13: A Handbook for Office Professionals**, 13th edition.*

Name _____ Date _____

Practice Guide 4

Instructions: Each of the exercise instructions provided below corresponds with a business letter or memorandum exercise in Part 2, Section 3 (pages 89–114), of this workbook. These business letters and memorandums reinforce the principles of capitalization contained in *HOW 13*. Use your word processing program to prepare the documents according to the instructions provided for each Reinforcement Letter, and supply the proper capitalization as you prepare the document. Use correct formats for business letters and memorandums, and balance all business letters vertically. Unless stated otherwise, use the current date.

1. **Capitalization, Proper Nouns and Adjectives, Reinforcement Letter 1 (page 92)**

   Modified block format, indented paragraphs, mixed punctuation

   Addressed to Ms. Janice Harris, 6923 Hughes Terrace, Apt. 1B, Detroit, Michigan 48208-5639

   Written by Travelwell Luggage, Leroy S. Speidel, Adjustment Department

2. **Capitalization, Abbreviations and Numbered or Lettered Items, Reinforcement Letter 2 (page 94)**

   Full block format, open punctuation

   Personal notation

   Addressed to Mrs. Denise R. Rice, Vice President, Leland Cole Cosmetics, 10400 Lafayette Street, Denver, Colorado 80233-4351

   Written by Arthur J. Anderson, Travel Agent

   Blind copy to be sent to Ms. Jane Hughes, Norris Travel Agency, New York City branch

3. **Capitalization, Personal and Professional Titles, Reinforcement Letter 3 (page 96)**

   Modified block format, indented paragraphs, mixed punctuation

   Delivery notation—fax confirmation

   Addressed to Mr. Vernon Ross, Chairperson, Committee for the Reelection of Councilman John Rogers, 630 South Figueroa Street, Suite 830, Los Angeles, California 90017-2073

   Written by Doris Chamberlain

4. **Capitalization, Literary or Artistic Works/Academic Subjects, Courses, and Degrees, Reinforcement Letter 4 (page 98)**

   Full block format, open punctuation

   Addressed to Dr. Maxine Carnes, Professor, School of Business and Economics, Jackson State University, 1325 Lynch Street, Jackson, Mississippi 39203-1023

   Written by Anthony T. Beller; signature line is Patricia R. Lowman, Editor in Chief

5. **Capitalization, Organizations, Reinforcement Letter 5 (page 100)**

   Modified block format, blocked paragraphs, mixed punctuation

   Addressed to Mr. Mark Smith, Manager, Accounting Department, Watson Corporation, 10420 Ninth Street, NW, Oklahoma City, Oklahoma 73127-1397

   Subject: Conclusion of Yearly Audit

Written by J. T. Rheingold, Chief Auditor, Gleason, Stone & Hale

Blind copy to be sent to John Jones, Vice President, Ryan Corporation

*The answers to this exercise appear in the **Instructor's Manual and Key** for **HOW 13: A Handbook for Office Professionals**, 13th edition.*

Practice Guide 5

Instructions: Each of the exercise instructions provided below corresponds with a business letter or memorandum exercise in Part 2, Section 4 (pages 115–126), of this workbook. These business letters and memorandums reinforce the principles of number usage contained in *HOW 13*. Use your word processing program to prepare the documents according to the instructions provided for each Reinforcement Letter, and supply the proper number formats as you prepare the document. Use correct formats for business letters and memorandums, and balance all business letters vertically. Unless instructed otherwise, use the current date.

1. **Numbers, General Rules, Reinforcement Letter 1 (page 118)**

   Full block format, mixed punctuation
   Delivery notation—fax confirmation
   Attention: Ms. Sally Fields, Order Desk
   Addressed to Johnson Furniture Manufacturing, Inc., 2400 North Elm Street, Greensboro, North Carolina 27408-3124
   Written by Mayo Department Stores, David Seigel, Manager, Furniture Department

2. **Numbers, Related Numbers, Reinforcement Letter 2 (page 120)**

   Modified block format, indented paragraphs, mixed punctuation
   Addressed to Mr. Robert Bradley, Arrangements Chairman, New Jersey Information Processing Association, 260 Ridgewood Avenue, Newark, New Jersey 07108-9214
   Written by Gloria McKimmey, President

3. **Numbers, Money and Percentages/With Nouns and Abbreviations, Reinforcement Letter 3 (page 122)**

   Full block format, open punctuation

   Addressed to Wards and Company, Plumbing and Heating Supplies, 1105 East Madison Street, Springfield, Illinois 62702-3242

   Attention: Mr. George Black, Manager

   Subject: Damaged Electric Motors

   Written by Gino P. Scopesi, Manager, Adjustment and Claims Department

   Blind copy to be sent to Phil Hernandez, Chicago Branch Office

4. **Numbers, Weights and Measures/Dates and Periods of Time, Reinforcement Letter 4 (page 124)**

   Modified block format, blocked paragraphs, mixed punctuation

   Addressed to Mr. and Mrs. Anthony Reed, 438 Penny Lane, Unit 2, Austin, Texas 78758-6921

   Written by Sunset West, Inc., James Bennett, Vice President, Sales

*The answers to this exercise appear in the **Instructor's Manual and Key** for **HOW 13: A Handbook for Office Professionals**, 13th edition.*

Name _____ Date _____

Section 3   Employment Application Documents
Online Career Centers (13-13)

Practice Guide 1

Instructions: The Internet has a variety of career centers devoted to assisting job applicants and employers. A listing and brief description of the most popular Internet career centers follows. Select a site from this listing from which you will explore job opportunities. You may need to visit more than one site before you find the site you would like to use for this project.

Once you have located a site, select the geographical area where you wish to work and the category that best describes the career for which you are preparing or are qualified. Peruse the jobs posted and note the qualifications listed for the jobs. From the jobs posted, select one that you think you would be qualified for now or when you have completed your education. **Print the detailed job posting, which includes the duties and qualifications.** Handwrite your name in the upper right corner. Staple this worksheet to the front of your printout.

1. *CareerBuilder*. http://www.careerbuilder.com. This Web site posts job openings, posts résumés, and provides career information for job seekers. This Web site strives to be a valuable source to both the employer and the job seeker. No fee; registration required for résumé posting.

2. *Monster*. http://www.monster.com. This popular Web site for job seekers offers a variety of services. The *Monster* network posts job openings, posts résumés, and provides career advice. No fee; registration required for résumé posting.

3. *MonsterCollege*. http://college.monster.com/. *MonsterCollege*, a division of *Monster*, specializes in listings for recent college graduates. It assists recent college graduates and college students to get started in their career. This site provides entry-level job listings, internship listings, job search tips, an opportunity to post a portfolio, and a career contact network. No fee; registration required.

4. *TrueCareers*. http://www.truecareers.com. *TrueCareers* connects educated, diverse job seekers with employers who want well-educated, diverse candidates. This Web site posts job openings and résumés. It also provides career advice. No fee; registration required.

*The answers to this exercise appear in the **Instructor's Manual and Key** for **HOW 13: A Handbook for Office Professionals**, 13th edition.*

Practice Guide 2 (13-12)

Instructions: From the job posting you printed in Practice Guide 1, locate at least 10 keywords in the description of duties and qualifications furnished for each job.

Job Posting Keywords

1. _____

2. _____

3. _____

4. _____

5. _____

6. _____

7. _____

8. _____

9. _____

10. _____

Incorporate the keywords you identified in a series of phrases to prepare a Summary of Qualifications. Use only the number of blanks needed to summarize the keywords into a profile of your qualifications.

1. _____

2. _____

3. _____

4. _____

5. _____

6. _____

7. _____

8. _____

9. _____

10. _____

*The answers to this exercise appear in the **Instructor's Manual and Key** for **HOW 13: A Handbook for Office Professionals**, 13th edition.*

Online Career Centers

Name _____ Date _____

Résumés

Practice Guide 3 (13-1 Through 13-8, 13-14)

Instructions: For this exercise you will prepare a résumé in ASCII format suitable for posting at an online career center or at a company online career site. Use your word processing program to prepare a chronological résumé as described in Sections 13-1 through 13-8 in *HOW 13*. Use the following categories, as appropriate, for your résumé:

1. Main Heading (name, address, telephone number, cell number, fax number [if applicable], and e-mail address)

2. Objective or Career Objective

3. Education, Educational Background, Academic Preparation, or Professional Training

4. Employment, Experience, or Employment Experience

5. Skills and Abilities

6. Activities; Honors and Awards; or Honors, Awards, and Activities

Follow exactly the formatting guidelines in Section 13-14 of *HOW 13* to prepare your résumé. Use *Save As* to save your résumé as an ASCII file by selecting *Plain Text* or *ASCII* from the *Save as type:* drop-down menu box. Print your ASCII-formatted résumé.

Your ASCII-formatted résumé will permit you to copy and paste your résumé or portions of your résumé to résumé templates and résumé builders on the Internet.

*The answers to this exercise appear in the **Instructor's Manual and Key** for **HOW 13: A Handbook for Office Professionals**, 13th edition.*

Practice Guide 4 (13-1 Through 13-8, 13-11)

Instructions: From the ASCII résumé you created in Practice Guide 3, compile a paper résumé that will be scanned. You will need to include a Summary of Qualifications after the main heading, which contains your contact information. Based on the information in your ASCII résumé, use the blanks below to compile at least ten keywords to include in your Summary of Qualifications.

1. _____   6. _____

2. _____   7. _____

3. _____   8. _____

4. _____   9. _____

5. _____   10. _____

Use your word processing program to prepare the scannable résumé. Follow the guidelines in Section 13-11d to format your résumé so that it will easily be read by scanners. Select the résumé type that best highlights your qualifications. Print your scannable résumé.

*The answers to this exercise appear in the **Instructor's Manual and Key** for **HOW 13: A Handbook for Office Professionals**, 13th edition.*

Practice Guide 5 (13-1 Through 13-8, 13-10)

Instructions: Based on the information you included in your ASCII-formatted résumé and your scannable résumé, use your word processing program to create a résumé using conventional formats. Serious job seekers should plan to create three different résumé formats—all for different audiences: a conventional résumé, a scannable résumé, and a résumé suitable for online transmission.

For the résumé that will be mailed but not scanned, the appearance of your résumé creates a first impression, the one a prospective employer has of you. Résumés that are well designed and well written are more likely to be read and generate an interview. Follow these guidelines to prepare your conventional résumé:

1. Use 24-pound high-quality white paper, and ensure that the print quality is minimally that of a laser printer.

2. Strive for 1-inch left, right, top, and bottom margins, but use no less than 0.75 inch for any of these.

3. Select a font that is easy to read and no smaller than 11 points.

4. Use headings for the major categories.

5. Use font attributes to make your résumé more attractive and easily comprehensible.

6. Single-space items within a category, but double-space between categories.

Refer to Section 13-10 of *HOW 13* for a detailed explanation of these guidelines. Review the chronological résumé examples in Section 13-8 as you prepare your own conventional résumé. Print your conventional résumé.

*The answers to this exercise appear in the **Instructor's Manual and Key** for **HOW 13: A Handbook for Office Professionals**, 13th edition.*

Part 4

Name_____ Date _____

Section 1 The Internet and Its Resources

Accessing Web Resources (14-6 Through 14-13)

Practice Guide 1

Instructions: Access the Internet. Follow the specific instructions given for each exercise.

1. Visit *XE The World's Favorite Currency Site* at http://www.xe.com/ to convert the following foreign
    currencies to United States dollars (USD).

    a. 1,084 EUR—Spain, Euro (EUR)   _____

    b. 374 GBP—Britain (United Kingdom), Pound (GBP)   _____

    c. 15,800 MXN—Mexico, Peso (MXN)   _____

    d. 650 AUD—Australia, Dollar (AUD)   _____

    e. 1,300 JPY—Japan, Yen (JPY)   _____

2. The search site *Google* has a built-in calculator. By entering query calculations in the search box,
    you can obtain answers to math problems, measurement conversions, and physical constants. Use
    Google (www.google.com) to obtain answers to the following measurement conversions. Use the
    wording suggested for each query, and write your answers in the blanks provided.

Question	Query and Answer
a. How many miles are in 327 kilometers?	a. 327 kilometers in miles
	_____
b. What is the Fahrenheit equivalent for 310.15 degrees Kelvin?	b. 310.15 degrees Kelvin in Fahrenheit
	_____
c. How many square meters are in 12 square feet?	c. 12 square feet in square meters
	_____
d. How many nautical miles equal 7 miles?	d. 7 miles in nautical miles
	_____
e. How many liters equal 6 gallons?	e. 6 gallons in liters
	_____
f. How many acres are in 7 hectares?	f. 7 hectares in acres
	_____

Information Sources   Accessing Internet Web Sites   325

3. Access the U.S. Senate site at www.senate.gov. This Web page provides a link at the top of the page (Senators) to the page containing the names, addresses, e-mail addresses, and links to the home page of senators currently serving in the U.S. Congress. Use the drop-down list to locate the state.

a. List the names of the two senators from Montana.

_____

_____

b. Visit the home page of one of the senators from Montana. List the senator's name. Describe the contents of the home page, noting briefly any links to other sites.

Senator _____

_____

_____

_____

_____

4. Use a search site to locate the information requested below about United States cities. Indicate in the blanks following these instructions the Web sites from which you obtained the information and the date of access.

Web Site Address   **Access Date**

_____   _____

_____   _____

_____   _____

_____   _____

Information Requested   **Answer**

a. How many United States cities have populations of more than one million?

_____

b. What city in the United States has the fourth largest population?

_____

c. How many United States cities have populations ranging between 500,000 and 999,000?

_____

d. How many United States cities have populations numbering 400,000 or more?

_____

e. Which United States city has the largest land area? Provide the name of the city, the state in which it is located, and the number of square miles it occupies.

_____

f. What is the land area of Atlanta, Georgia? State your answer in square miles.

_____

5. A number of Web sites provide driving directions from a starting point to a destination within the United States. One such popular site is *MapQuest*. Access *MapQuest* at www.mapquest.com and request driving directions from your home or school address to a destination at least 20 miles from your point of departure. Print the directions using the printer-friendly option at *MapQuest*. Staple your printout to this worksheet.

*The answers to these exercises appear in the **Instructor's Manual and Key** for **HOW 13: A Handbook for Office Professionals**, 13th edition.*

Name _____ Date _____

Practice Guide 2

Instructions: Access the Internet. Follow the specific instructions given for each exercise.

1. Access *Merriam-Webster OnLine* at www.m-w.com. Locate the definitions for *millennium*. Briefly summarize the contemporary meanings.

   _____

   _____

   _____

   _____

   Use the Merriam-Webster Dictionary search box to obtain definitions for the following words. Write one definition for each word in the blanks that follow the word.

   synchronize _____

   _____

   redundant _____

   _____

   cumbersome _____

   _____

2. Access *Merriam-Webster OnLine* at www.m-w.com. Note the *Word of the Day*. Provide the date of access, the featured word, and a brief definition of the featured word.

   Date _____

   Word _____

   Definition _____

   _____

   _____

3. Access *Merriam-Webster OnLine* at www.m-w.com. Use the Merriam-Webster Thesaurus search box to obtain three synonyms for the following words. Write the synonyms in the blanks that follow each word.

   coordinate (verb) _____   _____   _____

   redundant (adjective) _____   _____   _____

   concise (adjective) _____   _____   _____

4. Access another online thesaurus, *Thesaurus.com,* at http://thesaurus.com. Search for the noun *job* as it relates to *employment*. List ten words that could be used as substitutes.

   _____   _____   _____   _____   _____

   _____   _____   _____   _____   _____

5. Access *Acronym Finder* at www.acronymfinder.com. Search for the acronym *DARE*; **do not** include periods or spaces in your search. List only the most popular meaning for this acronym.

_____

6. For this exercise you will visit the Web site *Netlingo*, an online dictionary of Internet terms. Access www.netlingo.com and click on the link to use *Dictionary*. Press the letter that begins the first letter of the word you are looking up. Locate the following terms. Write a brief definition in the blanks provided.

a. domain name _____

_____

b. mirror _____

_____

c. spam _____

_____

d. browser _____

_____

e. ISP _____

_____

f. cookies _____

_____

7. For this exercise you will locate the nine-digit zip codes at the United States Postal Service Web site for six addresses within the United States. Access the U.S. Postal Service Web site for locating zip codes at www.usps.com/zip4.

a. 3624 West 59th Place
   Los Angeles, California

   a. _____

b. 900 Bagby Street
   Houston, Texas

   b. _____

c. 78 North Street
   Pittsfield, Massachusetts

   c. _____

d. 9205 South Tacoma Way, Suite 106
   Tacoma, Washington

   d. _____

e. 250 South Fifth Street, Suite 300
   Boise, Idaho

   e. _____

f. 100 North Tryon Street, Suite 3500
   Charlotte, North Carolina

   f. _____

*The answers to these exercises appear in the **Instructor's Manual and Key** for **HOW 13: A Handbook for Office Professionals**, 13th edition.*

Name _____ Date _____

Practice Guide 3

Instructions: Access *USA TODAY* online at www.usatoday.com. Select an article from the links provided. Provide the date of access, the title of the article, and a summary of its contents.

Date _____

Title _____

Summary _____

_____

_____

_____

_____

_____

_____

_____

_____

_____

_____

_____

_____

_____

_____

_____

_____

_____

_____

Practice Guide 4

Project—Planning a Business Trip Through the Internet

Instructions: Assume you are required to plan a business trip from your city to a city assigned by your instructor. Write the name of your destination city in the blank below.

_____

The business trip is scheduled to begin on Tuesday four weeks from the current week; you will depart from your nearest commercial airport in the morning hours. You will return from the destination city on the following Friday in the late afternoon or early evening.

For this business trip, you will use Internet resources to make airline reservations, hotel reservations, and car rental arrangements. You will plot your route from the destination airport to your hotel using the Internet site *MapQuest*. You will also use the Internet to select two or three restaurants to which you could take clients for dinner. Search the Internet for major attractions and events in the city. The day before you are scheduled to leave, check *AccuWeather* for a five-day weather forecast.

1. To receive the best airline rates, you will need to obtain airline fares at least three weeks in advance of your departure date. For the airline reservations, select an airline that provides the most direct route to your destination city. Plan to travel in coach class (economy); look for the most reasonably priced tickets available considering the time of day and the number of stops. Visit at least two sites before making your choice. Submit printouts from at least two of the different sources you visited.

   For the departing flight and the return flight you have selected, write in the tables shown at the end of these instructions (a) the name of the airline and the flight numbers, (b) the flight schedules, (c) the cost of the airline tickets, (d) any meal services (if available), (e) the Internet address from which you obtained your information, and (f) the last date of your Internet site visitation.

2. You will also need to book hotel reservations for your stay in the destination city. Plan to stay in a hotel in the downtown or financial area of the city. Rates will vary according to your destination city, but try to keep your per-night stay below $200. Consult at least two different sites before making your choice; submit printouts from at least two of the different sources you visited. Do not use any of the sources you used for your airline reservations.

   In the tables that follow these instructions, (a) record the name of the hotel you have selected, (b) the address of the hotel, (c) the telephone number of the hotel, (d) the fax number of the hotel (if available), (e) the dates of your stay, (f) the room rate, (g) the Internet address from which you obtained this information, and (h) the last date of your site visitation.

3. While you are in your destination city, you will need a rental car. Please make reservations beforehand—using Internet resources. Visit at least two sites before making a decision, and submit printouts from two sites. Use different sites from those you used to make airline and hotel reservations.

   Determine the car rental agency you will use, and then complete the information in the tables that follow these instructions: (a) the name of the car rental agency, (b) the dates you will be using the car, (c) the class of car you wish to rent, (d) the rate you will pay, (e) the Internet address of the site from which you obtained this information, and (f) the date on which you obtained the information.

4. Visit *MapQuest* at www.mapquest.com to plan your driving route from the destination airport to your hotel. Use the *Printer-Friendly* icon to print the driving directions and accompanying maps. Include this printout with the others for your airline, hotel, and car rental reservations.

5. Search the Internet to locate two restaurants to which you could take clients for dinner. Do not select specialty-food restaurants; keep your choices within the mainstream of typical American cuisine. Look for restaurants in which dinners *average* between $18 and $28 per person. To do so, you will need to locate menus for these restaurants. Print the Internet pages containing information about your restaurant selections, including at least one page showing typical entrées. Submit two printouts from different sources, and do not use any of the sites you used to obtain airline, hotel, and car rental reservations.

6. Search the Internet to locate attractions and events in your destination city. Look especially for events that will occur while you are there. If there are none, locate special attractions in the city. Print any relevant pages. Submit two printouts from different sources; use only sites you have not used previously.

7. The day before you are scheduled to leave on your simulated business trip, access *AccuWeather* at www.accuweather.com to obtain a forecast for the days you will be in your destination city. At the home page, place the city and state in the search box, and click *Go*. At the next Web page, click the link to obtain a five-day forecast. Use the print preview option of your browser to print pages containing only the five-day forecast.

8. Organize your printouts in the order in which they appear in these instructions. Complete the information in the following tables, and place the printouts behind the filled-in tables. Place the completed tables and the printouts in a folder for submission to your instructor.

Name _____ Date _____

Airline Reservations

FROM ORIGINATING AIRPORT TO DESTINATION CITY

From _____ to _____ (Fill in.)

Airline	Flight No.	Departure	Arrival	Meals

Any connecting flights required? Yes _____   No _____   If so, provide the following:

From _____ to _____ (Fill in.)

Airline	Flight No.	Departure	Arrival	Meals

RETURN FROM DESTINATION CITY TO ORIGINATING AIRPORT

From _____ to _____ (Fill in.)

Airline	Flight No.	Departure	Arrival	Meals

Any connecting flights required? Yes _____   No _____   If so, provide the following:

From _____ to _____ (Fill in.)

Airline	Flight No.	Departure	Arrival	Meals

Round-trip Fare	

Internet Site(s) Used	Date Visited

Hotel Reservations

HOTEL INFORMATION

Name	
Complete Address	
Phone	
Fax	
Dates	
Rate	

INTERNET REFERENCE(S)

Internet Site(s) Used	Date Visited

Car Rental Arrangements

CAR RENTAL RESOURCES

Rental Agency	
Rental Dates	
Car Class	
Rate	

INTERNET REFERENCE(S)

Internet Site(s) Used	Date Visited

*The answers to these exercises appear in the **Instructor's Manual and Key** for **HOW 13: A Handbook for Office Professionals**, 13th edition.*

Section 2 Indexing for Filing

Indexing and Alphabetizing (15-1 Through 15-5)

Practice Guide 1

Instructions: In the blanks below each name, write the name of the individuals in indexing order. In the *Alphabetized Listing*, write the numbers appearing before each name as they should appear in alphabetical sequence.

1. Mrs. Jo Lee R. McElvey

   _____ _____ _____ _____ _____

2. John G. Martin, Jr., MD

   _____ _____ _____ _____ _____

3. Wm. J. MacIntyre

   _____ _____ _____ _____ _____

4. Mary Lou Morton-Duben

   _____ _____ _____ _____ _____

5. Marly Louise Mason

   _____ _____ _____ _____ _____

6. John G. Martin, Sr., MD

   _____ _____ _____ _____ _____

7. Mrs. McKimmey

   _____ _____ _____ _____ _____

8. William J. MacIntyre

   _____ _____ _____ _____ _____

9. Mrs. Mary Morton

   _____ _____ _____ _____ _____

10. John G. Martin III, MD

    _____ _____ _____ _____ _____

Alphabetized Listing

___ ___ ___ ___ ___ ___ ___ ___ ___ ___
 1   2   3   4   5   6   7   8   9   10

Practice Guide 2

Instructions: In the blanks below each name, write the name of the organization in indexing order. In the *Alphabetized Listing*, write the numbers appearing before each name as they should appear in alphabetical sequence.

1.   The Fortune Cookie Café

_____   _____   _____   _____

2.   Dr. Forkner's Pet Clinic

_____   _____   _____   _____

3.   Ford & Young's Showcase

_____   _____   _____   _____

4.   F R T Worldwide Delivery

_____   _____   _____   _____

5.   Fast-and-Clean Linen Service

_____   _____   _____   _____

6.   Formann, Drake, Greco & Richards

_____   _____   _____   _____

7.   FBLA

_____   _____   _____   _____

8.   Fort Wayne Auto Leasing, Inc.

_____   _____   _____   _____

9.   D & D Pet Hospital

_____   _____   _____   _____

10.   Francois Fornier's French Cuisine

_____   _____   _____   _____

Alphabetized Listing

___ ___ ___ ___ ___ ___ ___ ___ ___ ___
 1   2   3   4   5   6   7   8   9   10

Practice Guide 3

Instructions: In the blanks below each name, write the name of the organizations in indexing order. In the *Alphabetized Listing*, write the numbers appearing before each name as they should appear in alphabetical sequence.

1. 7th Avenue Deli

    _____ _____ _____ _____ _____

2. A1 Financial Corporation

    _____ _____ _____ _____ _____

3. San Diego Cultural Center

    _____ _____ _____ _____ _____

4. Santiago Export & Import Co.

    _____ _____ _____ _____ _____

5. Sandy Beach Golf & Tennis Club

    _____ _____ _____ _____ _____

6. 7-11 Minimart

    _____ _____ _____ _____ _____

7. The San Marcos Inn

    _____ _____ _____ _____ _____

8. SDSU

    _____ _____ _____ _____ _____

9. Seventh Street Wholesalers, Inc.

    _____ _____ _____ _____ _____

10. Sandy Beech's Nail Boutique

    _____ _____ _____ _____ _____

Alphabetized Listing

___ ___ ___ ___ ___ ___ ___ ___ ___ ___
 1   2   3   4   5   6   7   8   9   10

Practice Guide 4

Instructions: In the blanks below each name, write the name of the government entity in indexing order. In the *Alphabetized Listing*, write the numbers appearing before each name as they should appear in alphabetical sequence.

1. Arizona Department of Justice (state)

   _____ _____ _____ _____ _____

2. Phoenix Police Department (city)

   _____ _____ _____ _____ _____

3. Federal Bureau of Investigation (national)

   _____ _____ _____ _____ _____

4. San Bernardino Board of Supervisors (county)

   _____ _____ _____ _____ _____

5. Department of Justice, Immigration and Naturalization Service (national)

   _____ _____ _____ _____ _____

6. Arizona Department of Highways (state)

   _____ _____ _____ _____ _____

7. Phoenix Department of Sanitation (city)

   _____ _____ _____ _____ _____

8. Glendale Department of Health and Safety (county)

   _____ _____ _____ _____ _____

9. Navy Department (national)

   _____ _____ _____ _____ _____

10. Glendale Commission on Disabilities (county)

   _____ _____ _____ _____ _____

Alphabetized Listing

___ ___ ___ ___ ___ ___ ___ ___ ___ ___
 1   2   3   4   5   6   7   8   9   10

*The answers to these exercises appear in the **Instructor's Manual and Key** for **HOW 13: A Handbook for Office Professionals**, 13th edition.*

Name _____ Date _____

Practice Guide 5

Instructions: In the blanks below each name, write the name of the government entity in indexing order. In the *Alphabetized Listing*, write the numbers appearing before each name as they should appear in alphabetical sequence.

1. Arizona Department of Justice (state)

   _____ _____ _____ _____ _____

2. Phoenix Police Department (city)

   _____ _____ _____ _____ _____

3. Federal Bureau of Investigation (national)

   _____ _____ _____ _____ _____

4. San Bernardino Board of Supervisors (county)

   _____ _____ _____ _____ _____

5. Department of Justice, Immigration and Naturalization Service (national)

   _____ _____ _____ _____ _____

6. Arizona Department of Highways (state)

   _____ _____ _____ _____ _____

7. Phoenix Department of Sanitation (city)

   _____ _____ _____ _____ _____

8. Glendale Department of Health and Safety (county)

   _____ _____ _____ _____ _____

9. Navy Department (national)

   _____ _____ _____ _____ _____

10. Glendale Commission on Disabilities (county)

    _____ _____ _____ _____ _____

Alphabetized Listing

___ ___ ___ ___ ___ ___ ___ ___ ___ ___
 1   2   3   4   5   6   7   8   9   10

*The answers to these exercises appear in the **Instructor's Manual and Key** for **HOW 12: A Handbook for Office Professionals**, 12th edition.*

Answer Keys

Key to Familiarization Exercise for *HOW* (pages 3–10)

	Answer	Section
1.	b	2-32
2.	b	1-37
3.	c	6-12
4.	c	10-12
5.	c	14-3
6.	c	12-20
7.	a	8-10b
8.	d	pages 218–219
9.	c or d	12-9 *or* 11-19b
10.	d	9-10, 9-11, 9-12
11.	b	2-33, 2-41e
12.	c, d	3-15e
13.	b	4-2
14.	b, c, d	4-1d, 5-4a, b
15.	a, c, d	1-16b
16.	b, d	1-21
17.	a, c, d	3-16
18.	e	3-6
19.	c	2-15a, d *or* 2-47, 2-54
20.	b	2-2
21.	b	10-2b *or* 11-17c
22.	b, c	1-4b
23.	c, d	page 221

24. a   6-12 *or* inside back cover

25. c, d   1-14f

26. c, d   11-1

27. d   4-8

28. d   11-13

29. b, c   5-5g, h

30. b, d   3-5a, c, d

31. b   page 258–259

32. b, c   3-4

33. d   2-5a

34. b, c   5-2a, b, f, h

35. b, d   11-16

36. b, c   15-3a

37. b   11-30b

38. a   14-2d

39. d   10-12

40. a, d, e   11-14b, c

41. a, e   1-8c

42. a, d   3-13, 3-14

43. d   11-27a, 11-39e

44. c   4-3

45. a, c   9-7a

46. d   3-6b

47. a, d   4-1

48. d   2-19

49. b, d   1-5a, c, d, h *or*
            2-55a, c, d, e

50. b, c   page 252

342

Key to Practice Exercises

Section 1 Grammar and Usage

Grammar Overview (1-1)

Practice Guide 1 (page 13)

1. Noun	10. Noun	19. Verb
2. Verb	11. Pronoun	20. Preposition
3. Pronoun	12. Conjunction	21. Adverb
4. Conjunction	13. Adverb	22. Adjective
5. Adjective	14. Preposition	23. Pronoun
6. Interjection	15. Adjective	24. Adjective
7. Adverb	16. Interjection	25. Noun
8. Preposition	17. Conjunction	
9. Verb	18. Noun	

Practice Guide 2 (page 14)

1. The <u>committee</u> <u>has met</u> several times this week.
2. <u>Hamburgers and french fries</u> <u>are served</u> daily from 6 a.m. until 12 midnight in this McDonald's location.
3. The yellow <u>copy paper</u> in the supply room <u>has been placed</u> on the wrong shelf.
4. The new <u>laptop</u> for our department from Toshiba <u>was damaged</u> during transit.
5. Either the <u>office manager or her</u> <u>assistant</u> <u>should have</u> this information on her computer.
6. Our <u>son-in-law</u> <u>will take</u> an active part in the business.
7. How many gallons of water <u>should</u> <u>I</u> <u>place</u> in the tank?
8. The <u>carload</u> of fresh oranges <u>will be delivered</u> tomorrow morning.
9. <u>Brad and Melissa</u> <u>have moved</u> their offices to the new building.
10. Please <u>answer</u> these e-mail inquiries this afternoon. (Subject <u>you</u> understood.)
11. Our <u>agency</u> <u>is</u> proud of its reputation for excellent service and dependability.
12. Three <u>members</u> of the Board of Directors <u>agreed</u> to support our proposal.
13. <u>E-mail</u> me the meeting agenda as soon as possible. (Subject <u>you</u> understood.)
14. This <u>information</u> <u>should be kept</u> confidential between you and me.
15. Our new <u>clothing line</u> <u>was designed</u> by one of Mr. Simonian's students.
16. The <u>agent</u> <u>sent</u> separate contracts to Mark and me.
17. How <u>did</u> <u>you</u> <u>respond</u> to his question?
18. Please <u>audit</u> these accounts before March 1. (Subject <u>you</u> understood.)
19. In my estimation, <u>Ms. Garcia</u> <u>is</u> the best-qualified person for the position.
20. <u>You</u> certainly <u>have made</u> great progress during the past month.
21. Your <u>understanding</u> of our new medical plan benefits <u>is</u> different from mine.
22. The <u>architect and</u> the <u>builder</u> <u>did (not) fulfill</u> their contracts.
23. <u>Were</u> <u>you</u> <u>angry</u> with John for not approving your budget request?
24. During the past year, our <u>sales and profits</u> <u>have declined</u> steadily.
25. Our new breakfast and lunch <u>menus</u> <u>have attracted</u> more dining customers.

Noun Plurals

Practice Guide 3 (page 15)

1. policies
2. churches
3. radios
4. lives
5. Montgomerys
6. tomatoes
7. curricula
8. statistics
9. mumps
10. brigadier generals
11. yeses and noes
12. cupfuls
13. bookshelves
14. brothers-in-law
15. bases
16. pants
17. 9s
18. roofs
19. attorneys
20. waltzes
21. altos
22. cargoes
23. thises and thats
24. monkeys
25. analyses

Practice Guide 4 (page 16)

1. alumni
2. per diems
3. counties
4. boxes
5. Koltzes
6. A's
7. parentheses
8. lessees
9. father figures
10. fathers-in-law
11. valleys
12. RNs
13. Mses. Ross *or* Ms. Rosses
14. data
15. Mickey Mouses
16. goings-over
17. t's
18. jockeys
19. Japanese
20. Messrs. Ramirez *or* Mr. Ramirezes
21. embargoes
22. yourselves
23. chassis
24. halves
25. Germans

Practice Guide 5 (page 17)

1. Valleys
2. cargoes
3. halves
4. mice
5. bills of lading
6. OK
7. 7s
8. crises
9. IOUs
10. parentheses
11. freshmen
12. W-4s
13. companies
14. IDs
15. OK
16. mosquitoes
17. zeros
18. themselves
19. alumni
20. economics

The answers to Practice Guide 6 appear in the *Instructor's Manual and Key for HOW 13: A Handbook for Office Professionals*, 13th edition.

Noun Possessives

Practice Guide 7 (page 19)

1. son-in-law's
2. children's
3. Everyone else's
4. week's
5. personnel managers'
6. Rosses and Lópezes'
7. girls'
8. Mr. Beaty's
9. Dora's and Phil's
10. company's
11. ladies'
12. months'
13. Mary's
14. Mrs. Jones's
15. chief of police's
16. Alumni's
17. ITT's
18. expiration date of the lease
19. men's, boys'
20. Martha and Don's

Practice Guide 8 (page 20)

1. women's
2. The CD/RW drive of this computer needs
3. Jesse and Sue's
4. company's
5. OK
6. stone's
7. Bob's
8. students'
9. brother-in-law's
10. Ms. Walsh's
11. Adam's and Barbara's
12. moment's
13. attorney's
14. Mr. Stevens'
15. company's, company's
16. OK
17. editor in chief's
18. week's
19. managers
20. truck engines

The answers to Practice Guide 9 appear in the *Instructor's Manual and Key for HOW 13: A Handbook for Office Professionals*, 13th edition.

Verbs

Practice Guide 10 (pages 23–24)

1. client *paid*
2. Joleen *called* all
3. we *will ship* your
4. also *teaches*
5. after *we had* already
6. OK
7. Region *have* increased
8. has *lain* idle
9. are *using*
10. OK
11. have *grown*
12. will *choose*
13. sale *began* on
14. have *laid* the
15. decorator *hung*
16. credit union *lends*
17. to *lose* any more
18. have *spoken*
19. *lying* around
20. anyone *verified*

Practice Guide 11 (pages 25–26)

1. Pork and beans *is*
2. supply . . . *is* rapidly
3. OK
4. staff and president *are* planning
5. Someone . . . *needs* to
6. check *or* credit card number *is* all you need
7. Most of the salespersons . . . *have* been
8. OK
9. There *are* at least four . . . .
10. OK
11. The number . . . *is*
12. If I *were* you
13. Nearly 60 percent . . . *need*
14. The secretary-treasurer . . . *approves*
15. Everything . . . *needs*
16. OK
17. Each . . . *has* been
18. detailed description . . . *is* included
19. Neither . . . *has* submitted
20. An unusually large number . . . *have* requested

Practice Guide 12 (pages 27–28)

1. Have you <u>written</u> e-mail messages congratulating the two new agents on their sales for the first quarter?
2. The *tract* of these new homes <u>was</u> laid out to attract buyers with growing families.
3. Our client has already <u>spoken</u> to an agent in your firm.
4. The patient asked if he could <u>lie</u> down on the cot.
5. <u>Have</u> the criteria been ranked in the order of their importance?
6. There <u>are</u> several *alternatives* you may wish to consider.
7. *Neither* of them <u>wishes</u> to postpone his vacation until August.
8. OK
9. Dr. Sanders is one of those *doctors* who <u>know</u> a great deal about law.

345

10. Our *stock* of felt-tip pens <u>has</u> disappeared from the supply cabinet.
11. He had <u>forgotten</u> about his doctor's appointment until his assistant reminded him.
12. Until yesterday the sign-in book had <u>lain</u> on top of the reception area counter.
13. All the *water* in the coolers on the second and third floors <u>has</u> been drunk.
14. OK
15. Neither you nor the other accountant <u>has</u> been absent once this year.
16. *Each* sofa, chair, and table in the reception area of our hotel <u>needs</u> to be replaced.
17. The staff <u>were</u> arguing loudly about who was responsible for the $110,000 error in overpayment of commissions. (*or* The staff members <u>were</u> . . . .)
18. *One* of the mothers <u>has</u> agreed to bring donuts for the class to celebrate the third-grade students' high scores on the English proficiency examination.
19. All our bills for this month have already been <u>paid</u>.
20. OK
21. <u>Has</u> the Board of Directors approved this purchase?
22. There <u>are</u> still a number of options we need to explore before we can institute a new loan-tracking system.
23. Andrew has <u>driven</u> nearly 15,000 miles during the past three months calling on all the doctors in his territory.
24. OK
25. The stock market has <u>sunk</u> 107 points within the past two days.
26. I e-mailed you this information after the 2013 financial information <u>had been</u> compiled.
27. Bob <u>has worked</u> in our Research Department since 2005.
28. <u>Has</u> the committee submitted <u>its</u> report?
29. None of the antiques <u>were</u> damaged during the earthquake.
30. OK

The answers to Practice Guide 13 appear in the *Instructor's Manual and Key for HOW 13: A Handbook for Office Professionals*, 13th edition.

Pronouns

Practice Guide 14 (pages 31–32)

Part 1

1. We
2. me
3. he
4. I
5. she
6. us
7. he
8. me
9. her
10. I

Part 2

1. Between you and *me*, ...
2. . . . was *she*?
3. . . . to be *she* . . . .
4. . . . have been *he*.
5. . . . Paul and *me*.
6. . . . Teri and *me* . . . .
7. OK
8. . . . Bob, Arlene, and *I* . . . .
9. If you were *I*, . . . ?
10. OK

Part 3

1. who	6. who	11. Whoever
2. whom	7. Whom	12. who
3. who	8. whoever	13. whom
4. who	9. who	14. whom
5. Whoever	10. whom	15. who

Practice Guide 15 (pages 33–34)

1. she	8. me	15. who
2. us	9. its	16. us
3. OK	10. OK	17. their
4. she	11. I	18. whom
5. whoever	12. us	19. I
6. person who	13. him	20. company that
7. I	14. Ms. Lloyd herself	

Practice Guide 16 (pages 35–36)

1. *their*	8. of *its*	15. praising *their*
2. submit *his or her*	9. guarantee *its*	16. guaranteed *its*
3. OK	10. introduce *its*	17. return *his or her*
4. clear *his or her*	11. solve *their*	18. completed *his or her*
5. *their* free time	12. OK	19. provide *them*
6. to *her.*	13. at *their* high	20. read *her*
7. refer *him or her*	14. list *it*	

The answers to Practice Guide 17 appear in the ***Instructor's Manual and Key for HOW 13: A Handbook for Office Professionals***, 13th edition.

Adjectives

Practice Guide 18 (pages 39–40)

1. *a one-bedroom*	8. felt *worse*	15. *12-foot* fence
2. *a lighter* oak finish	9. feel *bad*	16. *an* eight-unit
3. any *other* programmer	10. anyone *else*	17. *most* popular
4. *most nearly full*	11. *a* historical	18. create *unique*
5. feel *well*	12. The *promptest* response	19. *more noticeable* every day
6. *an* hour	13. *a better* way	20. any *other* unit
7. OK	14. *out-of-state* cars	

Adverbs

Practice Guide 19 (pages 41–42)

1. less *carefully*	8. OK	15. working *well*
2. netted *nearly*	9. delivered *regularly*	16. *most* widely
3. OK	10. do *well*	17. *really* disappointed
4. looked *good*	11. more *slowly*	18. *any* information
5. company *the longest*	12. have *barely* scratched	19. run *more smoothly*
6. with *anybody*	13. We *can* hardly	20. to *evaluate carefully*
7. to *receive shortly*	14. feel *bad*	

347

Prepositions

Practice Guide 20 (pages 43–44)

1. *Among* the three
2. OK
3. different *from*
4. discrepancy *between*
5. identical *with*
6. plan *to expand* its
7. retroactive *to*
8. *All the* computers
9. *opposite* Westlake
10. *inside* the main
11. *off* this counter
12. hardly *help* hearing
13. OK
14. convenient *for you*
15. *Both* these recommendations
16. compliance *with*
17. angry *with*
18. *Among* themselves
19. OK
20. buy *from* Midtown Office Supply

Conjunctions

Practice Guide 21 (pages 45–46)

1. by *either* fax or e-mail.
2. but *becoming* one
3. OK
4. company *not only* manufactures
5. Neither Dana *nor* Shannon
6. and *a signed lease.*
7. look *as if*
8. and *preparing the agenda*
9. become *as* popular
10. and *returning it*
11. *assistance to not only* physically
12. OK
13. he scored well on *not only* the written
14. turn out *as we* had hoped
15. patience *nor the understanding* to work
16. by *either Parcel* Post or
17. affairs, you may
18. and *assisting* visitors
19. week in *April* because
20. just *as* the diagram illustrates

Section 2 Punctuation

Practice Sentences 1 (page 49)

1. Many doctors, dentists, and lawyers . . .
2. . . . word processing, spreadsheet, and presentation software.
3. . . . Arizona, Nevada, Utah, and Idaho.
4. . . . answer the telephone, greet callers, and respond to customer e-mail inquiries.
5. Trees, shrubs, and ground cover . . . .
6. Call Jeremy Andrews, offer him the job, and ask . . . .
7. . . . changed all the locks, barred the outside windows, and installed . . . .
8. . . . obtained a permit, purchased the building materials, and hired . . . .
9. Proofread the report, make three copies, and mail . . . .
10. . . . the office supply store, the post office, and the grocery store . . . .

Practice Paragraph 1 (page 49)

We must e-mail Mr. Jones regarding our projected sales, current expenses, and profit picture. Ask him to let us know how our high inventory, low sales volume, and declining profits during the last quarter will affect our status for the entire year. Write the e-mail, proofread it, and send it.

The answers to Reinforcement Letter 1 appear in the ***Instructor's Manual and Key for HOW 13: A Handbook for Office Professionals***, *13th edition.*

Practice Sentences 2 (page 51)

1. In fact, ...
2. . . . , nevertheless, ...
3. . . . , fortunately.
4. Yes, ...
5. No commas. (*Perhaps* flows smoothly into the rest of the sentence.)
6. . . . , in other words, ...
7. Between you and me, ...
8. . . . , therefore, ...
9. . . . , without a doubt, ...
10. No commas preferred. (Optional commas around *indeed*.)

Practice Paragraph 2 (page 51)

We, as a rule, do not employ inexperienced accountants. However, Mr. Williams had so many excellent recommendations that we could not afford to turn down his application. Perhaps you will wish to meet him personally before assigning him to a supervisor. I can, of course, have him stop by your office tomorrow.

The answers to Reinforcement Letter 2 appear in the ***Instructor's Manual and Key for HOW 13: A Handbook for Office Professionals***, 13th edition.

Practice Sentences 3 (page 53)

1. Brett, ...
2. . . . , class, ...
3. . . . , Mrs. Davis.
4. . . . , ladies and gentlemen, ...
5. . . . , Gary, ...
6. Yes, fellow citizens of Spokane, ...
7. No commas.
8. . . . , Dr. Bradley.
9. No commas.
10. You, friends and neighbors, ...

Practice Paragraph 3 (page 53)

Would you, Ms. White, please review the financial report. I would appreciate your doing so too, Ms. Smith. Gentlemen, please check with both Ms. White and Ms. Smith for their advice before making any further financial commitments.

The answers to Reinforcement Letter 3 appear in the ***Instructor's Manual and Key for HOW 13: A Handbook for Office Professionals***, 13th edition.

Practice Sentences 4 (page 55)

1. . . . , Stan Hughes, ...
2. . . . , the author of a best seller, ...
3. . . . , a member of the finance committee, ...
4. No commas.
5. . . . , "Skiing in Colorado," . . . ?
6. No commas.
7. . . . , our new assistant, ...

8. . . . , two prominent authorities on the subject of e-commerce.
9. . . . , Bill Thompson.
10. . . . , Kligman Industries, ...

Practice Paragraph 4 (page 55)

We have just learned that our president, Mr. Black, will retire next June. He has been president of Data Products, Inc., for the past ten years. My assistant received the news yesterday and believes that Stephen Gold, PhD, will be asked to fill the position. We will keep our employees informed of further developments through our monthly newsletter, *Data Jottings*.

The answers to Reinforcement Letter 4 appear in the ***Instructor's Manual and Key for HOW 13: A Handbook for Office Professionals***, 13th edition.

Practice Sentences 5 (page 57)

1. . . . February 28, 2013.
2. No commas.
3. . . . 8 p.m., EST?
4. No commas.
5. . . . Thursday, June 12, 2014.
6. No commas.
7. . . . November 4, 2012, ...
8. No commas.
9. . . . 8:40 a.m., CST.
10. On Wednesday, December 6, 2016, ...

Practice Paragraph 5 (page 57)

We will meet on April 1 to plan the opening of two new branch offices scheduled for Tuesday, May 3, and Thursday, May 19. These offices are the first ones we have opened since August 22, 2012. We will need to plan these openings carefully because we will be directly responsible for two additional openings in September 2015 and April 2016.

The answers to Reinforcement Letter 5 appear in the ***Instructor's Manual and Key for HOW 13: A Handbook for Office Professionals***, 13th edition.

Practice Sentences 6 (page 59)

1. . . . Publishing, 6200 Walnut Avenue, Salem, Oregon 97302.
2. . . . Lane, Los Angeles, California 90041-2027.
3. . . . London, England, and Paris, France, ...
4. . . . Honolulu, Hawaii.
5. . . . Albuquerque, New Mexico, ...
6. . . . Avenue, Knoxville, Tennessee 37912-5821.
7. . . . Stocker, Office Manager, Smythe & Ryan Investment Counselors, 3370 Ravenwood Avenue, Suite 120, Baltimore, Maryland 21213-1648.

8. . . . Box 360, Rural Route 2, Bangor, Maine 04401-9802.
9. Dallas, Texas, ...
10. . . . Madrid, Spain.

Practice Paragraph 6 (page 59)

We sent the information to Mr. David Hope, Manager, Larry's Clothing Store, 2001 Adams Street, SW, Atlanta, Georgia 30315-5901. The information should have been sent to Mr. Hope's new address in Columbus, Ohio. It is 2970 Olive Avenue, Columbus, Ohio 43204-2535.

The answers to Reinforcement Letter 6 appear in the *Instructor's Manual and Key for HOW 13: A Handbook for Office Professionals*, 13*th* edition.

Practice Sentences 7 (page 61)

1. . . . January, and two of them . . . .
2. . . . 3 p.m., but we had not . . . .
3. . . . office, or you may . . . .
4. . . . minute, nor can they . . . .
5. No comma. (Second clause incomplete.)
6. . . . publication process, and it will . . . .
7. No comma. (The words *and that* result in a dependent clause.)
8. . . . himself, or he will arrange . . . .
9. . . . Akron, nor will he have . . . .
10. No comma. (Second clause incomplete.)

Practice Paragraph 7 (page 61)

We have checked our records and find that you are correct. Our deposit was mailed to your branch office, but no record of this deposit was entered into our check record. Our records have been corrected, and we appreciate your help in solving this problem. We hope that we have not caused you any inconvenience and that we may rely upon your help in the future.

The answers to Reinforcement Letter 7 appear in the *Instructor's Manual and Key for HOW 13: A Handbook for Office Professionals*, 13*th* edition.

Practice Sentences 8 (page 63)

1. . . . pleasant, patient . . . .
2. No commas.
3. No commas.
4. . . . elegant, secluded . . . .
5. No commas.
6. . . . ambitious, greedy . . . .
7. No commas.
8. Your outgoing, cheerful . . . .
9. . . . wealthy, well-known . . . .
10. No commas.

Practice Paragraph 8 (page 63)

Your informative, well-written report was submitted to the board of education yesterday. You will certainly be permitted to purchase some inexpensive modern equipment on the basis of the facts presented. I am sure the board will agree that the present facilities do not reflect a realistic, practical learning environment for business students.

The answers to Reinforcement Letter 8 appear in the *Instructor's Manual and Key for HOW 13: A Handbook for Office Professionals*, 13th edition.

Practice Sentences 9 (page 65)

1. When you see Bill, ...
2. While you were in New York, ...
3. Before you leave for Denver, . . .?
4. As stated previously, ...
5. Because Mr. Logan wishes to move to Indianapolis, ...
6. If so, . . .?
7. While Ms. Smith was consulting with her attorney, ...
8. Provided we receive a budget increase, ...
9. If you are unable to keep your appointment, ...
10. As explained above, ...

Practice Paragraph 9 (page 65)

When you receive the material, please review it carefully and return it to our office within two weeks. If possible, note all changes in red. As soon as we receive your corrections, we will be able to submit the manuscript to the printer. We expect that if the current production schedule is maintained, the book will be released early in March.

The answers to Reinforcement Letter 9 appear in the *Instructor's Manual and Key for HOW 13: A Handbook for Office Professionals*, 13th edition.

Practice Sentences 10 (page 67)

1. To continue this project, ...
2. Seeing Tom's mistake, ...
3. After viewing the architect's drawings, ...
4. Near the top of the new listings, ...
5. No comma.
6. During the next month, ...
7. No comma.
8. To be interviewed for this position, ...
9. Until the end of the month, ...
10. No comma.

Practice Paragraph 10 (page 67)

For the past 100 years, our bank has served the needs of the people of Hartford. At the present time, we wish to attract more depositors to our institution. To attract new customers to the Bank of Connecticut, we have established a premium plan. Hoping that such an incentive will draw a large group of new depositors, we have provided a number of gift items to be given away with the opening of new accounts for $1,000 or more.

The answers to Reinforcement Letter 10 appear in the *Instructor's Manual and Key for HOW 13: A Handbook for Office Professionals*, 13th edition.

Practice Sentences 11 (page 69)

1. Mr. Sims, who is responsible for reviewing all appeals, will . . . .
2. No commas.
3. . . . article, which appeared in last Sunday's local paper, discusses . . . .
4. No commas.
5. . . . shipped, although I tried to cancel it.
6. No commas.
7. Mr. Young, who has attended many of our seminars, is . . . .
8. . . . report, which was distributed at the last meeting of department heads.
9. . . . Inn, regardless of its expensive meals and remote location.
10. . . . president, planning to make major organizational changes, first . . . .

Practice Paragraph 11 (page 69)

The new community library, which is located on South Main Street, is presently recruiting employees to serve the public during the evening hours. Mr. Harris is looking for staff members who would be willing to work from 5 to 9 p.m. on weekday evenings. He would be pleased to receive your recommendations if you know of any qualified individuals who would be interested in such a position. We would appreciate receiving your recommendations within the next few days since Mr. Harris must hire the evening staff by May 10, before the library opens on May 13.

The answers to Reinforcement Letter 11 appear in the *Instructor's Manual and Key for HOW 13: A Handbook for Office Professionals*, 13th edition.

Practice Sentences 12 (page 71)

1. The format, not the content, of . . . .
2. . . . forms, the sooner we can . . . .
3. . . . July 1, but only to . . . .
4. . . . Internet sites, the more adept . . . .
5. . . . report, not just a simple e-mail, outlining . . . .
6. . . . July 9; Jennifer, August 15; Michael, August 22; and Katelyn, August 29.
7. . . . suites; yesterday, three; and the day before, two.
8. . . . report; the Personnel Department, 12; and the other departments, 8.
9. . . . supplies; this month, only one.
10. . . . in 2015; three, in 2016; two, in 2017.

Practice Paragraph 12 (page 71)

Last week our agent sold six homes; this week, just four. Mr. Stevens maintains that our construction site is not appealing to home buyers. His argument is plausible, yet weak. Other builders in the area have been more successful in their marketing efforts. The more competition Mr. Stevens encounters, the more his sales efforts seem to decline.

The answers to Reinforcement Letter 12 appear in the *Instructor's Manual and Key for HOW 13: A Handbook for Office Professionals*, 13th edition.

Practice Sentences 13 (page 73)

1. . . . for many, many years.
2. A long time before, she had spoken . . . .
3. Whoever wins, wins a . . . .
4. Ever since, Mr. Salazar has kept . . . .
5. We were very, very disappointed . . . .
6. Students who cheat, cheat only . . . .
7. Three months before, our sales manager . . . .
8. Whoever skydives, skydives at . . . .
9. Even before, he had shown . . . .
10. After this, time will seem . . . .

Practice Paragraph 13 (page 73)

All the meeting was, was a discussion of Mr. Green's plan to move the plant. Mr. Green has presented this same plan many, many times. A few weeks before, another committee totally rejected his proposal. Ever since, he has looked for another group to endorse his ideas.

The answers to Reinforcement Letter 13 appear in the *Instructor's Manual and Key for HOW 13: A Handbook for Office Professionals*, 13th edition.

Practice Sentences 14 (page 75)

1. . . . sign," said Mr. Grey.
2. "How long," asked Ms. Foster, "will it . . . hard drive?"
3. No commas.
4. Mr. Hughes said, "Everyone must . . . ."
5. No commas.
6. "Are you finished," asked Scott, "with . . . ?"
7. The witness reaffirmed, "That man . . . ."
8. "Please . . . Friday, May 5," said . . . .
9. No commas.
10. "Mr. David Brown," said Ms. Burns, the Department of Human Resources head, "has . . . ."

Practice Paragraph 14 (page 75)

Mr. Dallas answered the reporter's question with a simple "yes." His philosophy appeared to be "A bird in hand is worth two in the bush." The reporter then asked, "Do you believe this labor contract will be ratified within the next week?" Mr. Dallas answered confidently, "I believe the terms of the contract will be accepted by a clear majority." "I am sure," added Ms. Hill, "that the employees will be especially pleased with the additional insurance benefits offered."

The answers to Reinforcement Letter 14 appear in the *Instructor's Manual and Key for HOW 13: A Handbook for Office Professionals*, 13th edition.

Practice Sentences 15 (page 77)

1. . . . Web site; we feel they . . . .
2. . . . reports; she wishes . . . .
3. Andrea collated, Kim stapled.

354

4. . . . e-mail message; I will review . . . .
5. . . . new project; he will be . . . .
6. I dusted furniture, Tim cleaned the showcase, Linda vacuumed—all just . . . .
7. . . . Thursday's meeting; he will work . . . .
8. . . . application today; the committee will make . . . .
9. The thief entered, he grabbed the jewelry, he exited swiftly.
10. . . . all-time low; they increased somewhat during September; November recorded . . . .

Practice Paragraph 15 (page 77)

We need someone to meet with the Atlas Corporation representatives. Please call Mr. Green; ask him to be in my office by 10 a.m. tomorrow morning. He knows Piedmont, he knows commercial real estate, he knows prices. Mr. Green would be my first choice for the job; Ms. Jones would be my second choice; my final choice would be Mr. Bruce.

The answers to Reinforcement Letter 15 appear in the *Instructor's Manual and Key for HOW 13: A Handbook for Office Professionals*, 13th edition.

Practice Sentences 16 (page 79)

1. James Hogan, who is originally from Nevada, has written a book about tourist sights in Las Vegas; and he plans to have . . . .
2. Cliff Lightfoot, our supervisor, has been ill for several weeks; but he plans to return to the office next Wednesday, November 19, in time . . . .
3. . . . for all the offices, and we expect . . . .
4. We cannot, Ms. Baron, repair the DVD player under the terms of the warranty, nor can we under . . . . (*or* . . . of the warranty; nor can we under . . . .)
5. Nevertheless, the committee must meet again next Friday, but today we will . . . .
6. . . . live nearby, and they . . . .
7. Unfortunately, . . . have mechanical problems; but according to the latest information we have received, they will be . . . .
8. I believe, Ms. Edwards, that the contract . . . .
9. You may, of course, keep your original appointment, or you may reschedule . . . .
10. . . . 9 percent return; but we cannot guarantee that our next program, or any other programs planned for the future, will do as well.

Practice Paragraph 16 (pages 79–80)

We were pleased to learn, Mr. Bell, that you have opened a new store on West Main Street, (*or* Street;) and you may be sure that we look forward to establishing a mutually profitable business relationship. Our new line of stationery, greeting cards, and other paper products should be of interest to you; and we will have our sales representative in your area, Jack Dale, phone you for an appointment to view them. He can leave a catalog with you, (*or* you;) or he can take you personally to our showroom, which is located only three miles from your store.

The answers to Reinforcement Letter 16 appear in the *Instructor's Manual and Key for HOW 13: A Handbook for Office Professionals*, 13th edition.

Practice Sentences 17 (page 81)

1. . . . substantially this year; therefore, we are . . . .
2. . . . next week's schedule; however, your hours . . . .

3. . . . for remodeling; on the contrary, we will be . . . .
4. . . . hospital wing; consequently, we will have . . . .
5. . . . math textbooks; moreover, they will . . . .
6. . . . proposed novel; then we will . . . .
7. . . . pencil sharpeners; however, we are . . . .
8. Mr. Cooper, vice president of Western Bank, will not be able to attend our meeting; consequently, we will need . . . .
9. . . . more than eight hours; thus the distribution . . . .
10. . . . Chicago area; therefore, they will . . . .

Practice Paragraph 17 (page 81)

Our order for 24 sets of china arrived yesterday; however, more than half the sets have broken pieces. These china sets are a featured item for our May sale; thus we would appreciate your sending an additional 14 sets to replace the broken ones. Please ship these replacements immediately so that they will arrive in time for our sale.

The answers to Reinforcement Letter 17 appear in the *Instructor's Manual and Key for HOW 13: A Handbook for Office Professionals*, 13th edition.

Practice Sentences 18 (page 83)

1. . . . in Miami, Florida; Houston, Texas; and Portland, Oregon.
2. . . . were David Stevens, president of North Hills Academy; Agnes Moore, assistant principal of Rhodes School; and Vera Caruso, director of Flintridge Preparatory School.
3. . . . new sales campaign; for example, we will . . . .
4. . . . this problem; namely, labor shortages, wage increases, and frequent strikes.
5. Joleen has done all the fact-finding for this case; Jim has verified her findings; and Paul will take the case . . . .
6. . . . from San Fernando, California; Phoenix, Arizona; and Reno, Nevada, plan to . . . .
7. . . . occurred on July 4, 1776; October 24, 1929; and November 22, 1963.
8. . . . former procedures; for example, we no longer . . . .
9. . . . this year; namely, Charles Brubaker, Dana Walters, Phillip Gordon, and Lisa Stanzell.
10. . . . Dayton, Ohio; sales territories will be expanded from eight to ten; and the position . . . .

Practice Paragraph 18 (pages 83–84)

Our next student travel tour will include visits to London, England; Madrid, Spain; and Frankfurt, Germany. Two years ago we received 200 applications for our European tour; last year we received nearly 400; and this year we expect more than 700 students to apply for this tour. This tour is one of the most popular ones we offer because the Smith Foundation underwrites many of the costs; namely, hotel accommodations, meals, and surface transportation.

The answers to Reinforcement Letter 18 appear in the *Instructor's Manual and Key for HOW 13: A Handbook for Office Professionals*, 13th edition.

Practice Sentences 19 (page 85)

1. . . . following supplies: bond paper, laser printer paper, and writing pads.
2. . . . you were out: Marguerite Rodriguez from Atlas Corporation, Robert Wong from the Accounting Department, Lynne Hale from Thompson Industries, and . . . .

356

3. . . . from every viewpoint: she has studied . . . .
4. . . . bills for January 4, January 8, February 1, and February 7.
5. . . . either of these catalogs: Spring 2014 or Summer 2014.
6. . . . February were Naomi Chahinian, Bertha Granados, and Kelly Crockett.
7. . . . spring line: shirts, jeans, shoes, belts, and jackets.
8. . . . past year: Belmont Industries . . . .
9. . . . are being discontinued: we have had . . . .
10. . . . spring sale; namely, 3 cashiers, 5 salespersons, and 6 inventory clerks.

Practice Paragraph 19 (pages 85–86)

New offices were opened in the following cities last year: Albany, Billings, Dayton, and Fresno. We had planned to add additional offices in Portland and San Antonio: the high cost of financing has delayed the openings of these offices until next year. Both the planning and the development of the new offices have been handled by five persons in our home office: Bill Collins, Brad Morgan, Susan Smith, Carol White, and David Williams.

The answers to Reinforcement Letter 19 appear in the **Instructor's Manual and Key for HOW 13: A Handbook for Office Professionals**, 13th edition.

Practice Sentences 20 (page 87)

1. Former employers and instructors—these are the only names . . . .
2. A number of urgent e-mail messages—one from Mary Thompson, two from Laura Woo, and two from Michael Benton—still need to be answered.
3. Several major factors—increased interest rates, higher property values, and a general business slowdown—have caused a real estate decline in this area.
4. The administrative staff—hoping to boost employee morale, increase sales, and raise profit levels—instituted a bonus-commission program.
5. Sunburst, Apollo, Courtyard, and Apple Blossom—these four china patterns . . . .
6. Any number of private delivery services—Federal Express, United Parcel Service, DHL, etc.—can provide you with overnight service to Cincinnati.
7. All our staff members—with possibly only one or two exceptions—are certified public accountants. (or . . . , with possibly only one or two exceptions, ...)
8. You may choose from a variety of colors—black, navy, gray, white, bone, red, pink, yellow, brown, taupe, emerald, and sky blue. (or . . . colors: black, ...)
9. Three commercial online service providers—AT&T, Time Warner Cable, and Verizon—are being evaluated by our manager.
10. Word processing, spreadsheet, and database—any applicant we interview must have recent training or experience in these kinds of software programs.

Practice Paragraph 20 (pages 87–88)

Crestview Wood Finishing—manufacturers of French doors and windows, main entrance doors, and window boxes—has been serving our community for more than 25 years. Our quality workmanship—which can be seen in the lustrous wood finish, elegant hardware, and precision fit of our doors and windows—is guaranteed for five years. Stop by our showroom to view our new display of French doors and windows. Single pane, double panes, beveled, or frosted—you may choose any of these glass types for your French doors or windows.

The answers to Reinforcement Letter 20 appear in the **Instructor's Manual and Key for HOW 13: A Handbook for Office Professionals**, 13th edition.

Section 3   Capitalization

Practice Sentences 1 (page 91)

1. Dr. Chu's, Medical Arts Building
2. Promenade Shopping Mall, Franciscan china
3. Caribbean, Viking Queen
4. Green Tree Bridge, Suwannee River
5. HP TouchSmarts
6. Caesar salad, beef Stroganoff
7. Montclair Hotel, City of Angels
8. venetian blinds
9. Dakota County Fair, Norfolk
10. John Sreveski, india ink

Practice Paragraph 1 (page 91)

In April we will meet in the Islands to discuss the reorganization of territories in Alaska, California, Hawaii, Oregon, and Washington. Reservations have been made for April 7 on an American Airlines flight to Honolulu. Either General Motors or Ford Motor Company cars may be rented from Budget Car Rental for those agents attending the meeting.

The answers to Reinforcement Letter 1 appear in the *Instructor's Manual and Key for HOW 13: A Handbook for Office Professionals, 13th edition*.

Practice Sentences 2 (page 93)

1. c.o.d., 2 p.m.
2. CPA, USC
3. AA Flight 82
4. Invoice 578391
5. page 28, Model 1738 DVD player
6. No. 347
7. Figure 3, page 23
8. paragraph 4
9. Policy No. 6429518-C
10. Model 17 desk

Practice Paragraph 2 (page 93)

The medical expenses resulting from your fall are covered by your policy, No. 846821. However, as stated in Section B, paragraph 3, the company will cover medical costs only after the $100 deductible has been satisfied. If your medical expenses since January 1 have exceeded the deductible amount, please have your doctor fill out Form 6B and return it in the enclosed envelope. If you have any questions, call me at (800) 759-6382 any weekday between 9 a.m. and 4 p.m.

The answers to Reinforcement Letter 2 appear in the *Instructor's Manual and Key for HOW 13: A Handbook for Office Professionals, 13th edition*.

Practice Sentences 3 (page 95)

1. governor
2. Professor Carlos Rodriguez
3. Mark Swenson, president of Georgetown Steel
4. vice president, Joshua Wooldridge
5. Professor
6. Mayor-elect Ann Brown
7. Byron Teague, assistant dean of instruction
8. director of human resources
9. Lieutenant Colonel Bruno Furtado
10. Barack Obama, the president,

Practice Paragraph 3 (page 95)

The purchasing agents' convention in Miami was well attended this year. After a welcoming speech by Mayor Frank Barnes, John Lang, the president of Williams Manufacturing Company, spoke on how inflation is affecting the inventories of many companies throughout the country. Also speaking on the same subject was Professor Roberta Holt.

The answers to Reinforcement Letter 3 appear in the **Instructor's Manual and Key for HOW 13: A Handbook for Office Professionals**, 13th edition.

Practice Sentences 4 (page 97)

1. . . . *A History of the Americas* . . . History 12 class.
2. . . . *A Music World of Wonder* . . . ?
3. Theresa Flores, PhD, . . . conversational Spanish class . . . .
4. Walt Disney's movie *The Lion King* . . . .
5. . . . Lisa Gartlan, MD, ...
6. . . . "A Look at Teenage Life in These United States" . . . *Outlook Magazine*?
7. . . . master of science degree in engineering.
8. . . . "Singing in the Rain" . . . .
9. . . . *The New York Times* . . . *The Wall Street Journal*.
10. . . . Theater Arts 23 . . . *Phantom of the Opera*.

Practice Paragraph 4 (page 97)

I plan to interview Fred Case, PhD, the author of the book *It's Easy to Make a Million Dollars*. This interview will be the basis for a feature article that will appear in the "People Today" section of the Sunday *Chronicle*. I am interested to learn whether the ideas outlined in his book came from actual experience, research, or both. I understand, too, that the newly released movie, *How to Make a Million Without Really Trying*, is based on Dr. Case's book.

The answers to Reinforcement Letter 4 appear in the **Instructor's Manual and Key for HOW 13: A Handbook for Office Professionals**, 13th edition.

Practice Sentences 5 (page 99)

1. National Fund for the Protection of American Wildlife
2. Senate
3. company
4. Accounting Department, Payroll Department

359

5. Advertising Department
6. county
7. Department of Human Resources
8. government
9. Board of Directors
10. National Council of Teachers of English

Practice Paragraph 5 (page 99)

Bill Hughes has recently been promoted to head our Public Relations Department. As a former president of both the chamber of commerce and the Rotary club, he is well acquainted with many members of the business community. One of his main responsibilities in his new position at Fairchild Enterprises will be to promote the company among his business contacts.

The answers to Reinforcement Letter 5 appear in the ***Instructor's Manual and Key for HOW 13: A Handbook for Office Professionals***, *13th edition*.

Section 4   Numbers

Practice Sentences 1 (page 117)

1. 27
2. six
3. Thirty-six
4. ten
5. five

6. 38
7. Eighty-six
8. 3 million
9. 25
10. 12

Practice Paragraph 1 (page 117)

Mr. Wells requested that we send him 75 copies of our latest catalog. He is conducting three separate workshops at Eastern Business College and believes that more than 20 (*or* twenty) business teachers will sign up for each course. So that the business teachers can become acquainted with the materials we have available, Mr. Wells would like to give each teacher a copy of our catalog.

The answers to Reinforcement Letter 1 appear in the *Instructor's Manual and Key for HOW 13: A Handbook for Office Professionals, 13th edition.*

Practice Sentences 2 (page 119)

1. 3
2. 1,000,000
3. 2
4. 11, four
5. 7

6. 382, 9
7. two
8. 8
9. 1 million, 1.5 million
10. five

Practice Paragraph 2 (page 119)

We appreciate your order for 8 digital cameras, 22 DVD players, and 6 portable television sets. At the present time, we have only 9 DVD players in our Dallas warehouse. We will check with our three branch offices and our two retail stores to determine whether they have available the remaining 13. In the meantime, we are shipping you 8 digital cameras, 9 DVD players, and 6 portable television sets.

The answers to Reinforcement Letter 2 appear in the *Instructor's Manual and Key for HOW 13: A Handbook for Office Professionals, 13th edition.*

Practice Sentences 3 (page 121)

1. page 7
2. Policy 83478
3. No. 3
4. Number 1886
5. paragraph 8
6. $4
7. 6 percent
8. $.20

9. 8 percent
10. 85 cents
11. $1,000,000
12. $4 million
13. 22 percent
14. 30 cents
15. 0.4

Practice Paragraph 3 (pages 121–122)

A copy of your homeowner's policy, Policy 7832146, is enclosed. As you will note on page 1, line 6, the total company liability under this policy cannot exceed $200,000. Please submit this year's premium of $240. Because increasing costs have forced us to raise our premium rates, this premium reflects an increase of 8 percent over last year's.

The answers to Reinforcement Letter 3 appear in the *Instructor's Manual and Key for HOW 13: A Handbook for Office Professionals, 13th edition.*

Practice Sentences 4 (page 123)

1. 9 pounds 12 ounces
2. 3
3. June 3
4. 6 p.m.
5. 8 inches
6. 4 pounds 2 ounces
7. October 25
8. 9 o'clock in the morning
9. 1st of January
10. 18
11. 30
12. 18
13. thirty-three
14. 125th
15. 63

Practice Paragraph 4 (page 124)

When we were in Phoenix from August 13 until August 24, the average high temperature reading was 116 degrees. On the 25th of August, the temperature reading dropped to 110 degrees. We did enjoy our 12-day vacation but wished our stay had been a cooler one.

The answers to Reinforcement Letter 4 appear in the *Instructor's Manual and Key for HOW 13: A Handbook for Office Professionals*, 13th edition.

Section 5   Hyphenating and Dividing Words

Practice Guide 1 (pages 127–128)

1. five-minute
2. OK
3. word processing
4. OK
5. alarmingly toxic
6. OK
7. three- and four-bedroom
8. Oklahoma University
9. newly acquired
10. kindhearted
11. 30-year
12. charge account
13. snow-white
14. OK
15. part-time
16. OK
17. interest-free
18. government sponsored
19. OK
20. air-conditioning
21. high and low selling prices
22. Main Street
23. OK
24. hit-and-miss
25. large- and small-scale
26. redeemable store coupons
27. Little League
28. OK
29. basic accounting
30. OK

The answers to Practice Guides 2–4 appear in the *Instructor's Manual and Key for HOW 13: A Handbook for Office Professionals*, 13th edition.

Practice Guide 5 (pages 135–136)

1. nov / elty
2. unde / sir / able
3. ND
4. 4397 Halstead / Street
5. ND
6. ND
7. Mary N. / Gomez
8. ND
9. 25 per / cent
10. Columbus, / Ohio / 43210
11. read / ers
12. criti / cal
13. tech / niques
14. San / Fran / cisco
15. Agri / cul / ture
16. Ms. Darlene / Jackson
17. 3942 East / 21st / Street
18. December 17, / 2014
19. pos / si / ble
20. con / nec / tion
21. brother- / in- / law
22. thor / oughly
23. Mas / sa / chu / setts
24. self- / reliance
25. ND

The answers to Practice Guide 6 appear in the *Instructor's Manual and Key for HOW 13: A Handbook for Office Professionals*, 13th edition.

Section 6   Abbreviated Forms

Practice Guide 1 (pages 139–140)

1. CST
2. 900 BC
3. CLU
4. OK
5. NBC
6. Dr.
7. OK
8. OK
9. Model No. 1683
10. c.o.d.
11. OK
12. Ext. 327
13. UK
14. NE
15. Brig. Gen. Ret.
16. etc.
17. OK
18. MD
19. Ralph T. Drengson Sr.
20. HP laptop
21. Esq.
22. 5 p.m.
23. OK
24. PhD
25. CD-ROM.

The answers to Practice Guide 2 appear in the *Instructor's Manual and Key for HOW 13: A Handbook for Office Professionals*, 13th edition.

Practice Guide 3 (page 143)

1. OK
2. I'm not
3. isn't
4. OK
5. You're
6. hasn't
7. OK
8. its
9. they're
10. OK

363

Section 7   Words Often Confused and Misused

Practice Exercises for Words *A/An* Through *Aisle/Isle*

Practice Guide 1 (pages 145–149)

A/An

1. an
2. a
3. a
4. an
5. a

A lot/Allot/Alot

6. a lot
7. allot
8. allot
9. a lot
10. allotted

A while/Awhile

11. a while
12. awhile
13. A while
14. a while
15. awhile

Accede/Exceed

16. exceed
17. accede
18. exceed
19. accede
20. exceed

Accelerate/Exhilarate

21. accelerate
22. accelerate
23. exhilarate
24. accelerating
25. exhilarated

Accept/Except

26. accept
27. except
28. except
29. accept
30. accepted

Access/Excess

31. access
32. excess
33. excess
34. access
35. access

Ad/Add

36. add
37. add
38. ad
39. add
40. ad

Adapt/Adept/Adopt

41. adopt
42. adapt
43. adept
44. adapt
45. adopt

Addict/Edict

46. addicts
47. edict
48. edict
49. addicts
50. edict

Addition/Edition

51. edition
52. additions
53. addition
54. editions
55. edition

Adherence/Adherents

56. Adherence
57. adherence
58. adherents
59. adherents
60. adherence

364

Adverse/Averse

61. averse
62. adverse
63. averse
64. Adverse
65. averse

Advice/Advise

66. advise
67. advice
68. advice
69. advice
70. advise

Affect/Effect

71. effect
72. affect
73. effect
74. affect
75. effect

Aggravate/Irritate

76. aggravate
77. aggravate
78. irritate
79. irritate
80. irritated

Aid/Aide

81. aid
82. aid
83. aide
84. aid
85. aides

Aisle/Isle

86. aisle
87. aisles
88. isle
89. isle
90. aisle

The answers to Reinforcement Guide 1 appear in the **Instructor's Manual and Key for HOW 13: A Handbook for Office Professionals**, 13*th* edition.

Practice Exercises for Words *All Ready/Already* Through *Appraise/Apprise*

Practice Guide 2 (pages 153–157)

All ready/Already

1. all ready
2. already
3. already
4. already
5. all ready

All right/Alright

6. all right
7. all right
8. all right
9. all right
10. all right

All together/Altogether

11. altogether
12. all together
13. all together
14. Altogether
15. altogether

All ways/Always

16. always
17. always
18. all ways
19. always
20. all ways

Allowed/Aloud

21. allowed
22. allowed
23. aloud
24. allowed
25. aloud

Allude/Elude

26. allude
27. elude
28. allude
29. eluding
30. allude

Almost/Most

31. Almost
32. Most
33. almost
34. almost
35. almost

Altar/Alter

36. alter
37. altars
38. altar
39. alter
40. alter

Alternate/Alternative

41. alternate
42. alternative
43. alternate
44. alternate
45. alternatives

Among/Between

46. among
47. between
48. between
49. between
50. among

Amount/Number

51. number
52. number
53. number
54. amount
55. number

Anecdote/Antidote

56. anecdotes
57. anecdote
58. antidote
59. antidotes
60. anecdotes

Annual/Annul

61. annul
62. annual
63. annual
64. annul
65. annul

Anxious/Eager

66. anxious
67. eager
68. eager
69. anxious
70. eager

Any one/Anyone

71. anyone
72. Any one
73. any one
74. Anyone
75. anyone

Any time/Anytime

76. any time
77. anytime
78. anytime
79. any time
80. anytime

Any way/Anyway

81. anyway
82. Any way
83. any way
84. any way
85. Anyway

Appraise/Apprise

86. apprise
87. apprised
88. appraised
89. appraise
90. apprised

The answers to Reinforcement Guide 2 appear in the **Instructor's Manual and Key for HOW 13: A Handbook for Office Professionals,** 13th edition.

Practice Exercises for Words *As/Like* Through *Bolder/Boulder*

Practice Guide 3 (pages 161–165)

As/Like

1. as
2. like
3. as
4. like
5. As

Ascent/Assent

6. ascent
7. assent
8. ascent
9. ascent
10. assent

Assistance/Assistants

11. assistance
12. assistance
13. assistance
14. assistants
15. assistants

Assure/Ensure/Insure

16. ensure
17. insure
18. ensure
19. assure
20. assure

Attendance/Attendants

21. attendance
22. attendance
23. attendants
24. attendance
25. attendants

Bad/Badly

26. bad
27. badly
28. badly
29. bad
30. bad

Bail/Bale

31. bales
32. bail
33. bail
34. bales
35. bales

Bare/Bear

36. bare
37. bear
38. bare
39. bare
40. bare

Base/Bass

41. bass
42. base
43. base
44. base
45. bass

Bazaar/Bizarre

46. bizarre
47. bazaars
48. bazaar
49. bizarre
50. bizarre

Because of/Due to

51. Because of
52. because of
53. because of
54. Because of
55. because of

Berth/Birth

56. berth
57. birth
58. birth
59. berths
60. berths

Beside/Besides

61. besides
62. beside
63. beside
64. besides
65. besides

Bi-/Semi-

66. semi- (semiweekly)
67. semi- (semimonthly)
68. Bi- (Bimonthly)
69. bi- (biweekly)
70. semi- (semimonthly)

Biannual/Biennial

71. biannual
72. biannual
73. Biennial
74. biannual
75. biennially

Bibliography/Biography

76. bibliography
77. bibliography

78. biography
79. bibliography
80. biography

Billed/Build

81. billed
82. build
83. build
84. build
85. billed

Boarder/Border

86. border
87. boarder
88. boarders
89. border
90. border

Bolder/Boulder

91. bolder
92. boulder
93. bolder
94. bolder
95. boulders

The answers to Reinforcement Guide 3 appear in the **Instructor's Manual and Key for HOW 13: A Handbook for Office Professionals**, 13th edition.

Practice Exercises for Words *Born/Borne* Through *Cite/Sight/Site*

Practice Guide 4 (pages 169–173)

Born/Borne

1. born
2. borne
3. born
4. borne
5. borne

Bouillon/Bullion

6. bouillon
7. bullion
8. bullion
9. bouillon
10. bouillon

Breach/Breech

11. breach
12. breached

13. breech
14. breach
15. breach

Bring/Take

16. bring
17. take
18. bring
19. bring
20. take

Calendar/Colander

21. colanders
22. calendars
23. calendar
24. calendar
25. colander

368

Callous/Callus

26. callous
27. callous
28. callus
29. callous
30. calluses

Can/May

31. may
32. may
33. can
34. Can
35. may

Canvas/Canvass

36. canvas
37. canvass
38. canvas
39. canvass
40. canvass

Capital/Capitol

41. capital
42. capitol
43. capital
44. capital
45. Capitol

Carat/Caret/Carrot/Karat

46. carat
47. karat, karat
48. caret
49. carrot
50. karat

Cease/Seize

51. cease
52. cease
53. seize
54. seize
55. cease

Ceiling/Sealing

56. sealing
57. ceiling
58. Sealing
59. ceilings
60. ceilings

Censor/Censure

61. censor
62. censure
63. censured
64. censors
65. censored

Census/Senses

66. senses
67. census
68. census
69. census
70. senses

Cent/Scent/Sent

71. cent
72. sent
73. scents
74. scent
75. cent

Cereal/Serial

76. serial
77. cereal
78. cereal
79. serial
80. serial

Choose/Chose

81. chose
82. choose
83. choose
84. chose
85. choose

Chord/Cord

86. cord
87. chord
88. cords
89. cord
90. cords

Cite/Sight/Site

91. site
92. cite
93. sight
94. cited
95. sites

The answers to Reinforcement Guide 4 appear in the **Instructor's Manual and Key for HOW 13: A Handbook for Office Professionals**, 13th edition.

Practice Exercises for Words *Close/Clothes/Cloths* Through *Decent/Descent/Dissent*

Practice Guide 5 (pages 177–182)

Close/Clothes/Cloths

1. close
2. clothes
3. cloths
4. close
5. clothes

Coarse/Course

6. course
7. course
8. coarse
9. course
10. course

Collision/Collusion

11. collusion
12. collision
13. collusion
14. collision
15. collusion

Command/Commend

16. commend
17. commended
18. commands
19. command
20. commend

Complement/Compliment

21. complement
22. complement
23. complement
24. compliments
25. compliment

Complementary/Complimentary

26. complimentary
27. complementary
28. complementary
29. complimentary
30. complimentary

Confidant/Confident

31. confidant
32. confident

33. confident
34. confidant
35. confident

Conscience/Conscious

36. conscience
37. conscious
38. conscience
39. conscious
40. conscious

Console/Consul

41. console
42. console
43. consul
44. console
45. consul

Continual/Continuous

46. continual
47. continually
48. continuous
49. continuously
50. continually

Convince/Persuade

51. persuade
52. persuade
53. convince
54. convince
55. persuade

Cooperation/Corporation

56. cooperation
57. corporation
58. cooperation
59. cooperation
60. corporations

Corespondent/Correspondence/Correspondents

61. corespondent
62. correspondence
63. correspondents
64. correspondence
65. correspondents

Corps/Corpse

66. corpse
67. corps
68. Corps
69. corpse
70. corps

Costumer/Customer

71. customer
72. customer
73. costumer
74. costumer
75. customers

Council/Counsel

76. council
77. counsel
78. council
79. council
80. counsels

Credible/Creditable

81. creditable
82. creditable
83. creditable
84. credible
85. credible

Deceased/Diseased

86. deceased
87. diseased
88. diseased
89. diseased
90. deceased

Decent/Descent/Dissent

91. descent
92. decent
93. Dissent
94. descent
95. dissent

The answers to Reinforcement Guide 5 appear in the **Instructor's Manual and Key for HOW 13: A Handbook for Office Professionals**, 13th edition.

Practice Exercises for *Defer/Differ* Through *Every Day/Everyday*

Practice Guide 6 (pages 185–190)

Defer/Differ

1. defer
2. differ
3. defer
4. defer
5. differ

Deference/Difference

6. deference
7. difference
8. difference
9. difference
10. deference

Deprecate/Depreciate

11. deprecate
12. depreciate
13. depreciates
14. deprecate
15. depreciate

Desert/Dessert

16. desert
17. dessert
18. desserts
19. dessert
20. desert

Device/Devise

21. devise
22. devise
23. device
24. devise
25. device

Dew/Do/Due

26. due
27. dew
28. do
29. due
30. due

Die/Dye

31. dye
32. die
33. die
34. dye
35. dye

Disapprove/Disprove

36. disapprove
37. disprove
38. disprove
39. disapproves
40. disapprove

Disburse/Disperse

41. disperse
42. disburse
43. disbursed
44. dispersed
45. disbursed

Discreet/Discrete

46. discreet
47. discreet
48. discrete
49. discreet
50. discrete

Disinterested/Uninterested

51. disinterested
52. uninterested
53. uninterested
54. disinterested
55. uninterested

Done/Dun

56. dun
57. dun
58. done
59. dun
60. dun

E.g./I.e.

61. i.e.
62. e.g.
63. e.g.
64. e.g.
65. i.e.

Elicit/Illicit

66. elicit
67. elicit
68. illicit
69. elicit
70. illicit

Eligible/Illegible

71. eligible
72. eligible
73. illegible
74. Illegible
75. eligible

Emigrate/Immigrate

76. emigrated
77. emigrated
78. immigrate
79. emigrated
80. immigrate

Eminent/Imminent

81. eminent
82. eminent
83. imminent
84. imminent
85. imminent

Envelop/Envelope

86. envelope
87. envelops
88. enveloped
89. envelops
90. envelopes

Every day/Everyday

91. Every day
92. Everyday
93. Every day
94. everyday
95. every day

The answers to Reinforcement Guide 6 appear in the *Instructor's Manual and Key for HOW 13: A Handbook for Office Professionals*, 13th edition.

Practice Exercises for *Every One/Everyone* Through *Flaunt/Flout*

Practice Guide 7 (pages 193–197)

Every one/Everyone

1. Everyone
2. Every one
3. everyone
4. everyone
5. every one

Example/Sample

6. sample
7. sample
8. sample
9. examples
10. example

Executioner/Executor

11. executor
12. executor
13. executioner
14. executioner
15. executor

Expand/Expend

16. expend
17. expand
18. expand
19. expend
20. expand

Expansive/Expensive

21. Expansive
22. expensive
23. expensive
24. expensive
25. expansive

Explicit/Implicit

26. explicit
27. Explicit
28. explicitly
29. implicitly
30. implicit

Extant/Extent

31. extent
32. extant

33. extant
34. extent
35. extant

Facetious/Factious/Fictitious

36. fictitious
37. facetious
38. factious
39. factious
40. facetious

Facility/Faculty

41. faculty
42. facility
43. faculty
44. facility
45. facility

Fair/Fare

46. fare
47. fair
48. fair
49. fair
50. fare

Farther/Further

51. further
52. farther
53. further
54. farther
55. farther

Feat/Fete

56. fete
57. feat
58. feats
59. fete
60. feted

Fever/Temperature

61. temperature
62. fever
63. fever
64. fever
65. temperature

Fewer/Less

66. fewer
67. fewer
68. less
69. fewer
70. Less

Finally/Finely

71. finally
72. finely
73. finely
74. finally
75. finally

Fiscal/Physical

76. physical
77. physical
78. fiscal
79. fiscal
80. fiscal

Flagrant/Fragrant

81. flagrant
82. flagrant
83. fragrant
84. flagrant
85. fragrant

Flair/Flare

86. flair
87. flair
88. flare
89. flare
90. Flared

Flaunt/Flout

91. flaunt
92. flout
93. flouting
94. flout
95. flaunting

The answers to Reinforcement Guide 7 appear in the **Instructor's Manual and Key for HOW 13: A Handbook for Office Professionals**, 13th edition.

Practice Exercises for *Flew/Flu/Flue* Through *Human/Humane*

Practice Guide 8 (pages 201–205)

Flew/Flu/Flue

1. flue
2. flu
3. flue
4. flew
5. flu

Foreword/Forward

6. forward
7. forward
8. foreword
9. foreword
10. foreword

Formally/Formerly

11. formally
12. formerly
13. formerly
14. formally
15. formally

Former/Latter

16. former
17. former
18. latter
19. former
20. latter

Forth/Fourth

21. fourth
22. forth
23. fourth
24. fourth
25. forth

Fortunate/Fortuitous

26. fortuitous
27. fortunate
28. fortunate
29. fortuitously
30. fortunate

Good/Well

31. well
32. well
33. good
34. good
35. well

Grate/Great

36. great
37. grate
38. grate
39. grate
40. great

Hail/Hale

41. hail
42. hail
43. hail
44. hale
45. hailed

He/Him/Himself

46. him
47. he
48. himself
49. he
50. him

Healthful/Healthy

51. healthful
52. healthy
53. healthful
54. healthy
55. healthy

Hear/Here

56. here
57. here
58. hear
59. hear
60. here

Her/Herself/She

61. herself
62. she

63. her
64. she
65. she

Hew/Hue

66. hew
67. hues
68. hue
69. hewed
70. hue

Hoard/Horde

71. horde
72. Hordes
73. hoard
74. hoard
75. hoard

Hoarse/Horse

76. hoarse
77. hoarse
78. hoarse
79. horses
80. horses

Hole/Whole

81. hole
82. whole
83. whole
84. holes
85. whole

Holy/Wholly

86. wholly
87. holy
88. wholly
89. wholly
90. wholly

Human/Humane

91. human
92. human
93. humane
94. human
95. humane

The answers to Reinforcement Guide 8 appear in the *Instructor's Manual and Key for HOW 13: A Handbook for Office Professionals,* 13th edition.

Practice Exercises for *Hypercritical/Hypocritical* Through *Lessee/Lesser/Lessor*

Practice Guide 9 (pages 209–213)

Hypercritical/Hypocritical

1. Hypercritical
2. hypercritical
3. hypocritical
4. hypercritical
5. hypocritical

I/Me/Myself

6. me
7. I
8. I
9. me
10. I

Ideal/Idle/Idol

11. idle
12. idol
13. ideal
14. idle
15. ideal

Imply/Infer

16. imply
17. imply
18. infer
19. inferred
20. implied

In behalf of/On behalf of

21. in behalf of
22. in behalf of
23. on behalf of
24. In behalf of
25. on behalf of

Incidence/Incidents

26. incidents
27. incidence
28. incidence
29. incidents
30. incidences

Incite/Insight

31. incite
32. incited
33. insight
34. insight
35. incite

Indigenous/Indigent/Indignant

36. indigenous
37. indigent
38. Indigents
39. indignant
40. indigenous

Ingenious/Ingenuous

41. Ingenious
42. ingenious
43. ingenuous
44. ingenious
45. ingenuous

Interstate/Intrastate

46. intrastate
47. interstate
48. interstate
49. interstate
50. intrastate

Irregardless/Regardless

51. regardless
52. Regardless
53. regardless
54. regardless
55. regardless

It's/Its

56. it's
57. its
58. it's
59. its
60. its

Later/Latter

61. latter
62. later
63. later
64. latter
65. latter

Lay/Lie

66. lie
67. lain
68. lain
69. lying
70. lies

Lead/Led

71. lead
72. lead
73. led
74. led
75. led

Lean/Lien

76. lean
77. leans
78. liens
79. lean
80. lien

Leased/Least

81. least
82. least

83. leased
84. leased
85. leased

Lend/Loan

86. loan
87. lend
88. lend
89. loan
90. lend

Lessee/Lesser/Lessor

91. lessor
92. lessee
93. lessor
94. lesser
95. lesser

The answers to Reinforcement Guide 9 appear in the *Instructor's Manual and Key for HOW 13: A Handbook for Office Professionals*, *13*[th] edition.

Practice Exercises for *Lessen/Lesson* Through *Ordinance/Ordnance*

Practice Guide 10 (pages 217–221)

Lessen/Lesson

1. lessen
2. lessened
3. lesson
4. lessen
5. lesson

Levee/Levy

6. levees
7. levy
8. levy
9. levee
10. levies

Liable/Libel/Likely

11. liable
12. liable
13. libel
14. libelous
15. likely

Lightening/Lightning

16. lightening
17. lightening
18. lightning
19. lightening
20. lightning

Local/Locale

21. Local
22. locale
23. locale
24. local
25. local

Loose/Lose

26. lose
27. loose
28. lose
29. loose
30. lose

Magnate/Magnet

31. magnet
32. magnate
33. magnate
34. magnet
35. magnetic

377

Main/Mane

36. main
37. main
38. mane
39. main
40. mane

Manner/Manor

41. manner
42. manors
43. manor
44. manner
45. manner

Marital/Marshal/Martial

46. marital
47. marshal
48. martial
49. marshal
50. marital

May be/Maybe

51. may be
52. Maybe
53. maybe
54. may be
55. may be

Medal/Meddle

56. meddle
57. medal
58. medal
59. meddle
60. meddle

Miner/Minor

61. minor
62. minor

63. miner
64. minors
65. minor

Mode/Mood

66. mood
67. mode
68. mode
69. mode
70. mood

Moral/Morale

71. morale
72. morale
73. moral
74. moral
75. morale

Morning/Mourning

76. morning
77. morning
78. mourning
79. morning
80. mourning

Naval/Navel

81. Naval
82. navel
83. navel
84. naval
85. naval

Ordinance/Ordnance

86. ordinance
87. ordinances
88. ordnance
89. ordnance
90. ordinances

The answers to Reinforcement Guide 10 appear in the **Instructor's Manual and Key for HOW 13: A Handbook for Office Professionals**, *13th edition*.

Practice Exercises for *Overdo/Overdue* Through *Pray/Prey*

Practice Guide 11 (pages 225–229)

Overdo/Overdue

1. overdue
2. overdo
3. overdo
4. overdue
5. overdue

Pair/Pare/Pear

6. pare
7. pear
8. pairs
9. pare
10. pair

Partition/Petition

11. petition
12. partition
13. petition
14. partition
15. petition

Passed/Past

16. past
17. passed
18. past
19. passed
20. past

Patience/Patients

21. patients
22. patience
23. patients
24. patients
25. patience

Peace/Piece

26. peace
27. peace
28. piece
29. peace
30. pieces

Peak/Peek

31. peak
32. peak
33. peak
34. peek
35. peek

Peal/Peel

36. peal
37. peals
38. peel
39. pealed
40. peeling

Peer/Pier

41. peer
42. peers
43. pier
44. peer
45. pier

Persecute/Prosecute

46. persecute
47. persecuted
48. prosecute
49. persecutes
50. prosecuted

Personal/Personnel

51. personnel
52. personnel
53. personal
54. personnel
55. personal

Perspective/Prospective

56. perspective
57. prospective
58. prospective
59. perspective
60. perspective

Peruse/Pursue

61. pursue
62. perused
63. peruse
64. pursue
65. pursue

Plaintiff/Plaintive

66. plaintiff
67. plaintiffs
68. plaintive
69. plaintiff
70. plaintive

379

Pole/Poll

71. pole
72. poll
73. poles
74. polled
75. polls

Populace/Populous

76. populace
77. populous
78. populous
79. populace
80. populace

Pore/Pour

81. pores
82. pore
83. pour
84. poured
85. poring

Pray/Prey

86. prey
87. pray
88. pray
89. prey
90. prey

The answers to Reinforcement Guide 11 appear in the **Instructor's Manual and Key for HOW 13: A Handbook for Office Professionals**, 13th edition.

Practice Exercises for *Precede/Proceed* Through *Scene/Seen*

Practice Guide 12 (pages 233–237)

Precede/Proceed

1. proceed
2. precede
3. precede
4. preceded
5. proceed

Precedence/Precedents

6. precedence
7. precedence
8. precedents
9. precedent
10. precedence

Presence/Presents

11. presents
12. presence
13. presence
14. presents
15. presence

Principal/Principle

16. principal
17. principle
18. principal
19. principle
20. principal

Propose/Purpose

21. propose
22. purpose
23. purpose
24. proposed
25. propose

Quiet/Quite

26. quiet
27. quite
28. quite
29. quiet
30. quite

Raise/Raze/Rise

31. rise
32. raze
33. raise
34. rose
35. razed

Rational/Rationale

36. rational
37. rationale
38. rational
39. rationale
40. rational

Real/Really

41. really
42. really
43. real
44. real
45. really

Reality/Realty

46. realty
47. reality
48. realty
49. reality
50. realty

Receipt/Recipe

51. receipt
52. recipe
53. recipes
54. receipt
55. receipts

Regime/Regimen/Regiment

56. regimen
57. regiment
58. regimes
59. regimen
60. regimen

Residence/Residents

61. Residents
62. residence
63. residence
64. residents
65. residents

Respectably/Respectfully/Respectively

66. respectfully
67. respectively

68. respectfully
69. respectably
70. respectively

Ring/Wring

71. wring
72. ring
73. rings
74. wring
75. wring

Role/Roll

76. Roll
77. role
78. roll
79. role
80. roll

Rote/Wrote

81. wrote
82. rote
83. wrote
84. rote
85. rote

Rout/Route

86. route
87. rout
88. route
89. routed
90. routes

Scene/Seen

91. seen
92. scene
93. scene
94. seen
95. seen

The answers to Reinforcement Guide 12 appear in the *Instructor's Manual and Key for HOW 13: A Handbook for Office Professionals*, 13th edition.

Practice Guide 13 (pages 241–245)

Set/Sit

1. set
2. sit
3. sat
4. setting
5. sitting

Sew/So/Sow

6. sow
7. so
8. sown
9. sew
10. sewing

Shall/Will

11. will
12. will
13. will
14. will
15. will

Shear/Sheer

16. sheer
17. sheer
18. sheared
19. sheer
20. shear

Shone/Shown

21. shone
22. shown
23. shown
24. shone
25. shone

Should/Would

26. would
27. should
28. should
29. would
30. should

Soar/Sore

31. soar
32. sore
33. soared
34. soaring
35. sore

Sole/Soul

36. sole
37. sole
38. soul
39. soul
40. sole

Some/Somewhat

41. somewhat
42. some
43. some
44. somewhat
45. some

Some time/Sometime/Sometimes

46. sometime
47. sometime
48. some time
49. Sometimes
50. some time

Staid/Stayed

51. stayed
52. staid
53. stayed
54. staid
55. stayed

Stationary/Stationery

56. stationery
57. stationery
58. stationary
59. stationary
60. stationary

Statue/Stature/Statute

61. stature
62. statue
63. Statutes
64. statue
65. stature

Straight/Strait

66. straight
67. strait
68. straight
69. Strait
70. straight

Suit/Suite

71. suite
72. suit
73. suite
74. suite
75. suit

Sure/Surely

76. surely
77. sure
78. surely
79. surely
80. sure

Tare/Tear/Tier

81. tare
82. tier
83. tear
84. tare
85. tier

Than/Then

86. than
87. than
88. then
89. then
90. than

The answers to Reinforcement Guide 13 appear in the **Instructor's Manual and Key for HOW 13: A Handbook for Office Professionals**, *13th edition.*

Practice Exercises for *That/Which* Through *Your/You're*

Practice Guide 14 (pages 249–253)

That/Which

1. that
2. which
3. which
4. that
5. that

Their/There/They're

6. they're
7. there
8. they're
9. their
10. their

Theirs/There's

11. There's
12. there's
13. theirs
14. there's
15. theirs

Them/They

16. they
17. they
18. they
19. them
20. they

Threw/Through/Thru

21. threw
22. through
23. through
24. threw
25. through

To/Too/Two

26. too
27. too
28. too
29. to
30. Too

Tortuous/Torturous

31. torturous
32. tortuous
33. torturous
34. tortuous
35. torturous

Toward/Towards

36. toward
37. toward
38. toward
39. toward
40. toward

Us/We

41. us
42. we
43. we
44. us
45. we

Vain/Van/Vane/Vein

46. vain
47. vane
48. vans
49. vain
50. vein

Vary/Very

51. very
52. vary
53. vary
54. very
55. vary

Vice/Vise

56. vise
57. vices
58. vices
59. vised
60. vice

Waive/Wave

61. wave
62. waive
63. waving
64. waived
65. wave

Waiver/Waver

66. waiver
67. waver
68. wavered
69. waiver
70. wavered

Weather/Whether

71. weather
72. whether
73. whether
74. weather
75. weather

Who/Whom

76. who
77. whom
78. Whom
79. Who
80. whom

Who's/Whose

81. who's
82. whose
83. whose
84. who's
85. who's

Your/You're

86. you're
87. your
88. your
89. you're
90. You're

The answers to Reinforcement Guide 14 appear in the **Instructor's Manual and Key for HOW 13: A Handbook for Office Professionals**, *13th edition*.

Additional Practice Exercises for *Affect/Effect*

Practice Guide 15, Part A (page 257)

1. effect
2. affect
3. affect
4. effecting
5. effect
6. affect
7. effect
8. effect
9. effect
10. effects
11. affect
12. affect
13. effect
14. effecting
15. effect

The answers to Practice Guide 15, Part B, and Reinforcement Guide 15 appear in the **Instructor's Manual and Key for HOW 13: A Handbook for Office Professionals**, *13th edition*.

Cumulative Practice Guides

Part A (pages 261–262)

1. an
2. accept
3. adapt
4. advice
5. affect
6. already
7. altogether
8. elude
9. Almost
10. among
11. anyone
12. as
13. ensure
14. badly
15. biannually
16. capitol
17. site
18. complements
19. continual
20. council
21. dissent
22. deprecate
23. devise
24. due
25. disperse

Part B (pages 262–263)

1. elicit
2. emigrated
3. imminent
4. every day
5. everyone
6. further
7. fewer
8. formerly
9. well
10. hoard
11. me
12. imply
13. indigent
14. interstate
15. its
16. lie
17. liable
18. loose
19. martial
20. Maybe
21. morale
22. overdo
23. passed
24. patience
25. persecuting

Part C (pages 264–265)

1. personal
2. prospective
3. proceed
4. precedence
5. principle
6. quiet
7. rise
8. really
9. realty
10. receipt
11. respectfully
12. route
13. set
14. sew
15. sheer
16. sometime
17. stationary
18. stature
19. surely
20. than
21. their
22. too
23. waver
24. whether
25. You're

The answers to Cumulative Practice Guides 2 and 3 and to Testing Your Understanding, Parts 1 and 2, appear in the *Instructor's Manual and Key for HOW 13: A Handbook for Office Professionals, 13th edition.*

Section 8   Elements of Writing Style

Practice Guide 1 (pages 279–280)

1. inform
2. inform
3. convey negative news
4. persuade
5. convey negative news
6. inform
7. persuade
8. convey negative news
9. inform
10. inform

Practice Guide 2 (page 281)

Answers may vary. Example solutions follow:
1. tell
2. increase
3. aid
4. many
5. ease *or* lessen
6. Because
7. regarding
8. If
9. until
10. for
11. are
12. Please
13. flight attendant
14. police officer
15. maître d'

Practice Guide 3 (page 282)

Example Solutions, Part A
1. Plan to attend the Sales Department meeting on Tuesday, July 18, from 1:30–3 p.m. in Room 3250.
2. Are funds available for me to attend the American Marketers Association national convention in Chicago from March 20 to 24?
3. Please let us know by May 10 when you will be able to FedEx us the records for the Cranston estate.
4. Please complete the enclosed forms and return them before or by April 20, at least four weeks before your cruise ship, the Sea Princess, departs for the Caribbean.
5. Your reservations for July 21–23 at the Fremont Hotel have been confirmed, but please let us know whether you need a room with a king-size bed or two double beds.

Example Solutions, Part B
6. a compelling, an attractive, a superb, a dynamic
7. an excellent, an outstanding, a favorable, an appropriate, a suitable
8. an expansive, an extensive, a major, a large-scale
9. industry, market
10. organization, offices

Practice Guide 4 (pages 283–284)

Example Solution, Part A
We have established a new toy manufacturing business, and we are interested in developing a Web site. The Web site should showcase our products, and it should invite visitors to purchase directly from our site. Visitors may hesitate to purchase from a small business Web site, but all credit card information for online purchases will be protected through a secure site. Can you assist us in developing such a Web site, or should we, on the other hand, consult another service?

Example Solution, Part B
Please send me your expense report by April 1, which is due in our district office by April 3. Since copies of receipts are not acceptable for reimbursement, include all the original receipts with your report. The district office will issue your reimbursement check, but sales representatives must submit their expense reports by April 1 to receive payment this month. Missing the deadline date will result in your reimbursement check being issued next month.

Example Solution, Part C
We have an opening for a tax accountant in our Accounting Department. Although more than 50 people have applied for the position, none of the applicants are qualified for the position we have available. We have advertised this position in newspapers throughout the area, but this source does not seem to target our desired audience. We have also contacted several employment agencies in our area, and they, too, have been unable to recommend qualified candidates. We have posted this job opening on several Internet career centers, but none of the postings on the career center sites have produced a qualified applicant. If you have any suggestions for recruiting qualified candidates, please let me know.

The answers to Practice Guides 5–8 appear in the *Instructor's Manual and Key for HOW 13: A Handbook for Office Professionals, 13th edition.*

387

Section 9 Spelling, Proofreading, and Editing

Practice Guide 1 (pages 293–294)

1. We are in the process of planning fund-raising activities for the college's proposed building program.

2. Since the exterminators must tent the building, all tenants will be required to vacate their apartments from August 3 through August 5.

3. Perhaps we should engage a freelance photographer to obtain professional pictures for the sales brochure of our new Willowbrook development.

4. During this 3-day Memorial Day sale, you can save up to 50% on regular items that have been reduced temporarily only for this sale.

5. For job listings, visit the web site of *Monster Healthcare* at http://healthcare.monster.com; this online career center posts résumés and lists job opportunities in a wide range of health-related occupations throughout the U.S.

6. New keys will be issued for the parking gates to all employees parking lots.

7. Before entering the premises, all visitors must stop at the kiosk to obtain a permit from the security guard.

8. Plan to register early for this conference; after November 2nd, registration fees will be $195.00.

9. You are among our preferred customers, and we are pleased to invite you to this special by-invitation-only sale.

10. We cannot accept any out-of-state or third-party checks; therefore, you will need to find another means for making this payment.

Practice Guide 2 (pages 295–296)

1. If you will fax me your contact information, including your e-mail address, I will let you know the date_s of the convention as soon as the executive board determines them.

2. Will you be able to attend the luncheon that has been scheduled for Thursday, September 20th, at 12 Noon?

3. Clini Share has been able to serve most of our patient's needs for medical equipment, medical supplies, and nursing care.

4. Ms. Deborah Martin has been appointed Manager of the Accounting department; she will assume this position on July 1.

5. According to the sign posted, "Vehicles not displaying a valid parking permit will be towed away at owners' expense."

6. Stocks, corporate bonds, mutual funds, unit trusts, government bonds, tax-free municipal bonds, and precious metals; all of these investment opportunities are available through T. R. Noble.

7. For reservations for the nights of April 19 and 20 at the Park Regency hotel in Atlanta, your confirmation number is JRK1892.

8. Copies of the agenda, last year's minutes, a list of advisory committee members, a campus map, and a parking permit are enclosed.

9. Do you foresee that these changes will affect our ability to market this high-end software to home computer users?

10. All of these grant proposals must be submitted to the appropriate offices in Washington, D.C., by March 31, or they will not be funded.

The answers to Part 2, Practice Guides 3 and 4, and to exercises in Parts 3 and 4 appear in the *Instructor's Manual and Key for HOW 13: A Handbook for Office Professionals*, 13th edition.